dear Mommy:
to another of the alltime great mothers
Happy Mother's Day
from your loving daughter
Nº. 2 ; Annie
XXX

MOTHERS

MATER
MUTTER * MODER
MŌDIR * MOEDER * MÃE
MÈRE * MAMĂ * MĀTE * MOTINA * MATKA
MAJKA * MATERINSKI * MATI * MÁTHAIR * AITI * EMÄ
ANYA * MADRE * MATYNA * AMIR * MOŬ
MAYKA * MAT * MOR
MUMMA * METER
MATÀR

Mother and Child
Sculpture by Henry Moore

Mothers

100 Mothers
of the famous and the infamous
by the
DIAGRAM GROUP

**PADDINGTON
PRESS LTD**

**THE TWO CONTINENTS
PUBLISHING GROUP**

母親

DEDICATION
To the mothers of
the DIAGRAM GROUP and
PADDINGTON PRESS

ACKNOWLEDGMENT
The publishers would like to thank the many personal contributions by
curators of private collections, directors of archives,
and persons who have known the mothers
or could relate incidents from their lives.
All of whose generous enthusiasm for their
subject has enabled this book to be compiled.

© Diagram Visual Information 1976

Compiled by
Bernard Moore
Edited by
Richard Ehrlich
Contributors
Dulcie M. Ashdown
Ken Ashen   J. A. Camacho
Carla Capalbo   Jean Cooke   Richard O. David
Lesley Gorden   David Heidenstam   Jeremy Kingston
Jane O'Neill   Peter Presence   Theodore Rowland-Entwistle
Penelope Vita Finzi

Picture research by
Enid Moore
Illustrations by
Jeff Alger   Trevor Bounford
Richard Hummerstone   Susan Kinsey   Pavel Kostal
Kathleen McDougall   Graham Rosewarne

ISBN: 0-8467-0114-6
Library of Congress catalog card number
75–22962

In the USA
Paddington Press Ltd.
Two Continents Publishing Group
30 East 42nd Street
New York
NY 10017

In the United Kingdom
Paddington Press Ltd.
231 The Vale
London W3 7QS

In Australia and New Zealand
Distributed by
Angus & Robertson Pty. Ltd.
P.O. Box 117
Cremorne Junction 2090
Sydney N.S.W.

In Canada
Distributed by
Random House of Canada Ltd.
5390 Amber Drive
Mississauga
Ontario L4W 1Y7

FOREWORD

George Bernard Shaw thought his mother "the worst mother conceivable." Mrs Capone, mother of one of the world's most ruthless gangsters, always thought that Al was "a good boy." Stalin's mother was a deeply religious woman who wished he had become a priest. During the American War of Independence George Washington's mother declared "I wish George would come home and look after his plantation."

MOTHERS sets out to tell briefly about the mothers of one hundred notable men and women. They have been chosen somewhat at random — there are, after all, many famous people — but always with a view to covering as wide a range of activities and as many nationalities as possible. Most of the subjects are household names — statesmen, soldiers, writers, artists, scientists, musicians, entertainers, criminals, kings and queens, saints and sinners. Some of their mothers turn out to be considerable personalities in their own right, some are almost nonentities. Many of our mothers never lived to see their child's triumphs. Others not only shared their success, but even contributed directly to it. Others, in turn, were obstacles rather than stepping stones to their children's achievements.

Fame usually comes late in life, and until it is achieved no one thinks or records very much about mother. Interestingly, this lack of information is often most acute when the famous person comes from a family of modest financial means: preserving records is, or at least was, a privilege of the wealthy and the bourgeois. More is known about the merchants whom Rembrandt painted than about his mother, whose husband was a miller.

We present the biographies with as little embellishment as possible. No thesis has been formulated, no opinion has been allowed (or so we hope) unduly to obscure or distort. The most obvious question — what effect does a mother have on her child? — we leave to the theorists. This book serves other purposes.

"Where is father?"
19th century sentimental illustration

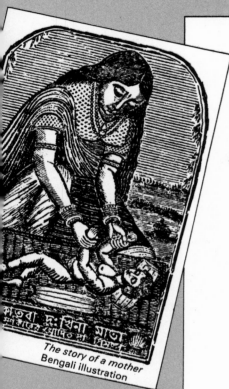

The story of a mother
Bengali illustration

*Tombstone to a mother
Ancient Greek bas-relief*

Eve. Russian popular print
(17 cent.)

Sending her son to war
Chinese Peoples Republic (1970)

Abigail May

LOUISA MAY ALCOTT
(1832-88)
American author, most famous for her novel *Little Women.*

Abigail May was the twelfth and youngest child of Colonel Joseph May, a military man of good New England stock. Little is known of Abigail's childhood; she is first described as an "energetic-looking woman, with a benevolent brow, satirical mouth, and eyes full of hope and courage."

Abigail married Amos Bronson Alcott, the Transcendentalist writer and educator who is one of the great eccentrics of American letters. Amos believed in vegetarianism and a radical version of the simple life: milk, butter, tea, salt, and spices were all useless luxuries to him. He also had some original ideas about education, and ran a school in Germantown, Pennsylvania, where he and Abigail spent the first years of their marriage. But his principles did not coincide with those of the people of Germantown, and the school failed. In 1834 he moved himself and his family to Boston, where he opened another school. This one also failed, with enrollment dwindling eventually to five, three of which number were the Alcotts' own daughters.

The daughters – Anna, Louisa May, Beth, and Mary – were all devoted to their idealistic and eccentric father. But it was Abigail's practical wisdom that held the household together. She struggled constantly to bridge the gap between her husband's idealism and the cruel necessities of material existence. She worked hard and saw to it that her daughters helped out. For their upbringing she had three simple precepts: "Rule yourself, Love your neighbors, Do the duty which lies nearest you." An early biographer of Louisa May said that the Alcott children were brought up in an atmosphere of "moral sunshine."

In 1840, after the closing of the Boston school, the family moved to Concord, Massachusetts. Nearby lived two family friends, Ralph Waldo Emerson and Henry David Thoreau. Thoreau occasionally gave the girls their lessons, and Emerson wrote fondly of evenings he spent with the whole family. It was just outside Concord that Amos joined with a Mr Lane in running a utopian community called Fruitlands. Fruitlands epitomized all Amos's ideals, including his extreme vegetarianism. Nothing must be used if it caused discomfort to any beast. Wool, silk, and leather were all forbidden on these grounds, although Abigail did manage to circumvent the prohibition of leather, declaring that neither she nor her daughters would ever go barefoot.

Abigail was one of only two women taking part in the community. The other, a Mrs Page, could or would not share the household drudgery. When asked how many beasts of burden there were at Fruitlands, Abigail replied: "Only one woman."

The Fruitlands experiment failed, like Amos's other projects, and the family moved back to Concord. In 1845 Abigail was able, with money left her by her father and with $500 lent by Emerson, to buy a small house called "Hillside." This house, later made famous in *Little Women,* was to serve as the family home for most of the next twenty-five years. Finances remained precarious for a time, but by the early 1870's Louisa May was successful enough as a writer to make the whole family financially secure.

Louisa May's success enabled her mother to spend the last years of her life in comfort. Abigail died in November, 1878, and was buried in Sleepy Hollow Cemetery. She served as the model for "Marmee" in *Little Women* and for the mother in all her daughter's books. But Louisa May claimed that Marmee, good though she was, was still "not half good enough" to do justice to the real woman who inspired her.

Right Portrait of Abigail in middle age.
Page 12 The Alcott homestead at Concord, and a page from Abigail's cookbook.

LOUISA M. ALCOTT'S ROOM, ORCHARD HOUSE

THE ALCOTT HOMESTEAD, "ORCHARD HOUSE"
CONCORD

Walpole 1856.
A. M. A.

Reciepts..
and
Simple remedies-
best way of doing
difficult things -
all tried, and
Proved

odetta lee grady clay

In about 1870, a Mr O'Grady left County Clare in Ireland and made his way to the American South. There he married a black woman, and his son eventually married a black woman too. Odetta Lee Grady Clay, the mother of Muhammad Ali, is a child of this marriage.

Her husband, Cassius Marcellus Clay Sr, is a descendant of a slave set free from the Clay plantation in Kentucky. He was a good husband in most ways. His sign-painting trade never lacked customers, and the family was always well provided for. Mrs Clay never had to buy on credit and always settled her bills promptly.

By the time Cassius Jr was born (on January 17, 1942) the family was well established in Louisville, Kentucky. When Cassius was about four years old they moved into a small house with a white porch and a tiny attic window overlooking a tree-lined street.

Mrs Clay took her sons to the Baptist Church every Sunday. She cared that they should have regular schooling but said little when she discovered them playing truant. Cassius Jr enjoyed dominating other children in his class, and his mother came to accept that the boy was fast developing into a man with a mind of his own. An early story about him gives an indication of things to come. When he was eighteen months old and still young enough to appreciate a good cuddle, his mother picked him up. One of his tiny fists shot up and hit her in the mouth. One tooth was loosened and, because she didn't see a dentist for some time, all her front teeth were affected. She now wears a dental bridge and says, "I can't smile too much these days."

Cassius started his boxing career at the age of twelve, when he and his brother were taken on by a trainer named Fred Stoner. For a time Mrs Clay was critical of Stoner: he kept her sons too late at the gym and was causing them to miss their sleep. She kept them away and only allowed them to return when Stoner worked out a new, healthier schedule.

Her son's success has enabled Mrs Clay to live a life of relative ease. Ali has tried to make up for the lean years by sharing much of his earnings with his parents. They have a new house in a nice neighborhood, and they follow Ali whenever they can. Mrs Clay still goes to his fights even though she is feeling the strain — not of traveling but of wondering whether he is going to be hurt.

Odetta Clay is a home-lover. She cooks and makes clothes and draperies, and she neither drinks nor smokes. Her once trim figure is now a thing of the past; she could be described as "heavyset." Her son, one of the great athletes of our time, calls her "Just another sweet little fat," homey mother."

MUHAMMAD ALI
(1942-)
Formerly Cassius Clay. American holder of the World Heavyweight Boxing title.

Page 14 Odetta wipes down her son after one of his "work outs."

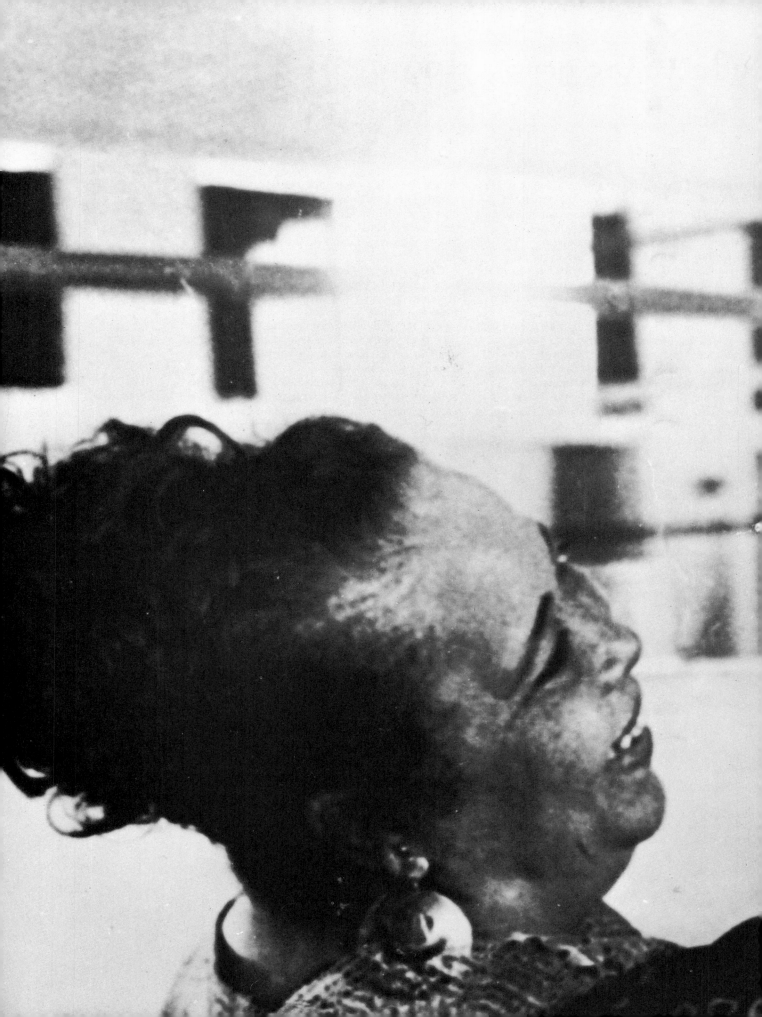

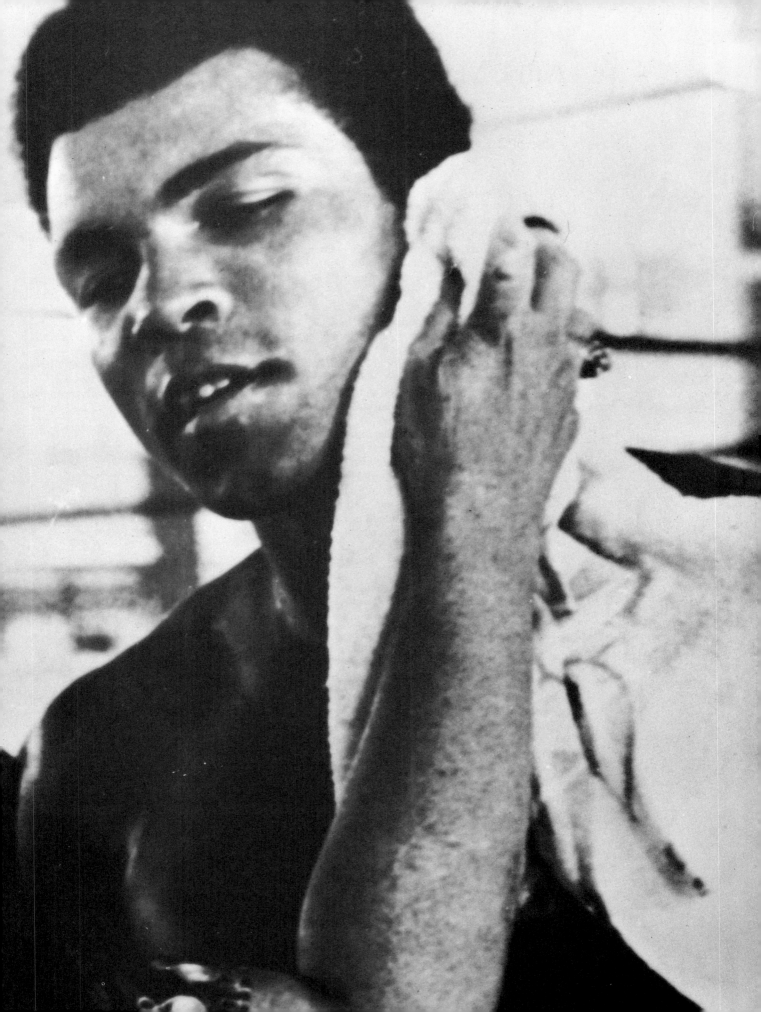

Anne Marie Andersen

HANS CHRISTIAN ANDERSEN
(1805-75)
Danish writer of children's stories, including *The Ugly Duckling* and *The Emperor's New Clothes.*

"In the year 1805 there lived at Odense, in a small mean room, a young married couple, who were extremely attached to each other; he was a shoemaker, scarcely twenty-two years old, a man of a richly gifted and truly poetical mind. His wife, a few years older than himself, was ignorant of life and of the world, but possessed a heart full of love."

In these words Hans Christian Andersen describes his parents Hans and Anne Marie. He understates the age difference – Anne Marie was fifteen years older than her husband – but otherwise the description is reasonably accurate. Hans Andersen the shoemaker was an intelligent man, with radical views on politics and religion. Although he had little formal education, he was an avid reader and questioned what he read. Anne Marie, on the other hand, was almost illiterate, able to read only block capitals, and those with difficulty. She could not write at all.

Anne Marie's childhood was a joyless one. Her mother had three illegitimate children by three different men. "When she was little," wrote Hans Christian, "her parents had hounded her out to beg, and when she couldn't do that, she had spent a whole day sitting weeping under a bridge. My childish imagination saw that so distinctly that I wept over it too." Six years before her marriage to Hans Andersen, Anne Marie had had an illegitimate daughter by a journeyman potter who deserted her and the child. Hans Christian's half-sister had been fostered out, and it is unlikely that the two knew each other in childhood.

In fact, Hans had little personal contact with his mother's family, and what contact he did have was very unpleasant: When very young he visited one of his half-aunts in Copenhagen and was welcomed rather unenthusiastically. It turned out that the woman ran a brothel, and a young boy was completely useless to her. Later in life, after he had made a name for himself, he lived in terror that one of his mother's kinsmen might acknowledge their famous relative.

Coming from such a background, Anne Marie determined to give Hans Christian a better chance in life than she had had: "I was their only child and greatly spoilt," he wrote. And certainly the picture he paints of his mother is of a contented, proud wife: "Our little room, which mother kept clean and neat, was decked with greenery and pictures. It was mother's pride that the sheets and the short little curtains at the window should always be snow-white." He describes Anne Marie's garden: "In the kitchen was a ladder leading to the roof and there in the gutter between our house and our neighbors' was a box of earth in which grew chives and parsley, and that was all my mother's garden." There is no doubt that she was a warm and loving mother, even if she did not understand her husband's questioning mind. When her husband one day closed the Bible, saying, "Christ was a human being like us, but a remarkable one," she was horrified and burst into tears. On another occasion, when he declared, "There is no other devil than the one we have in our own hearts," she feared for his salvation. With this unquestioning faith went a strong superstitious element in her character, so that when her husband appeared one morning with scratches on his arms, she believed that the devil had visited

Right Illustration from *She Was Good For Nothing,* a story by her famous son.

him in the night to prove his existence.

When Hans Christian was eleven, his father died and his mother went to work as a washerwoman. It was not long before she found another husband, a shoemaker like her first, though this one was more successful at his trade and the family was soon able to move into a more respectable area of Odense. It was from this house that Hans Christian set out to make his name in the world. His mother made him consult a fortune-teller before allowing him to leave, and only did so because the woman said he would be famous. "She loved me with her whole heart," Hans Christian later wrote of his mother, "but she did not understand my aspirations and hankerings." But when he came home to see her, she wept with joy at his acceptance by distinguished townsfolk "because I had been honored as if I had been a count's child."

Anne Marie's troubles did not end with her second marriage. She was widowed once again and she began to drink and to make increasing demands on Han Christian, who supported her financially so far as he was able. When he heard of his mother's death in 1834, his first reaction was to thank God that her misery was over; but later he was able to comfort himself: "Although I should never be able to make her last days bright and carefree, she had died in the happy belief of my good fortune, that I was *someone*."

MARY ANN ARMSTRONG

Mary Ann Armstrong's parents were almost certainly born in slavery. Louis maintained that he was of pure black African stock (rather than lighter-skinned Creole) and that his ancestors came from the west coast of Africa. Mary Ann, who was usually called Mayann, was probably born in the early 1880's. She spent her earliest years in Butte, Louisiana, and moved to New Orleans when very young. She later had a job as servant to a white family whose children she helped raise. If she had any formal education nothing is known of it, but she could just about read and write.

When Mayann was fifteen she married Willie Armstrong, who worked in a turpentine factory. Louis once said of his father that he stayed there so long he eventually had the power to "hire and fire the colored guys under him." This would suggest a foreman's job, but it must have come later because at the time of Louis's birth — usually acknowledged as 1900 — he was desperately poor.

The Armstrongs lived in a one-room wooden shack, entered by a side alley, in the Back O'Town district of New Orleans. This was a run-down area, and very rough; according to Louis, two people were shot dead nearby on the day he was born.

Although the photograph of Mayann gives the impression that she was stern and forbidding, she was, in fact, a fun-loving woman and extremely popular with her neighbors. But not with her husband. They were soon fighting and eventually they parted, leaving Louis to be brought up by Grandma Armstrong, who was also living in the one-room house. He loved her but always remembered the joyful moments in his boyhood when he was reunited with his mother. She and Willie were reconciled long enough to produce a daughter, Beatrice, but mostly they went their own ways. Louis had a succession of "stepfathers" and some writers have claimed that Mayann was a prostitute. Louis was noncommittal on the subject: "Whether my mother did any hustling I cannot say. If she did, she kept it out of sight."

Mayann was a very religious woman, and she tried to inculcate proper habits in Louis. She saw to it that he went to church, and the music he heard there had an important influence on his playing and singing. She also told him not to steal or fight, though these precepts were often difficult to stick to in the wild company he kept. He had minor brushes with the law and was sent to a reform school for firing a pistol into the air. Even this event was an accidental boon for his musical career. It was in the reform school that he learned to play the trumpet, since neither Mayann nor his grandmother had enough money to buy musical instruments. Mayann also told Louis to be "physic minded," which may account for his abiding obsession with his health.

Little more is heard of Mayann until Louis was playing with King Oliver in Chicago in 1922. After hearing that he was ill and down on his luck, she went from New Orleans to see him — only to find that he was in his usual robust health and starting to make a name for himself. She stayed in Chicago until she became homesick and returned to New Orleans where, she said, "My church is waiting for me."

About six years later, when Mayann was in her forties, her health began to deteriorate and she returned to Chicago to live with Louis and his wife, the pianist Lil Hardin. She died soon after, and when the lid was lowered onto her coffin, Louis Armstrong cried for the only time in his life.

LOUIS ("SATCHMO") ARMSTRONG
(1900-71)
American jazz musician, a great trumpeter and band leader.

Left Mary Ann with her son and daughter.

19

Cassandra Leigh

JANE AUSTEN
(1775-1817)
English novelist. Among her best-known novels are *Pride and Prejudice* and *Emma*.

Cassandra Leigh was born on September 26, 1739. She was the daughter of an Anglican clergyman and came from an eminent English family which had included a Lord Mayor of London in the days of Queen Elizabeth I. Though not a beauty, she was good-looking and had a noble nose of which she was a little vain. She considered herself sensible and was witty and bright.

Cassandra was twenty-five when she married the Reverend George Austen, a classical scholar whose social standing was slightly lower than hers. He was made rector of the small Hampshire village of Steventon, little more than a row of cottages in pleasant, wooded countryside. The rectory there was to be her home for thirty-seven years. Cassandra, who was an excellent horsewoman, loved the countryside and once described London after a visit as "a sad place. I would not live in it on any account." Her early married life was exclusively domestic. She bore the first seven of her children within ten years and in addition to overseeing the baking and brewing and the dairy, had the pupils at her husband's school to look after. The Austens were an affectionate and good-tempered family and the children appreciated their happy, talented parents and pleasant home. The parents taught all the children in the early years, and George taught the boys until they went to university. The two girls were sent away for a few years to school, where Jane nearly died of a "putrid fever", but she was back with her family by the time she was nine and was to live with her mother for the rest of her life.

The Rector's wife was not one to put on airs, and in later life the daughters expressed some embarrassment that visitors might find their strong-minded mother mending clothes and linen in the front parlor. She was an affectionate mother but never seemed very close to Jane, and as she grew older became something of a hypochondriac. In 1798 Jane wrote to her sister that her mother "complained of an Asthma, a Dropsy, Water in her Chest, and a Liver disorder." Despite all this she was to outlive Jane by a whole decade.

In 1801, when the Rector was sixty-nine and Cassandra sixty-one, ill health caused him to give up his living and to move to the then fashionable town of Bath "with what happy feelings of escape." The Rector died in 1805, leaving his widow and daughters badly provided for, and the following year Mrs Austen and her daughters moved back to their beloved Hampshire, to a cottage at Chawton, near the town of Alton. In this house (now a Jane Austen museum), the family resumed their happy rural life. Mrs Austen turned the domestic duties over to her daughters and, country-lover that she was, turned to activity in the garden. In these pastoral surroundings, while her mother was digging potatoes in the vegetable garden, Jane Austen found time from her domestic chores to write her novels. Jane died in her sister's arms at the age of forty-two. Her mother lived on at the Chawton cottage for another ten years and died when she was eighty-eight.

Right Steventon Rectory, Cassandra's home for 37 years; and a silhouette from the house at Chawton where Cassandra died.

Steventon Rectory, Hants.

Elisabeth Læmmerhirt

JOHANN SEBASTIAN BACH
(1685-1750)
German composer and organist.

Elisabeth Læmmerhirt came from a highly respected family of Erfurt, a city in Thuringia, now part of East Germany. The Læmmerhirts were a very musical family. They regularly held singing evenings, at which any member of the family — or friends who happened to be in the house — could join in. Elisabeth's father, Valentin Læmmerhirt, was a furrier who carried on his trade at the sign of the Three Roses. It was probably in this house that Elisabeth was born on February 24, 1644.

The Læmmerhirts were great friends with the Bach family. From an early age Elisabeth must have known the Bach twins, Johann Christoph and Johann Ambrosius, who were born in 1645. Christoph and Ambrosius (nearly all the Bachs had the first name Johann) were so alike that the people of Erfurt regarded them as great curiosities. Their father, also named Johann Christoph, was a member of the *Rathsmusik,* the town band. In 1653 the twins and their father moved to Arnstadt, and it was not until 1667 that Ambrosius returned to Erfurt to join the *Rathsmusik* as a string player. A year later, on April 8, 1668, he married his childhood friend Elisabeth.

Elisabeth's first two children were born in Erfurt. The first, a boy, Johann Rudolf, lived only

six months; but the second, Johann Christoph, survived. In October 1671, when her second baby was only four months old, Elisabeth and her husband moved to Eisenach, another Thuringian city about thirty-five miles west of Erfurt. There she was to have four more sons and two daughters, three of whom probably died in childhood. In addition to the cares of this large family, Elisabeth also had to help look after Ambrosius' elder sister, Dorothea Maria Bach, who was mentally retarded. Dorothea, however, died in 1679, before Elisabeth's three youngest children were born, so possibly life was not quite as difficult as it might have been.

Johann Sebastian, born March 21, 1685, was Elisabeth's youngest child. He began school in 1692, but his mother did not see much of his progress, for in May, 1694, when Sebastian was only nine years old, she died. Left with a young family on his hands, Ambrosius sought a new wife, and within six months he was married again, this time to Barbara Margeretha Bartholomäi, widow of a deacon of Arnstadt. Two months later Ambrosius too was dead, and his eldest son, Christoph, then aged twenty-four, took charge of the orphaned family in his own home in Ohrdruf, a small town some thirty miles from Eisenach.

Below The home of the Bach family in Eisenach, where Elisabeth gave birth to her last child, Johann Sebastian.

Maria Magdelena Keverich

Maria Magdalena Keverich was born in December 1746, in a village near Koblenz (now West Germany, then part of the Holy Roman Empire). Her father, Heinrich Keverich, was personal cook to the Elector at the palace of Ehrenbreitstein. On her mother's side of the family were merchants, councillors, and senators.

As a girl, Maria worked as a chambermaid in the homes of the nobility. In 1763, aged seventeen, she married Johann Laym, a valet to the Elector at Treves. He died two years later, and Maria married Johann van Beethoven, the son of the Choirmaster to the Archbishop-Elector of Cologne. Johann had a small salary as tenor in the choir, but most of his income came from his father. The father disapproved his son's marrying a chambermaid but continued to keep the young family in comfort. Maria had one son from her first marriage, and in 1770 she and Johann had another, whom they named Ludwig.

The young Maria van Beethoven was the perfect *Hausfrau,* addicted to knitting and sewing. A contemporary describes her: "rather tall, longish face, a nose somewhat bent, spare, earnest eyes and kind. A little colorless perhaps — raised to a passion only for the occasional quarrel with the neighbors. She was quiet and used to suffering, and never known to laugh."

But in 1773 Johann's father died, and the family's troubles began. Johann's talents were not enough to take him further in his musical career. He was weak-willed and overworked; when faced with poverty he began to drink, and as the habit grew his voice and character deteriorated. Maria's health suffered in turn, as poverty, conflict, and worry were added to the strain of frequent pregnancies. Between 1770 and 1786 she bore five more children, three of whom died in infancy.

Johann began to put his hopes on his son (it was an age that enjoyed being astonished by child musicians). But Ludwig was slow and rebellious — full of talent but no prodigy. He was strong and willful, and he was being pushed beyond his speed by an often drunken father. He grew to idolize his long-suffering mother — although there was probably no deep understanding between them. Maria was not stupid, but her intellectual endowments seem to have been modest. It was said of her: "She could give converse and reply aptly, politely, and modestly with high and low." That is not the portrait of a highly sensitive person, and she had too many ailing children to devote herself to one. It seems that the young Beethoven's love for her grew from pity, not intimacy.

In 1781 the eleven-year-old Ludwig was sent to Holland, in the care of Maria, to make his first concert appearances. It was so cold on the journey that she had to wrap up his feet and keep them in her lap. The visit was only a partial success — and Ludwig had obviously picked up some of his father's attitudes, for when they returned he said: "The Dutch are skinflints. I'll never go to Holland again."

Ludwig gradually took over the role of providing for the family, and in 1787 he traveled to Vienna to make contact with the musicians of the Imperial Court. His mother's final illness brought him back — so separating his development from the direct influence of Mozart. Maria died on July 17, 1787, aged forty, leaving a baby girl who also soon died. Beethoven wrote to a friend: "She was such a good loving mother, my best friend; oh, who was happier than I when I could still say the dear name 'mother,' and it was heard, and whom can I say it to now?" We have only one memorable sentence attributed to Maria: "What is marriage? At first a little joy, and then a chain of sorrows."

LUDWIG VAN BEETHOVEN (1770-1827) German composer and pianist.

Left The house in Bonn where Maria lived with her second husband, Johann.

Eliza Grace Symonds

Eliza Grace Symonds was born in 1809, the daughter of a surgeon in the British Royal Navy who served abroad the *HMS Osprey* during the naval war against Napoleon. She had three brothers, one of whom followed his father as a naval officer while the other two emigrated to Australia and rose to the upper ranks of the civil service.

When her father died, his widow retired to Edinburgh, Scotland, and Eliza went with her. Eliza was a talented painter of portraits and miniatures, and although somewhat deaf, played the piano well. Not until she was thirty-four did she meet the man, ten years her junior, who was to be her husband. This was Alexander Melville Bell, who had been living in the house in which she and her mother lived.

Bell was a teacher of elocution and was particularly interested in teaching deaf-mutes to understand speech. He invented the system of "Visible Speech." Eliza and Alexander were married on July 19, 1844. It is ironic that Eliza, deaf herself, had no faith in her husband's methods. Alexander Graham, who was to continue his father's work in communication with the deaf, wrote in later years: "It is a great grief when I come home to see her quiet resignation 'under the will of God,' because of an obstinate disbelief in the power of lip-reading."

Eliza's obstinacy was matched by her determination. She overcame her disability when playing the piano by fastening the earpiece of an ear trumpet to her ear and the mouthpiece on the sounding board of the piano. This was so successful that she was able to play duets with her husband, who accompanied her on the flute.

The Bells had three sons, of whom Alexander Graham, born in March, 1847, was the second. Eliza seems to have been an unusually good mother and wife: sweet-tempered, religious and patient, and much loved by her family.

The atmosphere of the Bell household had a profound effect on the boy Alexander Graham. Growing up around his father's work and his mother's deafness led to a lifelong preoccupation with the problems of sound. Indeed, the two older boys, inspired by Alexander Melville, invented mechanical talking babies and talking dogs.

Eliza was sixty when tragedy befell the family. The youngest son died from tuberculosis, and soon after, the eldest son died of the same disease. The doctors warned that Alexander Graham was also threatened. So the Bells decided to move to what was considered a healthier climate and, despite their age, packed up and moved to Canada where they settled at Tulato Heights, four miles from Brantford in Ontario. They were to live there for ten years before moving to Washington D.C. to spend the last years of their lives near their son, who had become a famous man.

Alexander Graham himself had married a deaf girl who had come to him as a pupil. He once wrote to her: "When I am with you dear, and speak to you freely by word of mouth, I often forget that you cannot hear — I never do so with Mamma." In fact he communicated with his mother by finger alphabet.

Eliza died in 1897, aged eighty-nine. Her husband wrote: "She was so kind, so gentle, so loving that during the fifty-two years of our companionship I never saw a frown on her sweet face."

ALEXANDER GRAHAM BELL
(1847-1922)
British-born American scientist who invented the telephone.

Pages 24-25 Eliza takes her usual back seat, while her son holds up her grandson for inspection. *Left* A family photograph of Eliza.

LEAH BALINE

IRVING BERLIN
(1888)
American popular song writer, famous for such hits as "Alexander's Ragtime Band" and "White Christmas."

Leah Baline lived in Temun, Siberia, with her husband, Moses Baline, who was the cantor in the local synagogue. Life was not easy: they had eight children and they were poor. Perhaps worst of all, they lived in constant fear of raids by the Cossacks.

Moses's cousins had emigrated to America, and the Balines had often talked of going there too. But it was a long, arduous journey and the decision to make it required immense courage. In 1892 circumstances helped them decide: their house was burned down and they felt that they had nothing to lose by tramping through the snow to the Baltic and getting on a boat to the United States. They did not take all their children because one, already grown, decided to stay; but among those who went off on the crowded boat was four-year-old Izzy — or, as he was later to become known, Irving Berlin.

Leah and Moses, like most immigrants, found that life in New York was difficult. Moses had few skills outside his religious qualifications, and work was hard to come by. Moses got a low-paid job in a Kosher slaughterhouse in New York and earned additional money by giving Hebrew lessons and acting as deputy cantor in the synagogue. But he, like Leah, was bewildered by their new way of life. Four years after the Balines arrived in America, Moses died. The exhausting effort of supporting his large family had sapped his energy.

How could Leah keep the family going? She could not speak English and there was little she could do to earn money. When she discovered that the local junkmen needed brass, she took her brass samovar from Siberia, broke it up into little pieces and sold them. But it was a harsh life. At night she used to sit on an old wood chair and spread out her apron into which her children threw such money as they had been able to earn from odd jobs.

Although Irving was only eight when his father died, he told his mother that he was no scholar and had decided to leave school. Soon he was earning money selling newspapers and somehow Leah managed to conceal their poverty, or at least to stop the situation from deteriorating. Irving Berlin once said that he was never aware of poverty in those days because he had never known anything else.

He had great affection for his mother and frequently told her that some day he would replace her battered old chair. But she was increasingly alarmed by his activities because, although he was still a child, he was performing in sleazy dives and saloons in the Bowery. Leah drew the line when he said that he was going to become a singing waiter, and he postponed the idea for a time until he decided that the only way he could do the things he wanted was to leave home. On one occasion, after neighbors had told her which dive he was working in, she tracked him down and took him home. Leah was much concerned with what other people would think. He stayed with her for one night, and then ran away again.

He soon made enough, however, to buy her a new rocking chair. By now, Leah realized that although Irving meant to go his own way, he was no wastrel. He had even taught himself to play the piano, at least on the black notes, though he never learned to read music.

Soon he was writing songs and they were being published, even if they didn't make much money. One of them, "Marie from Sunny Italy," had a misprint on the cover, naming him as I. Berlin instead of Baline. He kept the name and a few years later it was on the cover of "Alexander's Ragtime Band." Irving had made it and he didn't forget his old mother.

One night he drew up in a taxi outside the New York East Side apartment in which she was then living and took her to a magnificent house with servants in the rich Jewish area of the Bronx. He had bought her a new home.

Leah lived on for some years to enjoy her son's success. When she died she was buried in a Brooklyn cemetery.

Right A rare photograph of Leah.

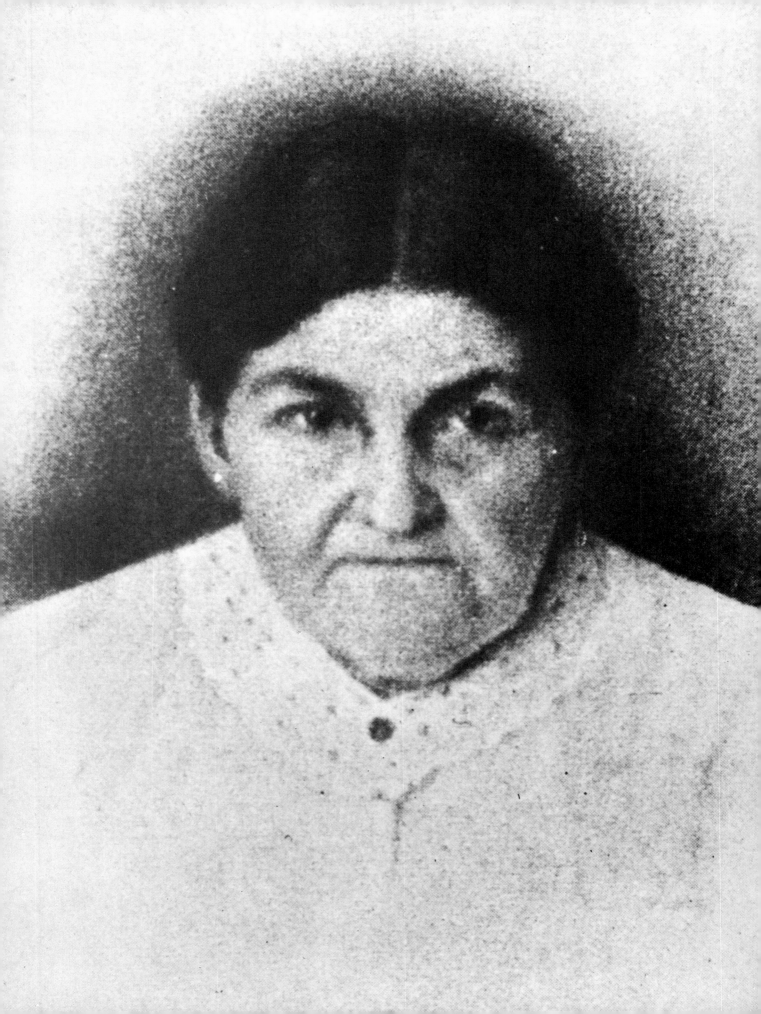

Louise Wilhelmine Mencken

OTTO VON BISMARCK
(1815-98)
Prussian statesman, known as
the "Iron Chancellor."

Louise Wilhelmine Mencken was a childhood playmate of the future King Frederick William IV of Prussia, though she herself was not an aristocrat. She came of an upper-class family that had produced professors and lawyers; her father was a senior Court official, an intelligent man with liberal views. She was born on February 24, 1790 and, while her father remained in office, was brought up in the atmosphere of the Court. Both her parents died when she was young, and at the age of sixteen she married Ferdinand von Bismarck, a landowner and aristocrat.

Wilhelmine's husband was typical of his class, having served as a cavalry officer before settling down to manage his estates. She bore six children – four sons and two daughters – but only three of them survived infancy. Otto, born in 1815, was her fourth child.

Wilhelmine is described as having a flair for elegance – she was a gay, handsome figure at the fashionable Berlin balls. But she was also an intelligent, serious-minded woman. She was very religious, and believed strongly in education and culture. (Higher education, she once said, would, "of its own accord, one day lead us to God.") She directed much of her attention toward Otto, for whom she had great ambitions and foresaw, with remarkable prescience, a career in diplomacy. She earned his lifelong resentment when she sent him away to school in order to "break his aristocratic pride."

Otto's subsequent behavior was perhaps a characteristic reaction to maternal pressures. He chose to go on not to a Prussian but to a Hanoverian University – at Göttingen – and there distinguished himself not only in heavy beer drinking and frequent fighting of duels, but by remarkable eccentricities of behavior. All this distressed Wilhelmine greatly, for she feared that her ambitions for her son were being dashed. Yet he did well in his examinations, became a lawyer, and entered the service of the State.

Wilhelmine died of cancer on New Year's Day, 1839, when Otto was not yet twenty-five. She did not live to see what would become of the dreams she had for her son.

Right A sentimentalized view of Wilhelmine, published long after her death.
Page 32 The room in which Wilhelmine gave birth to her son, Otto; Wilhelmine in a 19th-century popular press illustration; and an allegorical postcard of her son – the "Iron Chancellor" – forging the unity of Germany.

31

Bismarcks Geburtszimmer in Schönhausen.

Otto von Bismarck.

Maria Concepcion Palacios y Blanco

Doña Maria Concepcion Palacios y Blanco was born in Caracas, Venezuela, in 1759. She came of a highly aristocratic Creole family, with a former Captain General of Venezuela among her ancestors. When she married at the age of fourteen, Maria Concepción brought little to the marriage. The Palacios were no longer wealthy and her dowry consisted only of two young female slaves.

The man she married was forty-six-year-old Don Juan Vicente Bolívar y Ponte. He was a descendant of Simón de Bolívar, one of the first Procurators of the colony appointed by the King of Spain and ranked as a *conquistador,* in recognition of which his male heirs bore the title of *Capitán poblador* (Captain populator or settler). He brought to the marriage a fortune of over a quarter of a million pesos, in addition to many estates and plantations. From the export of the plantation produce and the import of manufactured goods which he then sold in his own warehouse and shop, his income was more than enough to maintain him as a leading member of the Creole aristocracy. But the shop was conducted under the name of its manager, for no aristocrat could sully his hands with trade.

It is not easy to recapture the atmosphere of colonial Caracas in the mid-1700s. The small enclosed society of Caracas, a city of some 40,000 people, was headed by the high officials sent from Spain and the Creole aristocracy, which looked down on the Spanish immigrants who were mostly traders. There were some 37,000 freemen, and a few thousand black slaves. Etiquette was rigid and deference to rank absolute.

Doña Concepcion, as she came to be known when she was married, was typical of her age and society. Her life was ruled by her Catholic faith and loyalty to the Spanish Crown. She occasionally attended morning receptions to kiss the hand of the Captain General and was part of his suite at High Mass in the Cathedral. As a child, her first duty every morning had been to kneel before her father and mother to receive their blessing and kiss their hands. She brought up her four children to do the same.

Her first daughter was born when she was eighteen; the next two years later. Her first son, named Juan Vicente after his father, was born when she was twenty-two, and her youngest, Simón José Antonio, two years later, in 1783. Her husband died in 1786. The family and the family fortune were left in her care and in the care of her father, Feliciano Palacios. From the age of

nearly six until he was nine, Simón was exclusively under the control of his widowed mother.

Doña Concepcion was a practical woman and managed the family estates well. But though firm of mind, she was poor in health. She died in July, 1792 at the age of thirty-three. Her father, Feliciano Palacios, remained in sole control of the Bolivar family and fortune. Doña Concepción's will was simple: she cared for the Palacios family, ensured adequate fortunes for her two daughters, and left the bulk of her husband's estate to her elder son, Juan Vicente. She had no cause to worry about Simón, her youngest child: his uncle, a priest who had baptized him, had willed to him all of a considerable fortune. Simón Bolívar was nine when his mother died. In 1825 he wrote to his sister concerning his wet nurse, a slave named Hipolita: ". . . give her all she wants and deal with her as if she were my mother; her milk fed my life, and I know no other father than she."

SIMÓN BOLÍVAR
(1783-1830)
Venezuelan revolutionary leader instrumental in freeing much of South America from Spanish rule.

Below The home in Caracas from which Doña Concepción controlled the family estates.

GIOVANNOZZA ·DEI·CATANEI·

LUCREZIA BORGIA
(1480-1519)
Infamous for her scandalous life, which involved incestuous relations, illegitimate children, and murder by poisoning.

When Giovannozza dei Catanei died in 1518 she left so much money to the church where she was buried that 200 years later the Augustinian monks were still saying Masses for her soul.

Vanozza (as she was always called) was born in 1442 into a middle-class Roman family. Some time between 1459 and 1475 she became the mistress of Rodrigo Borgia. Rodrigo was the nephew of Pope Calixtus III and a beneficiary of his nepotism. He was made a Cardinal at twenty-five, Vice-Chancellor of the Church of Rome only a year later, and in 1492 became Pope Alexander VI. Rodrigo was well known for his skill as a lawyer and administrator; for his worldliness, ruthlessness and dynastic ambition; and for his great love of women.

Historians disagree about how many children Vanozza had by him. Those positively identified are Cesare (born 1476 and made Duke of Romagna), Lucrezia (born 1480), Giovanni (second Duke of Gandia), and Goffredo (Prince of Squillace). She may also have had three other children previously, which would mean that she became Rodrigo's mistress before she was twenty. Their final break did not come until 1482, when she was already forty years old, and even then Rodrigo still honored her as the mother of his children. Their illegitimacy was no problem: it was an age of bastards.

During all this Vanozza had three or four husbands. The first was an elderly lawyer, another was apostolic secretary to Pope Sixtus IV. The last, Carlo Canale, was a Mantuan humanist of some note. Rodrigo found him for Vanozza after their own relationship was over. Canale was so proud of his position that he quartered the Borgia arms with his own.

As Vanozza's children grew up, they were first taken from her and then became caught up in Rodrigo's dynastic intrigues. Vanozza kept apart from this – or was kept apart from it – and was never a figure in Court or Vatican life. But she held her children's and Rodrigo's affection and with Rodrigo's help she purchased a vineyard and country villa, bought and sold houses, managed a large pawnbroking business, and became lessee of three popular Roman inns.

The last time Vanozza was in the limelight was in 1497, when her son, the Duke of Gandia, was killed. After a family dinner party at Vanozza's he vanished into the night with a masked man, and was found two days later when they dragged the Tiber. He had nine knife wounds, his throat was cut, his hands were tied, and a stone was bound to his neck. An Italian epigrammist flayed the worldly Spanish Pope who had just lost the center of all his hopes: "Lest we should not think thee a fisher of men, lo, thou fishest for thine own son with nets."

Like Lucrezia, Vanozza was genuinely religious. She spent much of her fortune on charity – though one litigant called her "a devilish woman." She suffered whenever the Borgia fortunes fell. The French looted her home in 1495, and in 1503, after Rodrigo's death, she had to leave Rome to flee from the Orsini family.

Vanozza died in 1518 and was buried in the same church as Giovanni, the murdered Duke of Gandia. The funeral was a magnificent affair: Pope Leo X sent his own Chamberlain, and Vanozza was carried in splendor almost worthy of a Cardinal. Her long life and piety had won her respectability. But later generations destroyed her tomb, and she was submerged again into the ugly Borgia legend. She wrote her own just memorial in her manner of signing her letters to Lucrezia: "The fortunate and unfortunate Vanozza Borgia de Catheneis." It was a more apt epitaph than that written by the University of Bologna on the diploma of their former student Rodrigo Borgia: "Died 1503. And buried in Hell."

Right A contemporary painting of Giovannozza.

Maria Branwell

THE BRONTE SISTERS
Three remarkable English sisters: Charlotte (1816-55), author of *Jane Eyre*; Emily (1818-48), author of *Wuthering Heights*; and Anne (1820-49), author of *The Tenant of Wildfell Hall*.

Maria Branwell was born on April 15, 1783, the third daughter of Penzance merchant Thomas Branwell and his wife Anne, who bore eleven children. Both Thomas and Anne were staunch Wesleyans.

In 1812, some years after her parents had died, Maria left Penzance to stay with her uncle, the Reverend John Fennell, in the West Riding of Yorkshire. It was there that the twenty-nine-year-old Maria met Patrick Brontë. Patrick, a big, striking-looking Irishman, had packed a wealth of experience into his thirty-five years. He had been a blacksmith's apprentice at twelve and had then worked as a weaver, a teacher, and a tutor before enrolling at St John's College, Cambridge when he was twenty-five. He received his B.A. in 1806 and then took holy orders.

Patrick was tall and strong, loquacious and confident, handsome and evidently vain. He was everything that Maria — gentle, unassuming, and plain — was not. They complemented one another perfectly. They also shared a talent for writing. Patrick's father had been a celebrated story-spinner in his county in Ireland, holding forth around the turf fire, spellbinding his family with weird and frightening tales. Patrick, who had something of his father's talent, wrote novels, poetry, sermons and pamphlets. Maria herself composed a religious tract called *The Advantages of Poverty in Religious Concerns*, which survived to be published a century afterwards.

Though Maria was quiet and refined, her feelings ran deep. "I am certain no one ever loved you with an affection more pure, constant, tender and ardent than that which I feel," she wrote to Patrick. "Surely this is not saying too much; it is the truth, and I trust you are worthy to know it. I long to improve in every religious and moral quality, that I may be a help, and if possible an ornament to you."

The newlyweds set up house in Hartshead, Yorkshire, where Maria had her first child and namesake in 1813, and a second daughter, Elizabeth, in 1815. Then they moved to Thornton, another parish near Bradford, where Charlotte was born in 1816, Branwell in 1817, Emily in 1818, and Anne in 1820.

In February 1820 the Brontës and their possessions arrived in a caravan of seven lumbering carts at Haworth, ten miles west of Bradford, to take up residence in the grey stone parsonage. Maria was never robust, and in the damp, bleak atmosphere of Haworth, she became seriously ill with cancer. She suffered for eight months' agonizing at the prospect of abandoning her precious children, and finally questioning the faith she and Patrick had always served. She died on September 15, 1821, aged thirty-eight. Maria's eldest sister, Elizabeth, came to Haworth and the Brontës' aid. Under her wing, the girls' talents blossomed, although Patrick suffered greatly from the loss of his wife.

Right The parsonage at Haworth, now a museum; and a portrait of Maria that may be seen there.

Agnes Broun

Agnes Broun was born on March 17, 1732. Her father, Gilbert, was a tenant-farmer at Kirkoswald near the coast in southwest Ayrshire (Scotland). When Agnes was ten, her mother died and the girl was left to cope with her father's household and his five younger children. Then two years later Gilbert remarried and Agnes went to live with her grandmother, a Mrs Rennie, at nearby Maybole. Grandma Rennie knew a wealth of old Scottish songs and Agnes, who had a good ear and a pleasing voice, doubtless passed many of them on to her own children.

Like most Scots girls of her class and time, Agnes was barely literate. She read with difficulty and she could not write at all. But she was shapely, personable, and shrewd, and she was a tireless worker about the house and farm. Her twinkling dark eyes concealed a hot and unruly temper which sometimes burst through the surface of her normally agreeable disposition. It was not long before a local ploughman, William Nelson, asked for her hand and was accepted. They were engaged for seven years, but eventually quarreled and parted.

Soon another admirer appeared. He was William Burns, head gardener on the neighboring estate of a wealthy Dr Fergusson. The articulate, austere, and ambitious William had quit his native Kincardine to find employment in the south. He was thirty-six and Agnes twenty-four when they married in December 1757. They lived in a clay cottage which his father had built for them with his own hands in the village of Alloway, a few miles south of Ayr.

In January, 1759 their first child, Robert, entered a hard world and a household plagued by debt and bad luck. The weather was inauspiciously stormy when he was born. A few days after his arrival high winds blew out part of the gable of their cottage.

In 1765 William, tired of tending a rich man's garden, leased Mount Oliphant farm, a few miles west of Alloway, but was unable to make it pay. By 1771 he and Agnes had seven young mouths to feed and a growing burden of debt. "We lived very sparingly," wrote Robert's brother Gilbert. "For several years, butcher's meat was a stranger in the house." Robert remembered their life at Mount Oliphant as: "The chearless [sic] gloom of a hermit with the unceasing moil of a galley-slave." After twelve years of unprofitable and joyless toil, the family moved to Lochlie farm ten miles to the northeast. But their ill-fortune moved with them and, on February 13, 1784, after a further seven years of failure and eventual bankruptcy, Agnes' husband was dead.

William's children had taken care to have their mother and themselves recognized as their father's employees. By this device they escaped responsibility for his debts and were even treated as preferential creditors. Robert and Gilbert were thus able to lease another farm from a friend, Gavin Hamilton, and to move from Lochlie with some cash in hand. As tenant-farmers, however, they were no more successful than their father.

Despite her lifelong family worries and privations, Agnes lived to the age of eighty-eight, sustained by an annuity of five pounds that Robert settled on her out of a loan he made to Gilbert. She died at Grant's Braes, Gilbert's home in East Lothian, in January 1820, and was buried in the churchyard of Bolton.

ROBERT BURNS
(1759-96)
Recognized as Scotland's national poet. Two of his poems – "Coming through the Rye" and "Auld Lang Syne" – are now better known as songs.

Left Probable likeness of Agnes (there is no verified portrait of the poet's mother).

CATHERINE GORDON

GEORGE GORDON, LORD BYRON
(1788-1824)
English poet, famous for such works as *Childe Harold* and *Don Juan*.

Even in youth, Catherine Gordon of Gight (Scotland) was no beauty. She was stout and small, long in the nose, and fleshy about the jowls. Her accent was coarse, her temper violent. But when Captain John Byron met the nineteen-year-old orphan early in 1784, she offered attractions more tangible than a pretty face and a mellifluous voice. She was worth £23,000, and he was penniless. His beautiful, titled wife had recently died in childbirth. What was worse, her £4,000-a-year income had perished with her.

The couple were married in May, 1784, and went to live at Catherine's estate in Aberdeenshire, Scotland. Here the dissolute Captain shocked the neighbors with his drunken revels, and the dumpy Catherine, decked in tasteless finery, inspired their derisive song:

> *O whaur are ye ga'en, bonny Miss Gordon?*
> *O whaur are ye ga'en sae bonny and braw?*
> *Ye've married, ye've married wi' Johnny*
>   *Byron,*
> *To squander the lands of Gight awa'.*

Catherine's fortune proved no match for her husband's reckless spending, and in 1787 the estate had to be sold.

To escape their creditors, they sailed to France. There John began a new round of profligacy while she strove to bring up his daughter, Augusta. When Catherine's own child was on the way, Augusta was placed in her natural mother's family and Catherine took lodgings in London. On January 22, 1788 her son, George Gordon, was born. All she had left of her money was £150 a year. It was enough for her own needs — but not for Mad Jack's as well. He was accumulating debts as recklessly as ever. Almost destitute, Catherine left London, and took rooms in Aberdeen.

George, handsome but lame, grew up there amid rows, reproaches and flying plates, as his mother became more embittered by poverty. Toward the end of 1790, his father fled back to France where, in the summer of 1791, he died. "I ever sincerely loved him," wrote Catherine to Augusta. Continuing poverty worsened Catherine's unpredictable humor. Young George suffered blows and kisses in quick succession.

In 1794 their fortunes took an unexpected upward turn when Lord Byron's son was killed in Corsica. Suddenly Catherine's son was heir to the peerage. In 1798 his great-uncle died. The title and the property were George's. Since George was a minor, his inheritance was administered by the Court of Chancery and, in spite of their new status, he and his mother still had only £150 a year. The family seat, Newstead Abbey, proved to be dilapidated and filthy. Catherine was obliged to take lodgings in nearby Nottingham.

Later she was granted a pension of £300 a year, and they moved to London where her whiskied breath, raucous speech, and fishwife's appearance repelled the elegant Earl of Carlisle, now George's guardian. The boy, highly sensitive, nurtured scorn for his fat, ugly little harridan of a mother. Barely a day passed without her cries and crockery ricocheting round the rooms. "Her conduct is so strange . . . her passions so outrageous," wrote George, "the evil quite overbalances her agreeable qualities."

After schooling at Harrow, George went to Cambridge University where he cut an extravagant figure but did little work. "That boy will be the death of me," his mother wrote, on hearing of his reckless spending. When he came home at the end of term she hurled the fire-tongs at him. He was over £3,000 in debt when, at twenty-one, he became master of his own fortune.

Leaving for the Continent, he stayed abroad for two years and returned to England only because creditors were threatening. Catherine, now forty-six, learned he was in London and remarked, "If I should die before Byron comes down, what a strange thing it would be!" A few days later, after a passionate protest over an upholsterer's bill, she had a stroke and died. It was August 1, 1811.

"My poor mother died yesterday," George wrote to a friend. "Peace be with her." Arriving at Newstead, he sat beside Catherine's body, sighing pitifully through the night. When a servant entered the room where he was keeping his vigil, Byron burst into tears. "I had but one friend in the world," he said, bursting into tears, to a servant who found him keeping his vigil, "and she is gone!"

Right Catherine Gordon of Gight.

TERESA CAPONE

Teresa Capone left Italy in 1893 with her husband Gabriel and their first son, to settle in New York City. There she brought up her family in an apartment on Navy Street, amidst the noisy confusion of Brooklyn's Italian colony. For rents of $3 to $4.50 a month, families lived in one-room apartments without bath or hot water. Teresa did some dressmaking and had a child about once every three years. Gabriel Capone first failed as a grocer, then succeeded with a barber shop.

Gabriel died in 1920, aged fifty-two, and Teresa's fourth son, Alfonse, took over the family's welfare. "Al" was beginning to be a success in the Chicago underworld, and he was soon able to bring his family — mother first — to live with him in Chicago. They lived in a large house that Al had built in a quiet suburb. The basement walls were of reinforced concrete one foot thick, and the windows had close-set bars. Al lived on the ground floor with his mother, two sisters, his wife and son. Upstairs lived his brother Ralph with his wife and children. Three policemen owned houses on the same block.

Like all the family, Teresa loved to make nostalgic trips back to Brooklyn. When she went back — an austere figure in black silk — Al arranged for one of his New York colleagues to provide her with a chauffeur, a bodyguard, and a bulletproof Cadillac.

The major crisis in Al Capone's life came in 1931, when the state managed to find a charge on which he could be brought to trial: tax evasion. When he was found guilty, his mother came down to see him with a huge dish of macaroni with tomato sauce and cheese. He was sent to the Atlanta Penitentiary, and when she visited him there she could only gaze at him and mumble a few broken words, because foreign languages were forbidden.

Later he was transferred to the new high-security prison at Alcatraz. When she first came to see him there, she set off the alarm buzzer every time she passed through the security check. Eventually they found the reason: the metal straps on her old-fashioned corset. Al Capone whiled away the time in Alcatraz learning to read music and improvise on the banjo. He composed a song called "Mother."

"He's mother's life," his sister Mafalda once said. Teresa was there when Al died — a free man and in bed — on January 25, 1947. She died in 1952, at the age of eighty-five, and was buried near the son about whom she had always insisted: "Al's a good boy."

AL CAPONE
(1899-1947)
A leading gangster in Chicago in the 1920s.

Left Teresa with her son, Al – a photograph from the files of the *Chicago Tribune.*

43

LINA GONZALES

In the sugar boom of the First World War, many Cubans left their homes to migrate across the island to the wild sugarcane country of the east. Among those who migrated was Lina Gonzalez, a girl from the town of Pinar del Rio whose parents had come to Cuba from Spain. She took work as a cook and serving-girl on the farm of Angel Castro y Argez, who had come to Cuba with the Spanish army in the Spanish-American war. His plantation was near the north coast of Oriente Province, fifty miles from Santiago de Cuba. Starting with nothing, he had somehow prospered in the confusion that followed the end of Spanish rule. He profited further from the Cuban revolution of 1917, when United Fruit Company land found its way into his plantation.

Angel had two children by his marriage to a schoolteacher, but this did not prevent him making Lina his mistress. She had five children by him. The third, born on August 13, 1926, was named Fidel.

Eventually his first wife died, and Angel married Lina. This may indirectly have been Fidel's doing. There is a story that, when he was six or seven, he threatened to burn down the house if he was not sent to school; his father found him a place in a Jesuit school, but had to marry Fidel's mother to placate the priests.

The plantation grew to 23,000 acres, with 500 employees. Fidel later called his father "a wealthy landowner who exploited the peasants." Angel died in 1956, before his son came to power. Lina was closely tied to her son emotionally, but matched her husband's conservatism and her love of possessions, and was also a pious Catholic. In 1957, while her son was still struggling through a difficult guerrilla war in the hills, Lina Castro made a visit to Mexico — and while she was there she complained to a group of her son's supporters that her cane fields, like many others, had been burned by the guerrillas. She asked for the plantation to be left alone; but they were not impressed when she said that the officers of Batista, then Cuba's President, sometimes called in for coffee.

She genuinely loved her son but she hated his politics. In 1959 she was enraged by the agrarian reform that nationalized all big estates, including that of the Castros. And in the most difficult years for Fidel's regime, 1962-63, she helped her youngest daughter Juana in doing as much damage to Fidel as she could. Despite all this, when she died in 1965 Fidel seems genuinely to have mourned.

FIDEL CASTRO
(1926-)
Communist leader of Cuba since 1959.

Left Protest march by the "mothers of Cuba" against the assassination of their sons during the dictatorship of Batista. Lina, however, hated the revolutionary politics of her son, Fidel.

45

Mrs Charles Hill Chaplin

CHARLES CHAPLIN
(1889-)
World-famous English
comedian and film director.
Among his many well-known
films are *The Kid, The Gold
Rush,* and *The Great Dictator.*

We do not know the maiden name of Charles Chaplin's mother. She was the daughter of an Irish cobbler and a woman who was half Gypsy. After leaving school she went on the stage and performed as a soubrette under the name of Lily Harley. At the age of eighteen, she eloped to Africa with a middle-aged man who was said to be a lord.

Despite a life of luxury, she soon returned to England and married Charles Hill Chaplin, with whom she had acted a year or two earlier. The marriage took place in 1886, and ended four years later. There were two sons, Sydney and Charles.

For while after her marriage ended Mrs Chaplin continued her stage career. She earned £25 a week, which was then big money, and Charles's very early years in south London were spent in middle-class comfort and prosperity. Unfortunately, his mother's voice had always been weak and now began to crack. Audiences who had once worshipped her now began to laugh and boo as she struggled, unable to control her voice, through her songs. At a theater in Aldershot, her performance was so bad that she had to leave the stage. Charles, then five years old, was waiting in the wings. He went on in her place, sang one of her songs, and brought the house down. It was his first stage appearance and his mother's last.

Mrs Chaplin's money soon ran out. She pawned her jewels and desperately sought some way of earning a living. But she knew about little other than the theater. She did have, however, one other skill. She had always made her own theatrical costumes, so she hired a sewing machine and made a pittance sewing blouses. And a pittance it was. One week she sewed fifty-four blouses and earned one shilling and sixpence. Alimony payments were erratic, and she and her two sons were so poor that sometimes the sewing machine was taken away because she was unable to pay the installments. For a time she hoped that her voice would improve, and that she would be able to return to the stage. But eventually it became obvious that this would not happen, and she finally admitted that her stage career was over when she sold all her theatrical costumes.

Despite poverty in an attic in south London, she was fun to live with. She entertained her children with impersonations of famous historical characters such as Nell Gwyn and Napoleon. She knew a great deal about acting technique and was fascinating on the subject of why various actors

and music hall artists were good or bad. She insisted that her children speak well and grammatically and, having become very religious herself, she took them regularly to church. She often managed to produce a cake or a few sweets from somewhere, and once a week she bought a penny's worth of flowers.

But she began to suffer from migraine; some days she was in too much distress to be able to work. Once more her sewing machine was taken away because of non-payment of installments, and now she was not merely poor but destitute. There was nothing she could do except report to the workhouse, where her children were separated from her and subsequently sent to a school for the children of impoverished families. In time she resumed her normal life, only to face an even worse problem — insanity. She was sent to an asylum but managed to recover sufficiently to be released. She immediately resumed her grim existence of sewing, poverty, and trips to the pawnbroker.

There was a modest improvement in the family's financial position when Sydney left school and found work as a telegraph boy, and soon Charles was earning a few coppers as well. But life was still harsh — so much so that Mrs Chaplin began to suffer from malnutrition. Perhaps this contributed to her insanity. Charles came home one day and was told that his mother was delivering pieces of coal at all the neighboring houses. She was put into an asylum and was there for eighteen months, some of the time in a padded cell. She was let out briefly but soon relapsed and was found wandering in the street, distraught and incoherent. This time she never recovered.

Charles and Sydney went to see her in the asylum, where she had again been confined to a padded cell, this time after a noisy phase of compulsive hymn singing. She had been treated with ice-cold showers, and her face was blue. Fortunately, her two sons were beginning to earn enough on the stage to be able to send her to a private institution. Eventually, Charles took her to the United States where she lived until her death in the late 1920s.

Right Mrs Chaplin in London before 1900.
Pages 48-49 Mrs Chaplin in Charlie's garden in the United States in the 1920s.

JEANETTE JEROME

WINSTON CHURCHILL
(1874-1965)
British statesman and author.
Prime Minister of Great
Britain during the Second
World War.

In August 1873, the cruiser *HMS Ariadne* was guarding the approaches to Cowes, on England's Isle of Wight, where the glittering Royal Regatta was in progress. As part of the festivities, the ship's officers gave a ball. Among the guests was Jeanette Jerome, then nineteen years old, the pretty and vivacious daughter of a wealthy American businessman. Jeanette, her mother and sisters had been living in Paris when the Franco-Prussian War broke out in 1870, and were almost the last to escape from the city before it was besieged. Another guest was Lord Randolph Churchill, second son of the Duke of Marlborough. They met, and the attraction was mutual and immediate: he proposed, and three days later was accepted. "She is as nice, as lovable, and amiable and charming in every way as she is beautiful, and by her education and bringing-up she is in every way qualified to fill any position," wrote Lord Randolph to his father. At first the duke opposed the match, but he later relented.

The couple were married at the British Embassy in Paris on April 15, 1874. Their first child, Winston, was born prematurely seven months later at Blenheim, the family seat,

following what Lord Randolph called Jeanette's "imprudent and rough ride in a pony carriage."

One of the conditions that the Duke had exacted for approving the marriage was that Lord Randolph should enter politics. Lord Randolph accordingly became Member of Parliament for Woodstock, where Blenheim stands. From that moment Jeanette was a politician's wife, using her attractive personality to further her husband's career and sometimes, by her impetuosity, to impede it. But her enthusiasm was infectious and effective. Once, when she was canvasing for her husband by touring his district in a tandem bedecked with his racing colors, she inspired the following rhyme:

> *And before me stopped her horses*
> *As she marshalled all her forces,*
> *And before I knew what had happened I*
> *had promised her my vote;*
> *And before I quite recovered*
> *From the vision that had hovered,*
> *'twas much too late to rally, and I had*
> *changed my coat.*

Something of this dazzling effect is evident in a description of Jeanette at a grand diplomatic function held in Dublin. All eyes were turned on

Right Jeanette, Lady Randolph Churchill, photographed as a nursing volunteer; and two photographs with Winston, the future Prime Minister.
Pages 52-53 Jeanette with Winston and his younger brother, John.
Pages 54-55 Jeanette in youth and troubled middle age.

THE MEDICAL STAFF ON THE HOSPITAL SHIP "MAINE"

50

"a dark, lithe figure standing somewhat apart and appearing to be of another texture to those around her, radiant, translucent, intense. A diamond star in her hair, her favorite ornament — its luster dimmed by the flashing glory of her eyes. More of the panther than of the woman in her look, but with a cultivated intelligence unknown to the jungle."

Lady Churchill had become a member of the British aristocracy. She was a celebrated hostess, entertaining members of the Royal Family and a wide variety of other celebrated figures. When George Bernard Shaw was a young man she invited him to one of her gatherings. He rather brusquely declined, saying that it would be contrary to his habits to attend. She wittily replied, by telegram, "Know nothing of your habits. Hope they are better than your manners." While Lord Randolph's political success continued (he eventually became Chancellor of the Exchequer) she also stayed abreast of political events, often attending the House of Commons herself.

It was normal in the British aristocracy to entrust the upbringing of children to nannies and governesses, and Jeanette's busy life meant that she paid very little attention to her sons, Winston and John. Once, Winston wrote to her pathetically from Harrow, where he was at school: "Please do do do do do do come down to see me . . . I have been disappointed so many times about your coming." But Winston seems to have overcome any bitterness about childhood neglect, for his future mother-in-law wrote: "His mother and he are devoted to one another, and I think a good son makes a good husband."

The last years of the Churchills' marriage were marred by Lord Randolph's declining health, and the exciting life ended some time before his death, at the age of forty-five, in 1894. Not long after, Jeanette startled society by marrying a young man of Winston's age. The Marlboroughs loyally turned out for the wedding, but the groom's family was represented by the groom alone. This marriage ended in divorce and Jeanette was to marry a third time.

Jeanette died in 1921, after an accident in which her ankle became infected. She was sixty-seven years old. Winston Churchill wrote that "she had the gift of eternal youth," and she was described by the Liberal leader Asquith as "an amazing reservoir of vitality and gay, unflinching courage. I call her the last of the Victorians."

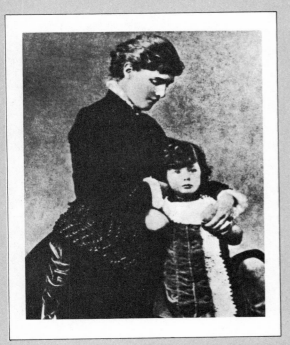

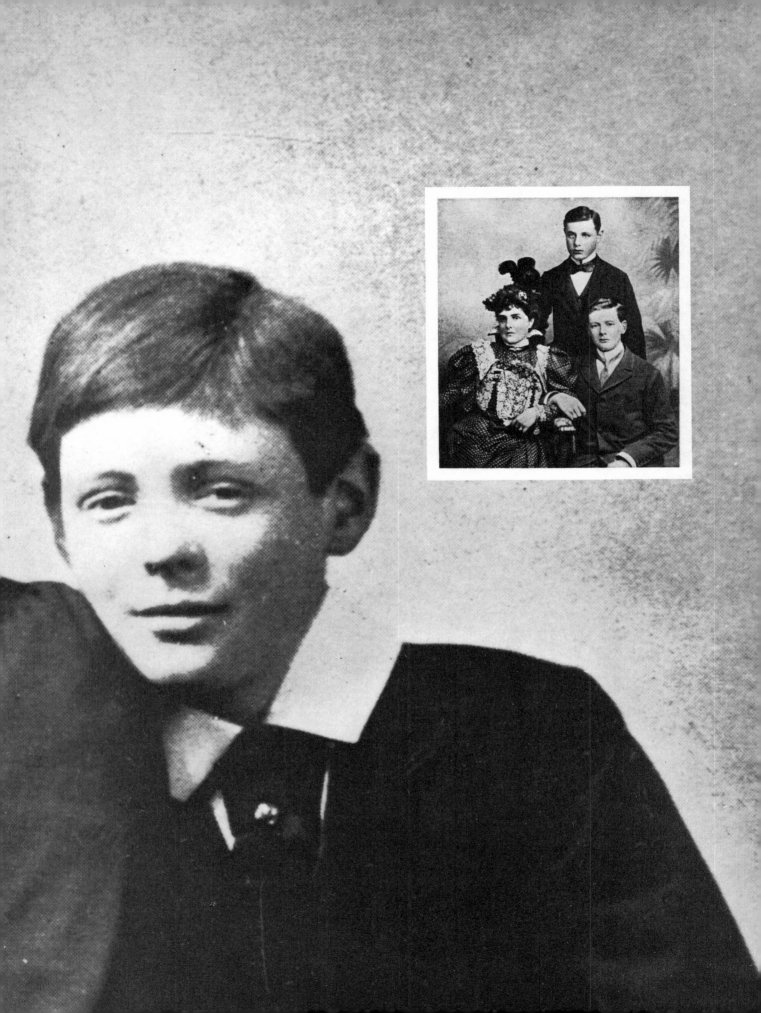

56

Adèle-Eugénie-Sidonie Colette

Few mothers of famous men and women have merited and received so much love and admiration from their offspring as Adèle-Eugénie-Sidonie did from her daughter Colette. Sidonie's parents died when she was still a child, and she spent the greater part of her girlhood with her married brothers in Belgium in a bohemian circle of journalists and artists. She was a lively and charming girl of eighteen when she met Robineau Duclos, a respectable French landowner. Duclos was an unlikely suitor for the young Sidonie: dour and taciturn, and much older than she. Nonetheless, in 1853 they were married and had two children — Juliette and Achille.

Sidonie was left a widow before she was thirty. She was still young and attractive, and in 1865 she was married again to a Captain Jules Joseph Colette, a *Zouave* officer who had lost a leg fighting against the Austrians in 1859. Captain Colette was passionately in love with the young widow and took her and her two children to live at a manor farm in Saint Sauveur en Puisaye some hundred miles southeast of Paris. There they lived in happiness and mutual love for a quarter of a century. They had a son, Léo, and in January 1873 a daughter, Sidonie Gabrielle, (the future writer Colette).

Sidonie admired her husband and later lamented that because his love for her was so great, he had neglected his talents to make her the center of his life. Sidonie loved and cared for her family with intense devotion. She also loved the natural beauty that surrounded her at Saint Sauveur. The more sophisticated pleasures of Paris attracted her but she could never live there, she said, unless she had a large garden.

Sidonie's letters also reveal a literary talent and, in later years, a capacity for literary appreciation and a sharp critical faculty.

But Sido (as she is sometimes known) was not without troubles. Her husband lost the family fortune, and in 1890 the manor farm at Saint Sauveur was sold. The family moved to the house of the eldest son Achille, by then married and established as a doctor in the nearby town of Châtillon Coligny. Sido and her family must have missed the house at Saint Sauveur, of which Colette wrote an almost lyrical description in *La Maison de Claudine.*

Within three years, Sidonie Gabrielle Colette had married Henri Gauthier-Villars of the firm of Gauthier-Villars et Fils, leading scientific publishers in Paris, with whom her father's interests brought him into contact. For Sido the departure of her daughter must have been a greater grief than the loss of the house at Saint Sauveur. But she was as resilient by nature as she was gay; and she was tolerant besides. There is no record of reproach when her daughter was divorced from Gauthier-Villars, or when she formed a scandalous relationship with "Missy," the Marquise de Belboeuf. But if Sido was tolerant of such "shocking" behavior, she was not so charitable toward narrow puritanical views. Before visiting her daughter Juliette and her son-in-law, she said that she dreaded staying in so restricted a circle with people "who believe in hell." She went on: "and, dear God, it is I who brought this child into the world."

In 1905 Captain Colette died, but Sido did not allow her grief to destroy her spirit. Her love of nature, for one thing, stayed with her to the end. When already over seventy and suffering from arthritis, she declined an invitation to visit Paris, not on account of her age and infirmities but because of a greenhouse cactus; it was said to flower only once in four years and was about to bloom. It might be, she wrote, the last chance she would have to see it.

Sidonie died in the autumn of 1912.

SIDONIE GABRIELLE COLETTE
(1873-1954)
French author who wrote under the name of "Colette". Her books include *Gigi* and *Chérie.*

Left
Adèle-Eugénie-Sidonie — affectionately called Sido by her famous daughter, Colette.

Marya Sklodowska (Marie Curie)

IRENE JOLIOT-CURIE
(1897-1956)
She and her husband,
Frédéric Joliot, won the Nobel
Prize for chemistry in 1935
for their work on radioactivity.

Marya Sklodowska was born in Warsaw, Poland, on November 7, 1867. She was the youngest of five children of Vladislav Sklodowski, a professor of mathematics and physics. Her mother died when she was eleven; this was a particularly grievous time in a childhood dominated by the hated rule of the Russians. Marya excelled at her school work. At the age of seventeen she took a job as a governess to help pay for her elder sister Bronya's medical studies. She stayed in this work for six years until Bronya, who was living in Paris, had passed her exams and was married. Then Marya too went to Paris, to begin her scientific studies.

In Paris Marya adopted the French form of her name, Marie. She studied all hours of the day and night, living in a small room without heat, light or water, and with the barest of furnishings. With only 100 francs a month to live on, she drank tea and ate bread and butter, and almost starved to death. During this period she met Pierre Curie, then engaged in teaching and research at the Sorbonne. He loved her at once, but Marie was dedicated to her work and scarred by an unhappy love affair in her governess days. She hesitated a long time before finally agreeing to marry him.

The Curies' marriage proved an ideal partnership. They were able to work together, sharing the triumphs and disappointments of research as soon as Marie had secured a fellowship that allowed her to work in France. For relaxation they spent hours on bicycles in the countryside. In 1897 Marie gave birth to their first child, Irène. Pierre's father, a doctor, delivered the child, and a few months later came to live with the couple. The following year Marie undertook doctoral study on the radiations produced by the substance that she was to name radium. In 1903 Marie received her doctorate and shared with Becquerel and Pierre the Nobel Prize for Physics. The following year Pierre became a professor at the Sorbonne, with Marie as his chief assistant. Their second child, Eve,

was born that year. The Curies hated fame, shunned company, and plunged deeper into their work. Then, sixteen months after Eve's birth, Pierre was struck and killed by a passing wagon.

Marie was desolated but still courageous enough to refuse a pension: "I am young enough to earn my living." The authorities at the Sorbonne enabled her to do so by breaking with traditional sex discrimination and appointing her to Pierre's post — no woman had ever before held such a post at the university. She was greatly helped at this time by her father-in-law, now aged seventy-nine but a tower of strength to her. During the next few years she isolated pure radium and published a fundamental treatise on radiation. Her work brought her the Nobel Prize for Chemistry in 1911 (she was the first person to receive two Nobel awards). In the next year she survived a serious illness and a spite of rumors about her morals. And in 1914 the Sorbonne completed building the Institute of Radium, constructed specially to provide a laboratory for this remarkable woman's work. Much of her earlier work had been carried out in a small, damp shed.

Marie Curie spent the First World War experimenting in the new science of radiology, X-raying wounded men, and teaching the technique to others. When the war ended, she devoted her energies to the Radium Institute, where she was assisted by Irène, now also dedicated to the study of radiation. In 1932 she had the satisfaction of seeing the Institut de Radium in Warsaw opened in her now liberated country, with Bronya as director. Honors and medals were showered on her, but Marie remained as she had always been — quiet, a little sad, and immersed in her work. She died in 1934 from leukemia which was brought on by exposure to the radiation she had given her life to studying. A few months earlier she had seen Irène and her husband, Frédéric Joliot-Curie, discover artificial radioactivity.

Right Work and pleasure
for Marie and Pierre Curie,
the discoverers of radium.
Page 60-61 Marie in her
laboratory in Paris.

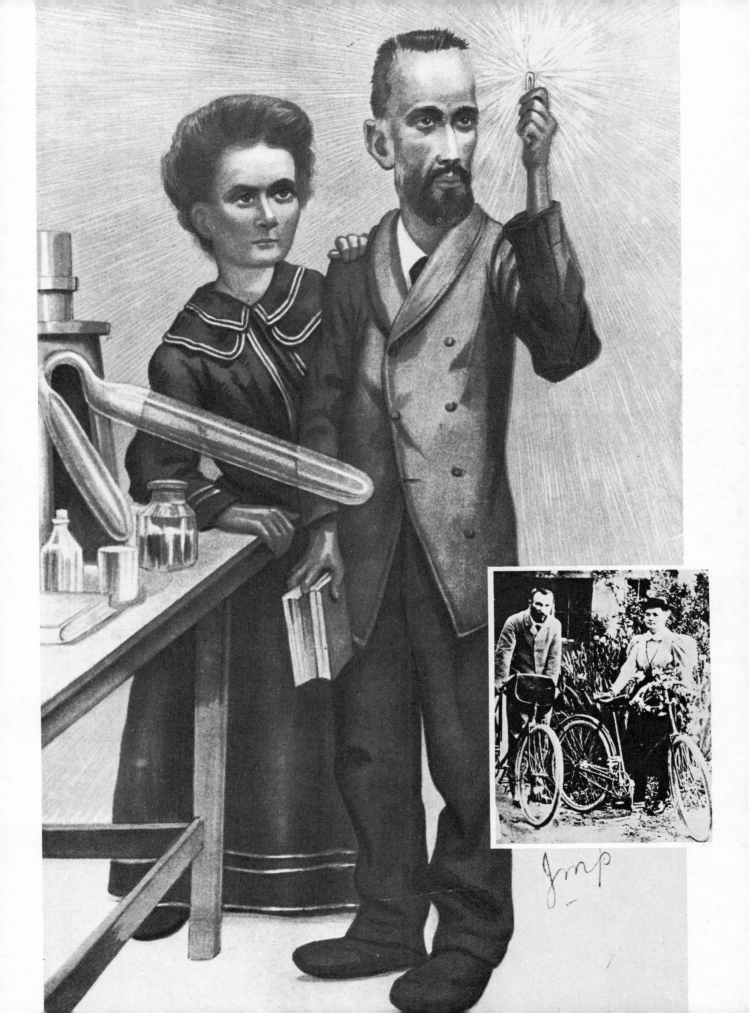

SUSANNAH WEDGWOOD

CHARLES DARWIN
(1809-82)
British naturalist whose books
The Origin of Species and *The Descent of Man* revolutionized thinking about evolution.

Susannah Wedgwood was the eldest daughter of Josiah Wedgwood, founder of the style of pottery that still bears his name, and Sarah Wedgwood, Josiah's third cousin. Susannah was born in 1765 and was followed by three sisters and three brothers.

Josiah and Sarah were loving, conscientious parents. They took great care in their children's education and created in their home an atmosphere of comfort and affection. A sense of this is conveyed in the family portrait, painted in 1785.

In 1796 Susannah married Robert Darwin, the youngest son of poet and naturalist Erasmus Darwin. The two families had been good friends for many years, and Susannah had known Robert from childhood. They had six children, all of whom were strong and healthy.

But childbearing seems to have strained Susannah's health, and after the birth of Emily, the youngest child, she became an invalid. From that time until her death in 1817 she took little part in family life. Charles Darwin, the great biologist, was eight when his mother died. He remembered almost nothing of her, "except her death-bed, her black velvet gown, and her curiously constructed night-table."

Right Painting by George Stubbs of the Wedgwood family (with Susannah riding side saddle).

ELIZABETH BARROW

CHARLES DICKENS
(1812-70)
English novelist. His works
include *Oliver Twist, David
Copperfield,* and *A Tale of
Two Cities.*

Elizabeth Barrow was about sixteen when she met her brother's friend John Dickens, who had a clerk's post in the Navy Pay Office in London. She was "small and pretty with bright hazel eyes, a strong sense of the ludicrous and a good mimic, cheerful and well educated." They fell in love and in 1809 were married. She was just twenty. John Dickens felt that he had moved up the social ladder, for his parents were domestic servants, while Elizabeth's father had an important post in the Navy Office.

At first, the Dickens family prospered. They lived for a time in Portsea, where Elizabeth gave birth to her first two children, Fanny and Charles. When Charles was born, in the dawn of February 7, 1812, Elizabeth had just returned from attending a ball. John was later posted to Chatham, where Elizabeth became the mistress of a three-story house and two servants.

John Dickens persistently lived beyond his income and, with the addition of three more children to the family, their financial situation became strained. In 1822 John was transferred back to London, and they had to move into a cramped little terraced house in Camden Town, at that time a suburban area.

The family's fortunes continued to decline. First books, then household articles were sold to pay tradesmen's bills, and eventually John Dickens was sent to Marshalsea Prison for debt. Some idea of Elizabeth's optimistic but scatterbrained character is gained from the fact that, to overcome their difficulties, she took a house at a high rent and opened a school. But as Dickens later sadly wrote, "Nobody ever came to the school, nor do I recollect that anyone ever proposed to come, or that the least preparation was made to receive anybody."

Charles, only twelve years old, was sent to work in a blacking factory for a few shillings a week. He was desperately anxious to continue his education, and he loathed the factory work. His father took him away from the factory but, wrote Charles, "I never shall forget that my mother was warm for my being sent back." This left a lifelong bitterness against her. Elizabeth, of course, failed to recognize her son's potential and emphasized the overwhelming importance to her, of his few shillings wages. When Dickens became successful, he many times paid off his father's debts and maintained his parents, but he wrote that "no mother's self-denying love, no father's counsel aided me."

Despite the terrible, wearing years of constantly threatening disaster, Elizabeth seems to have retained some of her youthful gaiety. Dickens wrote of her when she was sixty-four,

"My mother has a strong objection to being considered in the least old, and usually appears on Christmas Day in a juvenile cap which takes an immense time in the putting on." And three years before her death in 1863, he wrote bitterly, "My mother who was left to me when my father died (I never had anything left to me but relations) is in the strangest state of mind from senile decay: the impossibility of getting her to understand what is the matter, combined with her desire to be got up in sables like a female Hamlet, illumines the dreary scene with a ghastly absurdity that is the chief relief I can find in it."

From left to right Dickens family homes at Portsea, Chatham, and two in Camden Town, London (Ordnance Terrace and Bayham Street).
Pages 66-67 Painting and photographic portrait of Elizabeth — even in old age she loved to wear fancy clothes and hats.

NANCY ELLIOTT

THOMAS ALVA EDISON
(1847-1931)
American inventor, most famous for inventing the electric light. He patented more than 1100 inventions including the microphone and gramophone.

Below The house in Milan, Ohio, built for Nancy by her husband.
Right Nancy's portrait in the family home.

Nancy Elliott had unusual charm, strength of character, and courage in adversity. She was of Scottish, English, and Yankee descent, the daughter of the Baptist minister of the little township of Vienna in Ontario, Canada.

Nancy Elliott, as might be expected from the daughter of a Baptist minister, was deeply religious; her two brothers were also studying for the ministry. She taught in Vienna's little two-room school and had a deep love of learning. Marriage prospects in Vienna must have been limited, and Nancy's respectable family may have been a little startled when she was courted by and accepted the local tavernkeeper, Sam Edison. He was a Canadian, part Dutch and part English, who, before becoming tavernkeeper, had been a carpenter and a tailor.

Sam built a house with his own hands, and the couple spent the first years of their married life happily in Vienna. By 1836 Nancy had had four children, two girls and two boys. But in 1838 the family underwent a change, and a curious reversal of the Edison family's history took place. In that year some discontented colonists rebelled unsuccessfully against the government. Sam was one of the plotters, and troops were sent to arrest him. He, the son of Empire Loyalist who had fled from the United States, was forced to flee to that very country to take refuge.

There, in Milan, Ohio, he founded a lumber and grain business. It was only after a long separation that he was able to send for Nancy and the children. They crossed Lake Erie in a barge owned by Sam's friend Alva Bradley (from whom Thomas Edison got his second name). At Milan Sam built another house, in which were

born two more children who died in infancy, and, in February 1847, another son who survived. He was named Thomas Alva. Nancy was by then middle-aged, and adored her son from the moment he was born. He was declared to be very much like his mother in appearance, "with fair hair, large blue eyes and a round face."

When the boy was seven the family moved again, this time to Port Huron. Here Sam's business collapsed and Nancy took over the running of the family. Al, as Thomas Alva was called in the family, was sent to school, but his formal education lasted only about three months. One day he heard his teacher describe him as "addled" and was so hurt that he ran to tell his mother. Nancy was furious and told the schoolmaster that the child had more sense in his little finger than he had in his whole body, and took over the child's education herself.

There was a strong bond between mother and son, and she taught him to share her love of learning. She had the gift of making learning interesting, encouraged his intellectual curiosity and, soon realizing his interest in science, bought him a chemistry book when he was nine. She allowed him to conduct experiments in the cellar. Although she loved him dearly she did not spoil him, and Thomas was later to describe how she kept a birch switch behind the clock in the living room.

Thomas left home and made his own way in the world from the age of twelve, and he saw little of his mother from then on. But his love for her never waned. In 1870 he wrote to his parents: "I.C. Edison writes me that mother is not very well and that you have to work very hard. I guess you had better take it easy after this. Don't do any hard work and let mother have anything she desires. You can draw on me for money."

Nancy died, having declined into senility, at the age of sixty-two, on April 11, 1871. Edison knelt by her grave at the funeral. A childhood friend of his has left us this charming picture of her: "Mrs Edison loved every child in the neighborhood and used to meet us at the gate as we passed on our way to school with her hands full of apples, doughnuts, and other goodies."

A more profound tribute was paid by her famous son, who said in a newspaper interview: "With a mother of different mental caliber I should probably have turned out badly. But her firmness, her sweetness, her goodness were potent powers to keep me in the right path . . . . My mother was the making of me."

Pauline Koch

"Ulmenes sunt mathematici" ("The men of Ulm are mathematicians") says an ancient proverb. It was in Ulm, Germany that Albert Einstein was born in 1879.

He was descended from Swabian Jews, generations of small-town merchants and artisans. His maternal grandfather, Julius Koch-Berheimer, was a fairly prosperous grain merchant who rose to be Court Purveyor in the town of Bad Constatt. Julius's daughter Pauline was born on February 8, 1858. On August 8, 1876 she married Hermann Einstein, eleven years her senior and a businessman from the town of Ulm.

Hermann's family had lived in nearby Buchau until ten years before, and it was here that the two first set up home. Pauline was eighteen: a quiet, pleasant, broad-faced girl, with a mass of dark hair and no ambition for herself beyond the role of wife and mother. Nor could she have had great ambition for her husband. He was a very ordinary, good-natured, perpetually optimistic man, fond of beer and good food, and of country walks. But she did have ambitions for her son; she predicted always that he would be a great man.

After a year in Buchau the couple moved to Ulm. With money from Pauline's parents, Hermann set up a small electrical-engineering workshop. He and Pauline took an apartment at 135b Bahnhofstrasse, a nondescript four-story house, and here Albert Einstein was born on March 14, 1879. The house was destroyed by Allied bombing in 1944.

Hermann's business collapsed in 1880, and the family moved to Munich, where Hermann opened a small electrochemical works in partnership with his brother. They were to live here for fourteen years. In 1881 a daughter, Maja, was born. Hermann and Pauline quickly settled into a happy, devoted family routine. Both were freethinkers with little interest in traditional Judaism. Hermann spent his spare time on country walks and in taverns, and Pauline spent hers in artistic activities, especially music. She sometimes played the piano to entertain the engineers from Hermann's works.

From his mother Albert developed a precocious taste for classical music, and she started him on violin lessons at the age of six. Yet at other times she feared that her son was subnormal, for even by the age of nine his speech was not fluent. He also became, for a time, extremely religious. His religious enthusiasm passed when he discovered science, but the urge to go his own way remained.

When Albert was fifteen, in 1894, his father's business collapsed again. The family crossed the Alps to Italy and settled in Milan, leaving Albert behind at his school. He was expected to take his diploma, go to a university, and enter electrical engineering. Albert, however, didn't go along with this plan. He escaped from school after six months, joined his family in Milan, renounced his German citizenship, and then wandered and studied, a stateless person, before going to the Swiss Federal Polytechnic School at Zurich.

Pauline was living in Lucerne, Switzerland, when her son wired her the news of the first empirical confirmation of his theories. That was in September, 1919. By then he knew that his mother was dying of cancer. Later that year she went to Berlin to spend her last weeks with Albert and she died there early in 1920. Einstein, it seems, always felt too much at one with the processes of life ever to be afraid of death; and once, in his detachment, he had said that there was no one in the world whose loss would cause him pain. Yet at her death, an observer noted that he wept "like other men."

ALBERT EINSTEIN
(1879-1955)
German-Swiss physicist who became an American citizen. He is most famous for his theory of relativity.

Left Pauline Koch, always a firm believer in her son's great future.

Ida Stover

DWIGHT EISENHOWER
(1890-1969)
Supreme Commander of the
Allied Forces in Europe during
the Second World War, the
first military commander of
NATO, and 34th President of
the United States (1953-61).

Ida Stover was born on May 1, 1862, at Mount Sidney, Virginia, in the Shenandoah Valley. At the time of her birth "Stonewall" Jackson was rallying his army, only a few miles away, for the assault on Richmond, one of the critical points in the Civil War. By the end of the war, the Shenandoah Valley had been devastated – its farms burned and its pastures ruined by the battling armies.

Ida's mother died when she was only four years old, and her father died when she was eleven, so Ida's early years were spent mainly at the home of her maternal grandfather, William Link. Higher education for women was still a rare thing in the 1880s, but Ida had resolved to go to college. She supplemented her small inheritance by working for a year as a teacher in a local school, and gathered enough money to take her to Lane College in Lecompton, Kansas. It was a second-rate college, with low academic standards and meager funds, and her years there were important more for her meeting fellow-student David Eisenhower than for her education. They were married in the college chapel on September 23, 1885.

The Eisenhower family had emigrated to America from Germany in 1741, and in the 1880s David's father was a prosperous Kansas farmer, well able to afford the gift of a farm to his son. But David was determined to make his way in business rather than agriculture, and sold his farm to take a partnership in a shop in Hope, Kansas. Here Ida's troubles began. Times were hard, and David's partner absconded with their capital, leaving the Eisenhowers with many debts and a lifelong mistrust of financial entanglements. Ida studied law avidly, preparing for the day – which never came – when the faithless partner would be brought to account.

The family moved to Texas, where Ida's third son, Dwight, was born on October 14, 1890, but within two years they had returned to Kansas and set up house in Abilene. David Eisenhower took a succession of jobs, first on the railroad, then as an engineer in a creamery, then as the manager of a gas plant, and finally as the director of a savings group. There was never much money in the Eisenhower family, but David and Ida – still haunted by memories of heavy debts – would never ask for credit.

David Eisenhower left home for his work at six in the morning and didn't return until early evening, so it was Ida who governed the work and play of her sons. She was a firm but gentle disciplinarian, meting out punishment on the spot – only the worst cases of misbehavior were passed on to David. With little money and in a small house, Ida's work as the mother of six sons could have become intolerable, but she planned a schedule of shared chores which was followed by the whole family. She insisted that her children learn to become self-reliant.

Ida Eisenhower was deeply religious; family legend has it that she once won a prize for memorizing 1,365 verses of the Bible. Men of the sect to which she belonged – later to become the Jehovah's Witnesses – were all conscientious objectors to military service, but she never forced her beliefs, on her own sons. In 1911 Dwight entered the military academy at West Point. His mother, being a pacifist, disapproved, but she did not interfere with his chosen career.

After a lifetime of hard work, the Eisenhowers managed to save enough money for a comfortable retirement. All their money disappeared, however, when the stock market collapsed in 1929. Their sons then assisted them.

Ida Eisenhower was active until she was well into her eighties. She died in 1946, one year after the son whose military career she refused to oppose had helped lead the Allied forces to victory in World War Two.

Right Ida Stover, to whom her son showed a strong facial resemblance.

Anne Boleyn

ELIZABETH I
(1533-1603)
Queen of England from
1558-1603. Her reign is
synonymous with a great
period in English political and
literary history.

Anne Boleyn, the second of King Henry VIII's six wives was the youngest child of Thomas and Elizabeth Boleyn whose home was at Hever Castle in Kent. Her father was a lesser nobleman and although he was related to powerful families, his grandfather, then named Bullen, once Lord Mayor of London, had been a mercer by trade. Anne was born in 1507 and had two small deformities, a large mole on her neck and a tiny sixth finger on her right hand.

When Anne was seven she was sent to join her elder sister at the French court, then the most lively Court in Europe. In 1522, when she was fifteen, he returned to England to find that her father had become a wealthy and powerful court official and that her sister, who had been sent back from Paris in disgrace, was King Henry's mistress.

In appearance Anne was slender and dark-complexioned, with large dark eyes, a long neck, and a large mouth. She was mischievous, witty and high-spirited — strikingly different from Queen Catherine, to whose household she was attached. The Queen was white-faced and gloomy, and a devout Roman Catholic. At forty-one she was six years older than her royal husband and had failed to present him with the male heir he so desperately wanted.

Anne's lively elegance made her noticeable at Court, and she caught Henry's attention. At first he was annoyed with her for not accepting a marriage that had been arranged for her, but then he became very angry when she wanted to marry Lord Henry Percy, and forbade their marriage. Henry became infatuated with the young woman, sixteen years his junior. He wrote her passionate love letters and pleaded with her to become his mistress. Anne, however, had learned much in the French court, and was no doubt advised by her ambitious father. At one moment she led on her royal wooer, then withdrew to the country until the frustrated Henry was at last compelled to propose marriage. But to marry her meant that he must divorce Catherine, and this process was begun in 1527 and protracted over six years of struggling with the Pope. Meanwhile he made it clear that he wanted Anne as his Queen.

Anne very quickly began acting the part. She became unpopular not only at Court, where she

behaved arrogantly and ostentatiously, but among the general populace. Angry crowds gathered when she appeared in public. She also showed that she could be vicious and vengeful toward those who crossed her. In 1530 she brought about the fall and banishment of Cardinal Wolsey, the most powerful of the King's advisers, whom she hated for his part in destroying her romance with Henry Percy. By the next year she had succeeded in having the Queen herself banished from court and had moved into the Royal apartments. But by 1532 the divorce seemed no nearer. Anne, playing her last card, yielded to Henry's passion and soon became pregnant. Cranmer, newly appointed as Archbishop of Canterbury, ignored the Pope and proclaimed a legal divorce. Henry and Anne were married secretly at dawn on January 25th, 1533. In May this strong-willed young woman achieved her ambition with a magnificent coronation. At last she was Queen of England. But the English people continued to dislike her. Anne herself said of the procession from the Tower to Westminster that "the city was well enough, but she saw few heads bared."

On September 7 her child was born. To her and Henry's dismay, it was a daughter. Again Henry was denied a male heir. Anne was intensely maternal despite her disappointment, but at the age of three months the baby, named Elizabeth, was removed to Hatfield House in Hertfordshire, and there spent the greater part of the first ten years of her life.

Henry seems to have forgiven Anne for not giving him a male heir, but after two successive miscarriages his interest in her faded. She became shrewish and bad-tempered, even daring to mock the King in public. Henry began to gather evidence for an annulment of the marriage. In May 1536 Anne was taken to the Tower of London and charged with treason, adultery (with four men), and incest with her brother — charges she vehemently denied.

The result of her trial a fortnight later was no surprise. She had become a political liability, and she was found guilty and condemned to death. On May 19, 1536 she mounted the scaffold, smiling, and lifted her own headdress to be blindfolded. She was twenty-eight years old.

Right Painting of Anne Boleyn by Hans Holbein.

Queen Elizabeth, the Queen Mother

ELIZABETH II
(1926-)
Present Queen of Great
Britain and Northern Ireland
and Head of the
Commonwealth of Nations.
She succeeded her father,
George VI, in 1952.

Below Lady Elizabeth
Bowes-Lyon, aged seven.
Right Photograph with her
younger daughter,
Princess Margaret Rose.
Pages 78-79 A Royal
Family album of
memories.

Page 80-81 Three Queens
– mother, wife, and
daughter – at the funeral
of George VI.

Queen Elizabeth the Queen Mother is a
well-loved member of the British royal family.
There are many who remember her stalwart
service to the nation during the Second World
War, and today, in her seventies, she is still active
in royal duties.

The Queen Mother was born Elizabeth Angela
Marguerite Bowes-Lyon, daughter of Lord Claude
Bowes-Lyon and his wife Cecilia (*née* Cavendish
Bentinck), on August 4, 1900. She was four years
old when her father became Earl of Strathmore,
which gave her the courtesy title of "Lady."
Although she was born in England, at St Paul's
Walden Bury in Hertfordshire, the family estates
were in Scotland.

Of the ten Bowes-Lyon children, Elizabeth was
the ninth. She and her brother David, born in
1902, were very close, since their brothers and
sisters were between seven and eighteen years her
senior. She was educated mainly at home, by a
governess, but in 1912-13 spent eight months at a
private school in London. Elizabeth first saw her
future husband at a children's party in London.
She was five years old, he was nine; they did not
meet again for fifteen years.

The evening of August 4, 1914 found the
Bowes-Lyon family at a London theater,
celebrating Elizabeth's fourteenth birthday, but
by midnight Britain was at war with Germany.
Elizabeth spent most of the war years at Glamis,
helping her mother run a hospital for the
wounded, which was set up in the family castle.

Elizabeth was eighteen by the end of the war,
and ready for the excitement of a London
"season." At balls and parties she was
everywhere regarded as one of the most attractive
and popular debutantes of the year. It was at a
dance in May 1920 that she met Prince Albert
again – his father was now King George V. In the
spring of 1921, Prince "Bertie," now Duke of
York, told his father that he loved Elizabeth and
wanted to marry her. "You'll be a lucky fellow if
she accepts you," said King George. At that time
the Prince was not heir to the throne, but it was
still unusual for the son of a monarch to marry a
commoner. But on April 26, 1923, Bertie and
Elizabeth were married in Westminster Abbey.

For the next thirteen years the young couple
led a quiet life. They had two daughters:
Elizabeth, born in 1926, and Margaret, born in
1930. Both the Duke and the Duchess had many
royal duties to perform, but there was also plenty
of time for a home life. In 1936 George V died,
and Bertie's brother became King Edward VIII.
Almost immediately, however, the new King

The Duke of Windsor and Lady Elizabeth Bowes-Lyon 1923

Wedding day

Princess Elizabeth Alexandra Mary with the Duke & Duchess 19

April 23rd 1923

Royal christening 1926

1937

The Queen, Princess Elizabeth and Princess Margaret in 1934

...tion 1937

Princess Margaret · The Queen · Princess Elizabeth

Royal Wedding 1947

THE QUEEN

Christening of Princess Anne in October 1950

The Queen & Princess Margaret in 1951

made known his plans to marry Wallis Simpson, an American divorcee, and after only a few months he abdicated. Thus, the Duke of York became George VI, and so Elizabeth was Queen. At Buckingham Palace and at Windsor, she tried to keep her children free from ceremonial duties and to give them some stability despite their parents' frequent absences. She had complete trust in the Princesses' Scottish governess, Miss Marion Crawford.

Elizabeth was frequently separated from her children during the Second World War, when they were sent to safety in the country. The King and Queen remained in the capital and endeared themselves to the people by making excursions into the worst-bombed areas of London. Many a cockney had a story to tell of the Queen's kindness — as when she knelt in the mud to coax an old lady's dog out of a hole after it had been terrified by the bombing. When peace came and London thronged with thankful crowds, Buckingham Palace was surrounded by people calling for the King and Queen as well as for Winston Churchill, and Elizabeth and her husband spent many hours waving from their balcony.

But the war had taken its toll of George VI's strength, and he was frequently ill in subsequent years. He died on February 6, 1952. The Princess Elizabeth became Queen, and the new Queen Mother left Buckingham Palace for Marlborough House with her younger daughter, the Princess Margaret.

The Queen Mother has continued to play an active part in the duties of the royal family, and has also won success as the owner of many winning race horses.

MOLLIE McQUILLAN

F. SCOTT FITZGERALD
(1896-1940)
One of the best-known American writers of the years betwen the two world wars. His novels include *The Great Gatsby* and *Tender is the Night.*

When Mollie Fitzgerald died in 1936, and Scott Fitzgerald had the task of sorting through her belongings, he wrote to his sister: "It was sad, taking Mother from the hotel, the only home she knew for fifteen years, to die . . . Mother and I never had anything in common except a relentless stubborn quality, but when I saw all this it turned me inside out realizing how unhappy her temperament made her and how she clung to the end to all things that would remind her of moments of snatched happiness." His words reflect the sadness and disappointments of her life, but perhaps they underestimate the influence his mother had on him – that "old peasant" whom he described once "majestically dipping her sleeves in the coffee."

Mollie McQuillan was born in 1860 in St Paul, Minnesota. Her father was a self-made Irish businessman from County Fermanagh, who, at his death in 1877, left a large fortune which was to support her family in the hard times that followed. Mollie's mother was a devout Catholic, and the children were taken several times to Rome to see the seat of their faith. Mollie herself was an eccentric-looking character, with a wide, comical mouth, a round face, and flat features. She was given to romantic fantasies, fed by wide and rather indiscriminate reading; she was, unfortunately, more attracted to men than they were to her. As she approached thirty and was still unmarried, she accepted the proposal of Edward Fitzgerald, who had been courting her for several years. He too had his romantic fantasies, though they centered on the Civil War, the main event of his Southern youth. He was an elegant little man with a certain languor, and was curiously suited to the small wicker-furniture business which he found himself running in St Paul at the time of his marriage in 1890. His son loved him but found him difficult to respect.

The couple spent their honeymoon in Europe. From Nice Edward wrote home, "I have drawn a prize in a wife, one has to know her well to fully appreciate her." But their happiness was not to last long. Their first two children, both girls, died in epidemics just before Scott was born in September 1896. Less than two years after his birth, his father's business failed, and the family moved East. In 1908 his father lost his job, a blow from which he never recovered, and the family moved back to St Paul. From then on, they lived on the McQuillan family fortune – a fact that was to have a marked influence on the young Scott Fitzgerald. Her husband having failed her, all of Mollie Fitzgerald's hopes were centered on him. She supported the family and, in her turn, commanded Scott's reluctant respect. His maternal grandfather – the self-made Irishman who amassed the original fortune – became, in Scott's eyes, something of a hero.

Having lost her first two children (she never spoke of them, and a daughter born after Scott does not appear to have figured in her ambitious plans), Mollie was determined that Scott should want for nothing. She was equally determined that he should not be dragged down by his father's failure. She saw to it that he was accepted in all the best circles, though she and Edward remained on the fringes of society. She encouraged Scott's outgoingness, getting him to sing to company and even to the nuns when the Fitzgeralds visited the local convent. He was always dressed meticulously, though she herself dressed in an eccentric manner – "like the ark," somebody once said. Neighbors told their daughters to comb their hair or they would look like Mollie Fitzgerald. She had also been known to wear unmatching shoes. They called her witch and made fun of her sagging walk and drawling speech. Not only was Mrs Fitzgerald eccentric in her appearance; her tactlessness was famous. When a friend of the Fitzgeralds became ill and everyone was at pains to keep the seriousness of his condition from his wife, Mollie declared to her: "I'm trying to decide what you'll look like in mourning."

Right Mollie McQuillan, an eccentric dreamer.

HILDA ACHESON

MARGOT FONTEYN
(1919-)
A world-renowned prima ballerina, famous for her dancing partnerships with Rudolf Nureyev.

Right Two photographs from the family album — mother and daughter in the garden, and mother, father, and daughter at home in Shanghai.

Hilda Acheson was born on December 19, 1894 in Matlock Bath, Derbyshire, England. She was the daughter of a Brazilian father and an Irish mother. Her mother was very delicate and died when Hilda was seven. Her father then went back to his business in Brazil and left Hilda to be brought up by her maternal grandmother in Manchester, England.

Although she had been christened Hilda Morley Acheson Fontes, her grandmother sent her to school as Hilda Acheson, which she remained until she married Felix John Hookham in June, 1915. They had a son, whom they named Felix, in March, 1916. A daughter was born in May, 1919 and christened Margaret Evelyn Hookham but called Peggy for short.

At that time there was no ballet company in England but there were teachers of classical dancing and of musical comedy and tap dancing, and near her Ealing home Mrs Hookham found an excellent teacher to whom little Peggy went twice a week for five years. In 1924 a local paper reports "a remarkably fine solo dance" of hers that was "vigorously encored."

In 1927 Felix Hookham was posted to the United States by the tobacco firm for which he worked. Mrs Hookham and Peggy went too, leaving Felix behind at his school. From America they went to China where they spent much of the next five years, Mrs Hookham and Peggy visiting England periodically to see Felix. On one of these visits Peggy saw Alicia Markova dance and afterwards said to her mother, "That's what I want to do."

Back in Shanghai Mrs Hookham ensured that her daughter's dancing lessons continued. Peggy

did well but her mother knew that if she really wanted to become a ballet dancer she would have to return to England.

They came back to England in 1933 where Mrs Hookham managed, after much difficulty, to gain an interview with Princess Seraphine Astafieva, the teacher of Markova. The Princess, however, insisted that she could take no more pupils. Mrs Hookham persisted, declaring that she had brought her daughter all the way from Shanghai to be seen by the Princess. The Princess finally consented to "look" and was sufficiently impressed by what she saw to allow the girl to attend classes.

After six months of study with Astafieva, Mrs Hookham was anxious to know how her daughter was developing as a dancer and entered her for an audition at the Vic-Wells Ballet. The audition was successful and Peggy Hookham began her professional career as a dancer. She was just fifteen.

A change of name was requested and Margaret became Margot; for her surname she took the Brazilian family name, Fontes. The following year the head of the Fontes family learned of this and expressed his disapproval that the family name should become associated with the theater. Margot looked up Fontes in the telephone directory and chose the name next to it: Fonteyn.

At the age of fifteen Margot was already dancing leads; by the time she was sixteen Frederick Ashton was creating ballets for her. Her professional dancing career has now spanned an astonishing forty years, and Mrs Hookham has followed it with pride and happiness.

Mary Litogot

HENRY FORD I
(1863-1947)
American pioneer of cheap
automobiles based on
assembly-line production
methods.

Mary Litogot was born in Wyandotte, Michigan, in 1839 When she was three years old, she and her three brothers were orphaned by the death of their father; their mother had already died.

Not long after her father's death, Mary was adopted by Patrick and Margaret O'Hern, acquaintances of the Litogots from Dearborn, a settlement twelve miles to the southeast of Wyandotte. Her brothers stayed behind with friends. Patrick O'Hern, a native of Ireland, had come to America in about 1830, married, and settled down on a farm in the township of Dearborn. The O'Herns were childless, they gladly took Mary in, and a bond of mutual love and affection was quickly established between them and the little girl.

Mary went to school in the nearby Scotch Settlement – a community of exceptionally high cultural and moral standards. There she studied the "Sander readers", which contained such practical-minded lessons as "The Way to Become Wise" and "Read and You Will Know". Mary seems to have set a high value on her schooling, which was supplemented by tutorial assistance and philosophic guidance from Margaret O'Hern. Mary was later to provide the same kind of support for her own children.

Mary was twelve when William Ford, a sturdy young man of twenty-six, first came to work for Patrick O'Hern. Ford and his family had come to America from Ireland in 1847, when he was twenty-one. For several years he worked at clearing the forest land his father had bought. He had also made money working on the Michigan Central Railroad, which was extending its tracks westward.

During the next ten years, as William helped O'Hern with farmwork and carpentry, he watched Mary grow up. Early photographs of her show a dark-haired, dark-eyed young woman with a hint of a smile and an air of earnest integrity. William eventually fell in love with the vivacious Mary, and in 1860, when he had bought some land, he asked her to marry him. William was the only man in her life, and they were married on April 25, 1861, in the Episcopal Church in Detroit. The Fords took over the O'Herns' land and built a seven-room clapboard house to be shared by the two families. They

remained very close, and Mary eventually inherited everything the O'Herns had.

Mary's first child died in infancy. Henry, the second child, was born on July 30, 1863, a month after the Battle of Gettysburg. His three brothers and two sisters followed at two-year intervals. As the children grew up, they helped with work on the farm and around the house. Henry did not like the farmwork, but his mother taught him that self-discipline, courage, and patience were needed for disagreeable jobs, and that "The best fun follows a duty done."

Like many pioneer families, the Fords were isolated on their farm and had to be almost completely self-sufficient. Mary made her own pickles and jams, and their food was simple but wholesome. She also spun wool to make their clothes.

Mary Ford believed that it was as easy to keep a place clean as it was to keep it dirty. She was a diligent worker, and the farm was always kept spic and span. Herny later attributed the cleanliness of his motor factories to his mother's influence.

Henry was always very close to his mother. She taught him to read before he want to school, and he claimed that she knew him so well that she could read his mind. He also held that, unlike his father, his mother encouraged his interest in mechanics from the first. She exerted an influence on his character that remained with him forever. He inherited her belief in hard work, her love of the country and of simple pleasures, and her dislike of idleness and of all forms of self-indulgence. "I have tried to live my life as my mother would have wished. I believe I have done, as far as I could, just what she hoped for me."

In March 1876 Mary was expecting another child, her eighth. There was no reason for apprehension – at thirty-seven she was still young and healthy – but something went wrong. The child was lost, and twelve days later Mary died. Losing her devastated the family. Henry was not quite thirteen when she died, but as he later described it: "The house was like a watch without a mainspring." As a tribute to his mother, Henry Ford later restored the white homestead down to the most minute details of its furnishings. No one lived there: he kept it as a shrine to her memory.

Right An early
daguerreotype of Mary.

Catherine de' Medici

FRANCIS II
(1544-60)
King of France. Ascended the
throne in 1559, aged fifteen,
but reigned for only one year.
He was married to Mary
Queen of Scots.

Catherine de' Medici was born in 1519, the
daughter of a younger Lorenzo de' Medici and a
gay young French aristocrat Madeline de la Tour
d'Auvergne. Her mother died of puerperal fever
two weeks after her birth, and her father six days
later. At first the little orphan girl was looked
after by aunts, but from a very tender age she was
brought up in a series of convents. In them she
was supposed to be "protected" by her uncle,
Pope Leo X, and later by another relative, Pope
Clement VII. She was a commodity on the
marriage market, a helpless pawn in the pontiffs'
great European chess game.

In 1533, marriage was finally arranged
between Catherine and the Duke of Orleans, later
to become King Henry II of France. The match
was a good one for Catherine, though some of
Henry's supporters referred to her as "that
Florentine shopkeeper" (the Medicis made their
fortune as merchants). Ironically, the rumor was
circulated by her enemies that the young bride
(she was aged fourteen, as was her husband,
when they married) was not able to have children.
Catherine had the last laugh. She had ten. Three

of them became Kings of France, one Queen of
France, and one Queen of Spain.

At the time of her betrothal Catherine was
described as "small and thin; her features are not
delicate, and she has bulging eyes like most of the
Medici . . . she is lively and reveals an affable
disposition and distinguished manners." Later,
when she was Queen Mother and Regent of
France, she was to be described as "a plump little
woman with her white face and black clothes."
No mention then of an affable disposition, but
throughout her life she was a lover of good food.
She was also an enthuiastic horsewoman and
introduced the sidesaddle into France.

Her eldest son, Francis, was born in 1544 when
she was twenty-five. Three years later his father
became King of France and Francis thus became
the Dauphin or heir to the throne. While he was
Dauphin he married Mary, Queen of Scots.
Mary's mother was a member of the Guises,
powerful Roman Catholic French family. Mary,
who had been brought up among the French
aristocracy, seems to have shared the nobility's
contempt for her mother-in-law, whom she called

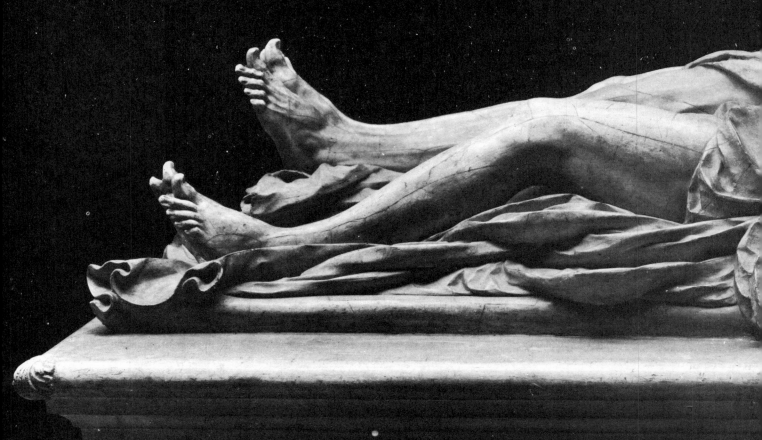

"that merchant's daughter."

Francis became King when he was only fifteen, died the following year and was succeeded by his young brother Charles. The new King was ten years old. Catherine, as Queen Mother and Regent of France, began to take control of the country. She ruled shrewdly and ambitiously, using every means at her disposal to protect the interests of her children.

Only a few years before, the Reformation had swept through Europe, and France was in a bitter struggle between Catholics and Protestants (Huguenots). Catherine played off one side against the other, but always with the interests of her children at heart. She married off her eldest daughter to the King of Spain, the most Catholic country in Europe. Hedging her bets, she married another daughter to King Henry of Navarre, one of the Protestant champions of France, who was later to become the first Bourbon King of France.

But her greatest claim to fame, or rather infamy, was her instigation of the Massacre of St Bartholomew's Day. Charles IX, who had succeeded Francis, was a weak and unstable man, completely dominated by his mother. Yet he became friendly with Admiral de Coligny, the Huguenot leader, whom he regarded as a father. Catherine suspected them of conspiring together, but persuaded her unstable son that he himself was the object of conspiracy and urged him to kill the Admiral. The massacre followed, with thousands of Huguenots being killed in brutal fashion. Although Charles later accepted responsibility, his brother, the Duke of Anjou, recorded that the inspiration was Catherine's.

Perhaps the most tolerant commentary on this strange woman was made by Henry of Navarre, her Protestant son-in-law who founded the line of Bourbon kings that was to continue until the French Revolution. "I ask you," he said, "what could she have done, the poor woman, left at her husband's death with five small children and two families in France — ours and the Guises — who hoped to get the crown for themselves? Wasn't it necessary for her to play some strange roles, to deceive each and everybody in order to defend her sons (as she did), who reigned in turn by the wise guidance of that wily woman? You are going to say that she did harm to France. The marvel is that she didn't do worse."

Below The tomb of Catherine and her husband, King Henry II of France – in the Abbey of Saint Denis, France.
Pages 90-91 Catherine (in the dark dress) watches a tournament held in honor of her husband.
Page 92 Catherine is married to the future King of France.

Abiah Folger

Very little is known about Abiah Folger, and most of what is known comes to us from her son, Benjamin Franklin. Abiah was born in 1667; her father was Peter Folger, one of the first settlers in New England.

Her husband, Josiah Franklin, had a small business as a tallow chandler and "sope boiler". His income was large enough to support his family but too small to buy anything but necessities. Indeed, Ben had to leave grammar school at the age of nine and go to help his father in the family business. He was one of thirteen children, the eldest of whom was over twenty-five when Ben was born in 1706.

Ben Franklin's *Memoir* says very little about his mother. But the overwhelming impression is that he loved and respected her; she wins his admiration for having "suckled all her ten children." He says that she had a strong constitution but makes no mention of her appearance, and after her death he wrote that she "lived a good life." But perhaps the most important thing Franklin wrote about his mother is the epitaph he composed for both his parents.

BENJAMIN FRANKLIN
(1706-90)
American statesman and inventor. He helped draft the US Constitution and was a signer of the Declaration of Independence.

JOSIAH FRANKLIN
and
ABIAH, his wife
lie here interred
They lived lovingly together in wedlock
fifty-five years
Without an estate, or any gainful employment
By constant labor and industry
with God's blessing
They maintained a large family
comfortably
And brought up thirteen children
and seven grandchildren
reputably.
From this instance, reader,
Be encouraged to diligence in thy calling
and distrust not Providence,
He was a pious and discreet man,
She a discreet and virtuous woman.

Left Book illustration of a popular story based on an incident in Benjamin Franklin's childhood.

THE WHISTLE

93

AMALIE NATHANSOHN

SIGMUND FREUD
(1856-1939)
Austrian physician who
developed the theory and
practice of psychoanalysis.

Amalie Nathansohn was born in 1835 in Brody, a small town then under Austrian rule and now part of the Ukraine. When she was a young girl her family moved to Vienna where, at the age of thirteen, she witnessed the riots of the 1848 revolution. Amalie is said to have been a slim, pretty, vivacious young woman.

When she was twenty years old, Amalie married Jakob Freud, a Vienna wool merchant. Jakob had been married once before; he was already a grandfather by a child from his first marriage when he married Amalie. Just ten months after their marriage they had their first child, a boy named Sigmund. Amalie was intensely proud of him and was convinced that he would be a great man. She gave him his first lessons and was able to send him off to high school at a very young age.

Jakob died in 1896, leaving Amalie a widow at the age of sixty-one. She continued to live in Vienna, and her daughter Adolfine – "Dolfi" to all the family – stayed at home and cared for her. Inflation during the First World War was too much for Amalie: she could not be made to understand that money was not worth as much as

it used to be. In 1918 Sigmund and his brother Alexander had to concoct a scheme for secretly providing Dolfi with funds to keep the household going, because Amalie made a scene every time she found herself having to pay out more than she thought proper.

In her later years Amalie spent summers in Bad Ischl, a health resort near Salzburg. There she would sit up late playing cards and talking with her friends. On her birthday the mayor of Bad Ischl always brought her flowers – a gift she found acceptable since it recalled the days of her youth.

Amalie retained her humor and lively spirits until the very end of her life. When she was ninety she turned down the gift of a shawl on the grounds that it made her look old. Not long before her death at the age of ninety-five she was shocked by a photograph of herself which she saw in a newspaper: "A bad reproduction – it makes me look a hundred!" Amalie Nathansohn Freud died on September 12, 1930, only nine years before the death of her famous son who, it has been observed, permanently altered the way we think about motherhood.

Right Amalie, aged 70,
photographed in the
mountains with her son,
Sigmund, and his wife.
Far right Amalie and
Sigmund.
Pages 96-97 The Freud
family – with Amalie
seated center.

PUTLIBAI GANDHI

MAHATMA GANDHI
(1869-1948)
Mohandas Karamchand
Gandhi, called "Mahatma"
(Great Soul) for his part in
winning Indian freedom from
British rule.

Not a great deal is known about the childhood of
the mother of Mohandas Karamchand Gandhi,
later known to the world as Mahatma Gandhi;
for among Hindus it is the duty of a girl or
woman to subordinate herself to her family and,
once married, to her husband and his family. She
must have come from a reasonably prosperous
family, however, for the man she married was of
great importance in the tiny princely state of
Porbandar, by the sea in western India. If her
adult life is any indication, she must have been a
well behaved and obedient little girl. Her home
was a deeply religious one in which the
observances of the Hindu religion were closely
attended.

She was born in 1839 into the Modh Bania
(trader) caste. It was the third caste in standing,
coming after the Brahmins (priests and learned
men) and the warriors. Among the more
successful Bania families, boys were given some
formal education but girls were never taught
anything beyond the rudiments and ritual of their
religion. Putlibai remained almost illiterate
throughout her life, though she was able to read a
little in her own native Gujerati tongue.

Putlibai married Karamchand Gandhi, a man
of her own caste. Gandhi was over forty, three
times a widower and the father of two daughters
by his earlier marriages. He came from a
prosperous family, and served for twenty-eight
years as Diwan, or chief minister, of the little
state of Junagadh.

After they were married, Putlibai and
Karamchand lived on the ground floor of a
sizeable three-story house shared with
Karamchand's five brothers and their families.
Putlibai devoted herself to her wifely duties but
inevitably, because of her husband's position,
came into contact with the ladies of the Court
where she won respect as a capable woman. She
gave birth to four children, two sons followed by
a daughter and, finally, another son named
Mohandas Karamchand, who was born on
October 2, 1869 when Putlibai was thirty
years old.

Putlibai's life was austere by her own choice.
Unlike most of the women of her age and
standing, she had no interest in fine clothes or
jewels. She was an intelligent woman and gave
her children exceptional care, particularly when
they were sick. All of them survived to adulthood,
which was unusual in nineteenth-century India.
She devoted herself also to religion: fasting
frequently, making many vows, and dividing her
time between her home and the temple. She was
strictly orthodox in her observance of the
traditional customs of her faith. She found
difficulty in answering the questions of her
enquiring youngest son Mohandas, who could
not understand why it was wrong to witness an
eclipse or how it could harm him to come into
contact with Uka, the "untouchable" household
sweeper. Nevertheless, her faith and austerity left
a lasting impression on the young Mohandas.

When Putlibai was thirty-seven, her husband
had a disagreement with the ruler of Porbandar
and left for Rajkot, where he was at once
appointed Diwan. But Karamchand lived only
ten more years, and Putlibai was left a widow in
1886. Mohandas matriculated a year later. By
then he was flirting with atheism, and he smoked
and ate meat outside his home, all sins in the
Hindu religion. Putlibai knew none of this, but
she was greatly disturbed when Mohandas
decided to study in England. She was horrified
when the elders of the Modh Bania caste declared
that a journey to England would be contrary to
the Hindu religion. Her mind was set at rest when
a monk sanctioned the journey provided that
Mohandas make a vow to touch no wine, women,
or meat while he was away. The money was
provided by his elder brother, and Mohandas
sailed in 1888. Putlibai never saw her youngest
son again, for she died in 1891 before he returned
to India.

Right Putlibai, mother of
the Mahatma.

Anna Gustafsson

GRETA GARBO
(1906-)
Swedish-born film star, famous for her performances in such Hollywood productions as *Ninotchka* and *Camille*.

The renowned secrecy of the great, exquisite, and legendary Garbo also extended to her family background. When she went to Hollywood, a reporter asked her the usual questions about where she was born and what sort of upbringing she had, only to receive this daunting answer: "I do not want it printed that I was born in this house or that – that my mother was this or my father that. They were my mother and father. That is enough. Why should the world talk about them?"

Nonetheless, a little is known about her parents. Her mother, Anna, was brought up in the Swedish countryside before moving to Stockholm. In 1896 she married Karl Alfred Gustafsson, who also had a farming background. They had three children, Alva, Sven, and finally Greta, who inherited something of her looks from both parents. From her father she got her sensitive, finely chiseled features. But when she first went to Hollywood, she had something of her mother's plumpness. Indeed, she was initially considered fat and clumsy, and she was told to take up riding in order to lose some weight.

The Gustafssons lived in a working-class part of Stockholm called Söder. Greta's father had no skills that fitted him for a city life and was condemned to poorly paid, humdrum jobs. The family lived in a four-room apartment with no hot water. Anna had a perpetual struggle to make ends meet, but she was a good seamstress and her children always had adequate, if not luxurious, clothes. There was no money for entertainment and summer holidays. The family's chief recreation was visiting their allotment on the outskirts of Stockholm every Sunday. Here they grew vegetables, and Greta and the other children enjoyed themselves in the fresh air.

But in 1919 life became even more difficult. Karl became very ill and was unable to work. Anna, Alva, and Sven now became the breadwinners while Greta stayed at home and nursed her father. A year later he died.

Greta was now fourteen, and the death of her father more or less coincided with the end of her formal education. She began to ease the burden on Anna by earning a little money as a lather girl in a barber's shop – a common occupation for a young girl in Sweden at this time. But Greta's real love was acting and soon, to her mother's consternation, she was trying to meet actors and directors in order to find out how to get the training for a stage career. Once, after she had been backstage at a local theater, Anna told her sternly that she was too young for that sort of thing. But her mother was no match for Greta's consuming passion. Soon she had acquired some dramatic training and was making films in Sweden. Then her director, Mauritz Stiller, took her to Hollywood. Anna often received letters from Greta, usually saying that the life of a film star was not all it was reputed to be. Finally, Greta, now world-famous, went home for a rest. But it was a difficult time for both herself and her family since she was pursued by reporters all the time. Anna, naturally, was proud of her daughter, though she was none too happy about the way Greta kissed in some of her films.

Anna still lived in the street in which Greta was born, despite the fact that Greta regularly sent money to her. Most of it was put in a bank and never spent. Greta also bought her mother an apartment with a magnificent view. But as Mrs Gustafsson could have moved long before she did, she seems to have shared some of her daughter's indifference to fame and fortune.

Right Anna welcomes Greta on a visit to Sweden after finding fame in Hollywood.

Rosa Raimondi

Rosa Raimondi was born in 1770 in Loano, near Genoa, Italy. Her husband, Domenico Garibaldi, was also from a town near Genoa but the couple lived in Nice, which was then part of the kingdom of Piedmont. Domenico was a merchant seaman, the owner of a twenty-nine-ton ship called the *Santa Reparata*.

Rosa and Domenico had six children over a period of twenty years. Giuseppe, born in 1807, was the third. He and his brothers and sisters were loved and well cared for, even though the family did not have much money. Giuseppe was later to say that his parents had been "overprotective," and the evidence we have bears out this contention. This overprotective tendency may have intensified after the death by fire of Rosa and Domenico's youngest child, Teresa. This took place in 1820; in 1799 the eldest child had died, also in infancy. Rosa was an extremely religious woman. She made her children go to church every Sunday and her first hope for Giuseppe was that he become a priest. She and Domenico hired three tutors – two priests and one layman – who were to teach him the standard academic subjects. Giuseppe, however, was more interested in becoming a sailor like his father and grandfather. He taught himself mathematics, astronomy, geography, commercial law, and other subjects necessary for his chosen career. Rosa never completely approved of Giuseppe's aspirations – and her disapproval may have increased as, with age, she became more religious. But she never tried to stand in her son's way, and even packed his bags for him when, at the age of fourteen, he left for his first sea voyage. Three years later she insisted that he join the crew of his father's ship: if he had to go to sea, she reasoned, it was better to go with his father.

Giuseppe disagreed with his mother as strongly about religion as he did about his profession. He was strongly anticlerical throughout his life. Yet he always spoke of his mother's religious views with the greatest respect, acknowledging the influence they had on him as well as the comfort they gave. He attributed his love of country and of humanity to his mother's compassionate nature. And he once wrote that "at the most difficult moments of my stormy life . . . I seemed to see my loving mother bending and kneeling before the Infinite, a suppliant for the child of her womb."

Giuseppe last saw his mother in the autumn of 1849, when he stayed in Nice before going into exile for the second time. Domenico had died in 1843, but Rosa was still living in the old family house. She had never completely accepted her son's chosen career or everything he did; but the reunion was a happy one nonetheless. Giuseppe left soon after. He was at sea in March 1852 when, during an attack of rheumatism, he had a blurred vision of his mother in a funeral procession. On that night, he later learned, his mother had died in her sleep.

He wrote later: "One of the bitter things of my life, and not the least bitter, has been and will be not to have been able to make her happy, but, on the contrary, to have saddened and, indeed, made painful the closing days of her life."

GIUSEPPE GARIBALDI
(1807-82)
Italian patriot whose army of Red Shirts played a significant part in gaining Italian independence and unification.

Far left The house in Nice where Rosa lived for over 50 years.

Left A sentimental portrait of Rosa from the biography of her son by Alexandre Dumas.

JEANNE MAILLOT-DELANNOY

CHARLES DE GAULLE
(1890-1970)
French soldier and statesman.
He formed the Fifth French
Republic in 1958, and then
became President.

Jeanne Maillot-Delannoy was a native of Lille (France), but on her marriage to her cousin Henri de Gaulle in 1886 moved to Paris, where he taught in a Jesuit school. It was only because she wished to bear her second child under her mother's care that Charles de Gaulle was born in Lille.

The five de Gaulle children – Xavier, Charles, Jacques, Pierre, and Marie-Agnès – were lively and imaginative, a close-knit group whose playmates were more often their cousins than outsiders. Xavier was the most intellectual of them, but Charles was a natural leader, displaying even from infancy a passion for war-games and thoroughly enjoying his mother's tales of his ancestors in "battles long ago."

But at the same time, they were brought up strictly, their parents leading "improving" conversations at meal-times and insisting on the children's being thoroughly abreast of the political events of the day. Jeanne de Gaulle was intensely pious (two of her sisters were nuns), and imposed a strict religious observance on her children. She and her husband were also fervent patriots: Madame de Gaulle would often recount the horror of her own parents when France was defeated by the Germans in 1871. This combination of religion and patriotism, so firmly inculcated in him by his mother, was to be the cornerstone of General de Gaulle's whole life.

Madame de Gaulle had strong views on the importance of the united family, and her children were always closely in touch with each other when careers and marriage separated them – with Charles making his career in the army. With the coming of the Second World War, the widowed Madame de Gaulle made her home with her eldest son's family in Brittany.

On June 18, 1940 the Germans began to pour into the locality, almost unchallenged. "Why does no one shoot?" cried Jeanne de Gaulle. "Are we going to let them take France like so many tourists?" But her shame for her compatriots was turned to hope when the parish priest burst in with the news that a French general had just spoken on the radio from London, swearing that France would continue to resist. "Whatever happens, the flame of the French Resistance must not and will not be put out." "Which general spoke?" someone asked. "General de Gaulle," replied the priest triumphantly. "That is my son!" cried Jeanne de Gaulle. "That is *my* son!"

A little less than a month later, on July 16, 1940, Madame de Gaulle died. As the mother of so famous a son, the Germans feared that the announcement of her death could be used as propaganda by the rapidly gathering Resistance, and forbade publication of the news. But it spread like wildfire. Soon Jeanne de Gaulle's grave at Paimport was covered with flowers, and visitors flocked to see it with its plain Maltese cross – some of them even taking away stones, like relics from a shrine. A Breton fisherman smuggled a photograph of the grave with its garlands across the Channel, and it was delivered to General de Gaulle at the headquarters of the Free French.

Right Jeanne, pious and
patriotic mother of
General Charles de Gaulle.

Katherina Elisabeth Textor

JOHANN WOLFGANG VON GOETHE
(1749-1832)
Poet, playwright, and novelist, recognized as one of Germany's greatest literary figures.

Katherina Elisabeth Textor was born in 1731 into a wealthy and established family of Frankfurt am Main. Her father was a member of the Frankfurt city council and became the Schultheiss, a combination of judge, chief magistrate, and mayor. Katherina Elisabeth was brought up in a large, rambling house with a substantial garden. Accounts of her childhood indicate that she was vivacious and talented.

Katherina Elisabeth was barely eighteen when she married the wealthy Johann Kaspar von Goethe, an ambitious lawyer more than twice her age. In spite of a rigorous application to study and no small idea of his own importance, Johann Kaspar achieved little success. His young wife bore eight children though only the two eldest survived: Johann Wolfgang, born in 1749, and Cordelia, born in 1750. Cordelia died before she was thirty.

Johann Kaspar ruled the household and insisted in the early years of their marriage that his wife spent her time writing, playing the clavichord, and singing. As a result of her musical studies, Katherina Elisabeth learned some Italian. In his autobiography her son describes her as "always cheerful and gay and willing to make others so." Later he writes of her as "a good woman, never without some mental interest, who found her dearest solace in religion." He also tells a story that reveals something of the atmosphere of his childhood.

When he and his sister were very young they slept by themselves and, fearful of the dark, would leave their rooms to find comfort with one of the maids. Their father would put his dressing-gown on inside out, waylay them, and frighten them back to their beds – which only increased their fears. It was their mother who solved the problem by promising the children ripe peaches if they remained in their beds until morning.

Johann Kaspar insisted on personally giving his children their early education, and Goethe learned Italian by hearing his father teach his sister Cordelia. Johann Kaspar centered all his hopes on his children's achieving the high social standing that he himself had failed to attain, and he certainly recognized the exceptional ability of his son. He was a hard taskmaster, and if his children's studies were interrupted by illness he intensified their work on recovery in order to keep up with his rigid schedules.

In 1765, at the age of fifteen, Goethe was sent by his father to study law at Leipzig. He remained there for three years, until illness forced him home. His return was a source of happiness to Katherina Elisabeth, who idolized her son. But her happiness did not last, for her husband soon decided that Goethe's education should be completed by travel. After his travels her son settled in Weimar, the city that would be his home for the rest of his life, and she saw him only rarely. Katherina Elisabeth, her vivacious nature much subdued, remained alone with her embittered husband after the marriage of Cordelia.

Even after Johann Kaspar's death in 1782 she saw little of Goethe. He rejected her suggestion that she join him in Weimar, and when he did invite her to come to him because the French Revolutionary Armies had invaded Germany, it was she who refused. (She did eventually accept his suggestion that she sell the family home and move into lodgings.)

In 1799 Goethe visited her in Frankfurt, with his wife and son, but only for a few days. Five years later her grandson, August, then fifteen, paid her an extended visit, and this led to perhaps the warmest letter she ever received from her son. In it he wrote: "We all send our fondest, best and most grateful love." Not long afterwards, she received another visit from her son, and they parted for the last time. Goethe records that the parting was "not without emotion, for it was the first time after so long that we had got used to each other again." Katherina Elisabeth died alone in Frankfurt in 1808.

Goethe never seemed to have, and certainly did not express, any great affection or warmth for his parents. In spite of his father's help with his education and the interest shown by both his parents in his advancement, Goethe always remained cold and distant. Katherina Elisabeth had to be content with the reflected glory of his greatness, and the knowledge that his relations with her were a little more cordial than those with his father.

Right Cameo portrait of Katherina Elisabeth.

Gracia Lucientes

The mother of the Spanish painter Francisco Goya was Gracia, or Engracia, Lucientes. Her family were landowning aristocrats but the man she married, Francisco de Paula José Goya, was the son of a notary. José was a gilder by trade but not a prosperous one. At first the Goyas lived in Saragossa, the main city of the province of Aragon, but when José's business failed they moved to the village of Fuentodos, where Gracia had a little property.

It was there, at 18 Caile de Alfondiga, that their son Francisco was born, on March 30, 1746. He grew up like any other peasant boy of the time, mainly in the open air, with plenty of hard work and rough play. But the Goyas — and more probably Gracia, whose former way of life gave her ambitions for her sons — insisted that their children go to school. When the family moved to Saragossa again, in 1760, the boys had lessons at the Escuela Pia del Padre Joaquin, and it was here that Francisco had his first formal instruction in painting.

While Francisco's talents were taking him to churches and salons throughout Spain, and even to Court, José and Gracia still lived in poverty. When José died in December 1781, a note was written on his death certificate: "He died without leaving a will, because he had nothing whatever."

But by that time Francisco was a successful painter, well able to provide for his family. He had already furthered his brother Camillo's career in the Church (and in return received several commissions to paint religious pictures) and could afford to bring his widowed mother to live with him. He brought her to Madrid, where he was living in some style, but Gracia soon became homesick for Saragossa and after a while returned there, to live on a pension provided by her son until her death.

Goya was proud of his mother's noble birth and, when he became famous, took her family's coat-of-arms as his own emblem.

FRANCISCO GOYA
(1746-1828)
Spanish painter famous for his portraits of the Spanish royal family and for his etchings depicting the horrors of war.

Left Gracia, a detail of a portrait by her son.

Hannah Simpson

ULYSSES S. GRANT
(1822-85)
Commanded the Northern
armies in the American Civil
War. 18th President of the
United States (1869-77).

Below Hannah's first
married home on the
banks of the Ohio River.
Right A studio portrait
with her husband, Jesse.

Hannah Simpson was born in Ohio, the daughter of a rich farmer, John Simpson, who had moved to that state from Pennsylvania. In June 1821 she married Jesse Grant, a tanner, and settled with him in a two-room house at Point Pleasant, on the Ohio River.

In 1822 when the Grants' first child was born, the Simpsons and Grants met together to decide what names he should bear. Hannah herself wanted to call him Albert after the famous Swiss-American statesman Albert Gallarin; an aunt suggested Theodore. Since no decision could be reached by agreement, the various members of the family drew lots. The Simpson grandparents won. Mr. Simpson chose Hiram; Mrs. Simpson chose the more fanciful name Ulysses. He was always called by the latter name, and his mother often contracted it to "Lys." (Hiram Ulysses Grant became Ulysses Simpson Grant at the age of seventeen. He was mistakenly registered in a military academy as "U.S." and never bothered to correct the error.)

Ulysses was followed by five brothers and sisters: Simpson and Orvil, Clara, Mary, and Virginia. Jesse Grant's tanning business prospered, and the Grant home was a comfortable one. Moreover, both parents took great care in the upbringing of their children.

While Jesse Grant ensured that his sons gained the learning he had never acquired, Hannah took care of all the children's moral education. She was a strong Methodist and always lived her faith to the fullest. While her husband was social and ebullient, though contentious and not always well liked, Hannah was greatly respected for her modest behavior. Friends declared that she never argued, boasted, or gossiped, and she despised an uncontrolled show of emotion. "I never saw her shed a tear in my life," a neighbor remarked in later years. Another praised Hannah's fortitude: "When Ulysses was sick, she gave him a dose of castor oil, put him to bed and went calmly about her work, trusting in the Lord and the boy's constitution."

In 1848 Ulysses married Julia Dent, whom he had long loved; it was only after a long wrangle with his parents that he managed to obtain their blessing on his choice of a wife, for Julia's parents were slave-owners while the Grants were fervent Abolitionists. The Grants refused to attend the wedding at Julia's home, but they were soon won over by her charm, and Julia and her children spent long periods in their home while Ulysses was away at war.

When her son came home after the Civil War, Hannah made no show before her neighbors, nor did she treat him any differently. She greeted him at the door in her apron, saying: "Well, Ulysses, you've become a great man, haven't you?" – and then went back to her work.

When Grant was inaugurated as President of the United States, his mother did not go to Washington to see the ceremony. Nor did she ever visit him when he was President, though she had an open invitation. Her husband did go to the White House, but he always stayed in a hotel for he loathed Julia's father, who lived with the family.

Jesse died, aged seventy-nine, in the first year of President Grant's second term in office. Hannah went to live with her daughter Virginia in Orange, New Jersey, and there was always great excitement in the small town when her son came to visit her, though she always refused to make a public show for him.

Hannah died in 1883, a much respected woman. Her husband had once said of her: "Her steadiness and strength of character have been the stay of the family through life," and her son Ulysses never ceased to pay tribute to his mother's sober virtues.

KLARA POLZL

Above Klara Polzl Hitler.
Right The Hitler family
home; and Alois and Klara
Hitler's tombstone.

Klara Polzl was born on December 12, 1860, in
the village of Spital, in what is now northwestern
Austria. It was then a poverty-stricken corner of
the Austro-Hungarian empire — a wooded
countryside of isolated peasant settlements. Klara
was the eldest daughter of Johann Baptiste Polzl,
an unsuccessful farmer, and a peasant woman
named Johanna Hiedler (also spelled Hitler). Of
eleven children, only she and two other daughters
survived.

Klara was a simple, uneducated girl: tall, with
brown hair and quite attractive. Since her parents
still had to support her younger sisters, Klara
went at the age of eighteen to be a servant in the
household of "Uncle" Alois Hitler, a middle-aged
customs official stationed at the village of
Braunau on the Austro-German border.

Alois Hitler was born in 1837, the illegitimate
son of a servant woman named Maria Anna
Schicklgruber. Maria later married Johann Georg
Hiedler, a wandering miller whom she had known
at the time of Alois' birth. (His surname, a
common one, was often spelled Hutler or Hitler.)
But the child had been brought up by Johann
Georg's brother, Johann Nepanuk Hiedler, who
was also the father of Johanna — Klara Polzl's
mother. This convenient arrangement made
Maria's son "Uncle Alois" to Klara Polzl.

Maria Schicklgruber ended up so poor that she
had to sleep in a cattle trough, but her son Alois
made more of a success in life. At thirteen he
went to be a cobbler's apprentice in Vienna. At
eighteen he joined the Imperial Customs Service.
On the surface he matched his rank: a dignified,
impressively whiskered man; passionate about
beekeeping and fond of his uniform; strict and
pedantic in his dealings. In 1877 he had his
surname changed to Hitler after a legitimization
ceremony in which the dead Johann Georg was
posthumously — and hardly legally — declared to
be Alois' father.

When Klara joined his household, in the late
1870s, Alois was separated from his first wife —
Anna Glass, a well-off widow fourteen years his
senior — and was living openly with his mistress,
Franziska Matzelberger, a servant in the inn
where he had lodgings. Franziska, hoping for
marriage and fearing a rival, demanded that
Klara leave the household. Klara's father could
not support her, so she journeyed to Vienna to
earn her living as a domestic servant.

She returned to Alois' household in 1884. Alois
had married Franziska, and there were two
children, Alois Jr and Angela. The son was born
sixteen months before the marriage, the daughter

112

three months after. Klara returned because Franziska was dying of tuberculosis. She had to look after the two young children, and often went to help nurse Franziska.

Franziska died in August, aged twenty-three, and Klara stayed on as niece, maid, nurse, and mistress. By autumn she was pregnant. Alois was ready to marry her, the children adored her, and her parents had no objection. But marriage would be illegal, for Alois' legitimization — spurious though it was — had made the two second cousins.

Alois applied for and received a papal dispensation which would allow them to marry. On January 7, 1885, Klara and Alois were married. The wedding meal was in Alois' lodgings. The only guests were the new maid, two customs men, and Klara's sister Johanna — a hunchback with an unbelievably foul temper. Before the day was over, Alois was back on duty at the customs station. Klara carried on her roles of stepmother, housemaid, and cook. For years she called her husband "Uncle Alois."

By September 1887, Klara had three children. By January 1888 they were all dead. Then, on April 20, 1889, when Klara was twenty-nine and Alois forty-nine, Klara gave birth to another son. They called him Adolf. The child was sickly and Klara was always afraid that he would die.

Both mother and father came to pin their hopes on this child. As Alois grew older, his emotional instability increased. He moved house endlessly; experimented briefly with the farm he had always dreamed of; and retired in 1895, only fifty-eight, to a suburb of the town of Linz. Here, after a lifetime of officialdom, he found himself trapped in a household of young people. The growing Adolf came under the influence of his restless authoritarianism, and Alois set about planning a career in the civil service for his son. At the same time, Alois' disappointment with life communicated itself to Klara; as she gave up her own hopes, so she built up those for her son.

Alois died in 1903, aged sixty-five. By then, Adolf was well on the way to complete academic failure. And his hatred of his father's plans for him had crushed his will to learn. By 1905, Adolf, aged sixteen, was living in his mother's apartment in Linz — unemployed, reading, drawing, dreaming of the artist's career.

In 1907, Klara became painfully ill with a breast tumor. She died on December 21, after a terrible final month. Adolf was in Vienna, where he had just been finally rejected by the Academy of Art. He did not return until after his mother had died. When he did return the family doctor commented that he had never seen a young man so broken by grief.

On March 17, 1938, the day the Third Reich took over Austria, Hitler crossed the border at his birthplace, and the next day laid a wreath on his parents' grave. Throughout the war, his private room at Obersalzberg contained two portraits. One was of his mother, the other was of his dead chauffeur.

ADOLF HITLER
(1889-1945)
Founder of the German Nazi Party, and from 1933-45 dictator of Germany.

MARICHEN ALTENBURG

HENRIK IBSEN
(1828-1906)
Norwegian poet and playwright. Among his best-known works are *Peer Gynt*, *A Doll's House*, and *Hedda Gabler*.

Marichen Cornelia Martine Altenburg was born in 1799 in Skien, a small trading center in southern Norway. Her father was a wealthy shipmaster. As a young girl, Marichen was gay and spirited. Her son's biographer, Michael Mayer, describes her as "small and dark-haired, with deep and sensitive eyes." She played the piano and painted watercolors, and she was very fond of the theater. She continued to play with her dolls until she was a grown girl.

In 1825 Marichen married Knud Plesner Ibsen, a merchant two years her senior. Knud's father had been a sea-captain, but in the year of Knud's birth he was lost at sea. Knud's widowed mother married Marichen's uncle, so the two children had grown up together.

For the first eight years after his marriage to Marichen, Knud's business prospered. He ran a general store that stocked dairy produce, hardware and glass, dolls from Germany, English cotton goods, and French wines. He distilled his own schnapps in a distillery that was the second largest in the town. In 1833 only sixteen citizens of Skien's population of 3,000 earned a higher income than he.

Ten months after the marriage, Marichen gave birth to her first son. He died at the age of eighteen months, one month after the birth of her second child, Henrik Johan. Over the next seven years were born three more sons and a daughter, Hedvig.

Their first house in Skien was a two-story wooden building in the main square, directly opposite the church.

The family later moved to a bigger house, where they entertained frequently, and in 1833 Knud bought a small country house with forty acres of land. The following year his business collapsed. He was unable to pay his debts, the distillery was closed, the Skien house was sold with all its contents, and the family retired to the country house.

Knud never recovered from this blow. For the next forty years he worked at a variety of odd jobs, borrowing money from relatives and friends. Financial ruin broke his spirit, and it broke Marichen's too.

After the family's ruin, Marichen became a melancholic recluse. Her husband, distraught over his failure, bullied the family. "Knud Ibsen scared the wits out of her," said an old lady who had known Marichen, "so that in the end she became a changeling."

The country house was spacious and had a fine view of the valley, but social disgrace never lifted from the family. (The theme of bankruptcy repeatedly features in Henrik Ibsen's plays.) In 1843 Knud moved the family back to Skien. There were frequent rows between him and Marichen, and there was so little money that sometimes the main meal of the day consisted of nothing but potatoes.

Two days after Christmas in 1843, fifteen-year-old Henrik set sail for a tiny coastal town a hundred miles to the south, where he was apprenticed to an apothecary. He may have been able to afford an occasional journey back to Skien, but in 1850 he paid his last visit to his family on his way to the university at Christiania (now Oslo). By now Marichen and her daughter had been converted to a strict pietist religion with which the young Henrik, teeming with revolutionary ideals, felt no sympathy.

Marichen never saw her eldest son again. He married, wrote plays, and went abroad where he was to remain for nearly thirty years.

Marichen's second son emigrated to California and is thought to have died in the goldfields. Another son also emigrated to America. Marichen died in 1869 – two years after the successful publication of *Peer Gynt* – having spent her first thirty-five years in affluence and the second thirty-five years in varying degrees of poverty. Hedvig wrote to Henrik informing him of their mother's death. His reply may have been his first contact with his family since he had left home, more than nineteen years before.

Right The house next to the church, where Marichen and Knud Ibsen began their married life. *Far right* A silhouette believed to be the young Marichen.

114

Mary Queen of Scots

JAMES I AND VI
(1566-1625)
James VI of Scotland from 1567, he succeeded to the English throne, as James I, in 1603. He was the first monarch to rule both these countries.

Right A court painting of Mary Stuart, Queen of Scots.
Pages 118-119 Mary's trial and execution; and a letter to Elizabeth 1 written during Mary's imprisonment.

Mary Stuart was born in 1542, the only daughter of King James V of Scotland. Her mother was a French princess, Marie de Guise. Her father died within a few days of her birth, and Mary was one week old when she became Queen of Scots. The Scottish Court, scene of tough rivalry between rough and jealous Scots noblemen, was a dangerous place for a child Queen and it was not surprising that, when she was six, she should be sent to Paris to be educated at the French Court.

Thirteen years were to pass before she returned to her kingdom, and during that time she had become briefly not only Queen of Scots but Queen of France, for she had married the Dauphin of France when she was aged sixteen. Her husband, on the death of his father, became Francis II of France in 1559 but died the next year. The young widow was nineteen years old when she returned to Scotland.

Herself a devout Roman Catholic, she found Scotland (particularly the Court) divided between Protestantism and Catholicism. Dark intrigues and bloody feuds were the order of the day, and Mary herself was far from averse to intrigue. She was clever, beautiful and gay, and "would lounge for days in bed and rise only at night for dances and music." At twenty-one she made a disastrous mistake that was to affect the whole of her life and lead eventually to her tragic death. She married her cousin, the handsome Henry Stuart, Lord Darnley. Both were descended from Henry VII, Tudor King of England, and were therefore in the line of succession to the English throne, then occupied by the childless Queen Elizabeth.

The marriage was disastrous both politically and psychologically. Mary, highly intelligent and strong-willed, soon discovered that Darnley was weak, vain, and dissolute. She came very quickly to hate and fear him. When her secretary was murdered she thought that Darnley was one of the conspirators and that he had similar plans for herself and her son James.

James, who was to become the first monarch to reign over both England and Scotland, had been born (with a caul over his head) on June 19, 1566. His christening in December that year, for which his godmother Elizabeth I sent a huge gold font, was to be the last state ceremony Mary would attend until her own execution.

A few weeks after the christening, Darnley was killed when his house was blown up. Suspicion fell on Mary's closest supporter, the robust Earl of Bothwell, and on Mary herself. Shortly afterwards, when Mary married Bothwell, these suspicions seemed to be confirmed. The marriage was a second fatal mistake. The outraged nobles rose against them. Bothwell was driven into exile, from which he never returned. Mary was imprisoned on the island of Lochleven and was made to abdicate in favor of her baby son.

In 1568 Mary managed to escape from her prison and raised a small army, but it was easily defeated and she fled to England for protection. But protection was to take the form of virtual imprisonment, even if she lived in regal comfort. For Catholic Mary was a dangerous rival to Protestant Elizabeth for the English throne. She became the center of plots against Elizabeth, who once wrote to her: "Your actions are as full of venom as your words are of honey."

Despite her imprudent actions, Mary had great political ability and charm. One historian wrote of her "beauty, exquisite grace of manners, her generosity of temper and warmth of affection, her frankness of speech, her sensibility, her gaiety, her womanly tears, her manlike courage." One of Elizabeth's envoys, perhaps a little too close to the situation to judge dispassionately, painted a very different picture when he wrote: "Whatever craft, falsehood and deceit is in all the subtle brains of Scotland is either fresh in this woman's memory or she can fetch it out with a wet finger."

Mary sought to return to Scotland by offering to share the Scottish throne with her son James, arguing, as she had always done, that her abdication had been wrung from her under duress. But James would have none of it, for while Elizabeth was childless he was heir to the English throne. He turned down his mother's offer and accepted from Elizabeth the then considerable sum of £4000 down and £4000 a year.

By 1586 the conspiracies against Elizabeth had become intolerable. Mary became involved in a plot to kill her — it had been rumored that Rome did not think this would be regarded as a sin — and was sentenced to death. On February 8, 1587 (a year before the Catholic King of Spain sent his great Armada against England) she was beheaded. Of her forty-five years of life, the last nineteen had been spent in imprisonment.

117

The Execution of Mary, Queen of

MARY ROBERTSON WALSH

In 1836, two young men who were disillusioned with Presbyterian teaching abandoned their studies at Princeton Theological Seminary. One of them, Hugo Walsh, took his friend to his family home in Washington Square in New York City, where his widowed mother, Mrs James Walsh, lived on the income from the business estates left by her father and husband. The elegant Georgian house had entertained the elite of New York society, and it contained two eligible daughters named Mary Robertson and Catherine. The name of the visiting friend was Henry James.

Mary Robertson was twenty-six. She and her sister were so impressed by the young men's religious eloquence that they resigned from the local Presbyterian church. Two years later Mary accepted Henry's marriage proposal. Their wedding was on July 28, 1840. It was a secular ceremony, conducted in the Washington Square house by the Mayor of New York. Henry James — a man of extrovert fancies and introspective idealism — had won himself a shrewd, firm, practical wife.

Not practical enough, though, to curb the restlessness his inherited wealth allowed. In the first months they lived in three different houses and in the Ascot House Hotel — the most luxurious in the country. William, the eldest son, was born here in January, 1842. During the next six years they made a trip to Europe and had four more children: Henry, Jr, born in 1843; Garth Wilkinson, 1845; Robertson, 1846; and Alice, 1848. In the 1850s they traveled in Europe twice more, returned to live in a house in Newport, Rhode Island, and finally in 1866 settled in Cambridge, Massachusetts. Through all this, Henry James, Sr — friend of Emerson, host to Thackeray — carried on his role of prophet and metaphysician, lecturing, writing, and pamphleteering.

Mary's intellect could not share in his thoughts, but she was sympathetic nonetheless. "All that he has to say seems so good and glorious, and easily understood to him, and it falls so dead upon the dull, so sceptical souls who come to hear him."

Henry was her favorite, and when he wrote of her it was always as the picture of self-sacrifice: "sweet," "mild," "gentle," "patient," "beneficent." But she was, as she wrote, "strong in the nerves and strong in the legs." William wrote that she worked even when ill, "like a little buffalo." Emerson's son, visiting, paled at the sight of her children's argumentative furies, which included brandished dinner knives. "Don't be disturbed, Edward," she said, "they won't stab each other." That licence, too, was deceptive. "Holding a firm rein," she wrote, "is especially my forte." She would give way, quickly and cleverly, when opposed; but behind a mask of serenity, she ruled the house. When her children grew up and scattered, she ruled by letter: letters that could make them feel subtly accused of extravagance or hypochondria. Here is part of a letter William wrote home in 1861: "Wilky read Henry's letter and amused me 'metch' by his naive interpretation of Mother's most rational request that I should 'keep a memorandum of all moneys I receive from Father.'"

Mary James died on January 29, 1882. Her husband wrote with his usual bluntness: "She was not to me 'a liberal education,' intellectually speaking . . . but she really did arouse my heart." He lived on only till December, 1882. Henry Jr wrote that he died "with entire simplicity, promptness and ease, for the definite reason that his support had failed."

HENRY JAMES
(1843-1916)
American writer who spent much of his life in Europe. Among his most famous novels are *The Turn of the Screw* and *The Portrait of a Lady*.

Left Mary Robertson — "Holding a firm rein," she wrote, "is especially my forte."

Jane Randolph Jefferson

THOMAS JEFFERSON
(1743-1826)
A prominent democrat, he became third President of the United States in 1801. He played a major role in the drafting of the Declaration of Independence.

One biographer of Thomas Jefferson has written of Jane Randolph Jefferson that "the mother of no great man is as singularly devoid of embodiment for posterity" as she.

Jane Randolph was born in England, in the London parish of Shadwell, on February 20, 1720. Her father, Isham Randolph, was a well-to-do farmer and public servant in Virginia, well able to afford a trip to England for himself and his wife, and it was during their holiday in London that Jane was born. The Randolphs could trace their ancestry back to England and Scotland, a fact of which they were very proud.

Jane was still only a child when she met Peter Jefferson, a friend of her family. He was trying to raise a tobacco crop on his plantation near her home and often sought advice from Isham Randolph. In October, 1739, Peter and Jane were married. Although a match with a girl of such an aristocratic family was a step up for Peter Jefferson, he certainly did not marry Jane for her money. Her father promised her a dowry of £200, but it was not paid until three years later.

The Jeffersons lived first in a small house on Fine Creek, and in 1743 they moved into the house that they named Shadwell after Jane's birthplace. It lay in a deeply wooded area in the foothills of Virginia's Blue Ridge Mountains. Not long after they had settled there, Jane's third child and eldest son, Thomas, was born, to be followed in the subsequent years by seven more children, two of whom died in infancy.

These must have been trying years for Jane. Her husband was by no means wealthy, though by hard work he managed to make a decent living from raising livestock as well as tobacco. But he was eager to take his place in the colonial government, and often Jane was left alone to supervise work on the estate and tend her children without his help. Shadwell was near the front lines of the French and Indian War, and in 1755, when Jane was carrying her twins, the family lived in fear of Indian raids.

In 1757 Peter Jefferson died. In his will he left about 10,000 acres of land, 60 slaves, 25 horses, 70 head of cattle, and 200 hogs. Shadwell was left to Jane, and ample provision was made for the children's education and the girls' dowries. But financial security could be of only limited help to the young widow left with so many children — the youngest not yet two years old.

There seems to have been little affection between Thomas Jefferson and his mother, though he was always anxious for the welfare of his brothers and sisters. While he made his own way in the world, Jane lived on at at Shadwell until the winter of 1770, when it burned to the ground.

Jane Jefferson did not live to see her son become a hero of the emerging United States or his election as President. She died in 1776, while the War of Independence was raging. Her son recorded her death precisely but without emotion in his account book: "My mother died about eight o'clock this morning, in the fifty-seventh year of her age."

Right "Tuckahoe," home of the Jefferson family when Thomas was a young boy.

AMY (CISS) HODGE

If Amy Johnson epitomized the spirit of adventure, her mother, Amy Hodge, could be said to have epitomized bourgeois respectability.

Amy Hodge's father, William Hodge, was Mayor of Hull, a seaport on the North Sea coast of England. The Hodge family — who were small industrialists — lived in some style amid the comforts enjoyed by well-to-do Victorian families. In 1881 Amy Hodge was born, but she was soon given the nickname Ciss, by which she was almost always known throughout her life. She was brought up in a warm family atmosphere and, as was usual in families such as hers, she had a governess and music lessons.

She is described as "gentle, petite and dainty, with refined tastes as well as great charm" and was very fond of music. But in her 'teens, thanks to her father's prodigality, the family's fortunes declined and its standard of living dropped. Nevertheless those early years were to have a strong influence on her later life and Ciss clung to the memories of the Victorian elegance of her childhood.

When she was twenty she was wooed by Will Johnson, who was five years older than she, and married him in September, 1902. He was a market salesman in a family fish business. It was a flourishing business but the marriage was, socially, something of a let-down for the Hodge family. The newlyweds lived first in a modest two-story terrace house in Hull and it was here that Amy, the eldest child, was born on July 1, 1903. A sister, Irene, was born eighteen months later. A third daughter, Molly, was born in 1912 when the family had moved into a rather better house.

Ciss was a busy, rather fastidious mother and housewife. Her love of music continued and she became the official organist at the Methodist chapel where the family worshiped. She was a devout Methodist, something that was later to lead to a rift between her and Amy.

The rift occurred when Amy, who was at school until she was nineteen and then went to Sheffield University, fell in love with a local Hull businessman, a Swiss, whose mistress she eventually became. He was a Roman Catholic and her parents became so concerned over her affair that her father told her that she must either give up her lover or leave Hull. Amy chose the latter and went to London, the first step on her road to fame.

Although it was her father who delivered the ultimatum it was probably Ciss who inspired it. Amy wrote to her lover, "I don't think Father would ever have acted as he did if it hadn't been for Mother. . . . I really and honestly believe that given the opportunity and an excuse Mother could kill you. She's one of that sort." In London Amy found a new love — flying. Her Swiss lover married someone else and good relations between Amy and her mother were restored.

When Amy was planning her first great solo flight Ciss was forty-nine and in ill health. She was consumed with anxiety over the perils of the coming adventure. Nevertheless she reluctantly gave her approval and, in fact, the Hodges put up £500 toward the purchase of Amy's airplane.

As Amy became world famous for her exploits, Ciss, whose health was deteriorating, faded into the background, but it is clear from Amy's letters that she continued to be anxious about her daughter. "No more flights for me, I'm afraid, so you can finish worrying," Amy wrote. And in 1937 when her American counterpart Amelia Earhart was lost over the Pacific she hastened to ease her mother's mind: "No more flights so no need to worry. Poor Amelia."

Ciss's fears were to prove justified when her daughter was killed in the Thames Estuary on January 5, 1941.

AMY JOHNSON
(1903-41)
English aviator who established records in the 1930s for flights to India, Australia, and South Africa. She was presumed dead after her airplane was lost over the Thames Estuary.

Pages 124-125 Ciss poses with her daughter after Amy's flight from Japan.
Pages 126-127 Ciss and Will smile with pride as Amy receives the gift of a car after her flight to Australia.

NAOMI CANTOR

AL JOLSON
(1886-1950)
Born Asa Yoelson in
St Petersburg, Russia. He
became a popular American
singer and actor. He was
famous for his song
"Mammy," performed in black
face.

Naomi Cantor was the daughter of Reb Asa Cantor, the President of the synagogue at Keidani in Russian Lithuania. Records of these times are nonexistent, but some time, probably in the 1870s, she met Moses Yoelson, a young man from the village of Srednik, who was applying to her father for a job. Moses eventually became the rabbi and cantor in Srednik. But before that, he and Naomi had fallen in love and within two weeks of their meeting, they were married.

Times were hard in Srednik, particularly after Naomi began to have children. There were five in all; the future Al Jolson was the youngest. One child, a daughter, failed to survive the cold Lithuanian winter. Naomi had a powerful personality and was the moving force in the home. With great resourcefulness, she somehow managed to keep her family clothed and fed.

But lack of money was not the family's worst fear. The Russian Jews lived in dread of persecution by the Tsarist government. Many Jews were emigrating to the United States, and after some Cossack raids in neighboring villages, Moses began to wonder if he ought to join them. It was a hard decision because he did not have enough money to take his family as well, and there was no guarantee that he could earn enough in America to send money so that they could join him. Moses discussed the matter endlessly and, finally, it was Naomi who made the decision that he should go.

The year was 1890 and Al Jolson — known then as Asa Yoelson — was about four years old. With his father away in the United States, he and the other children became even more attached to their mother. Managing as best she could, she had to support the family for four years before Moses had saved enough to enable his wife and children to join him. She became weak and ill.

At last the day came when she could take them to the United States. Moses, who had settled in Washington D.C., was overjoyed to see them all again. His delight was even more intense when he discovered that little Al had a fine natural singing voice, because it had always been his ambition that his sons should also become cantors.

Al and his elder brother Harry had other ideas. Washington was a very different place from Srednik. Above all, there was a new and exciting kind of music. Soon Al and Harry were singing songs like "Swanee River" and "My Old Kentucky Home." Their father was furious and chastized them, but Naomi took their side. They were strengthening their voices, she said, in preparation for the day when they would become cantors. Moses was unconvinced. Neither was he happy when his wife arranged for her two sons to have violin lessons. Despite her spankings when they were late for meals, she was her sons' favorite parent.

Then tragedy struck. Naomi's long years of hardship had sapped her strength, and a year after emigrating to the United States she died. Without the powerful influence of Naomi, the Jolson family disintegrated. Moses never grasped what her loss meant to the children, who had been utterly dependent on her during their formative years. Even less did he understand their liking for American popular music. One cuff round the ear followed another as he watched his children absorbing a new life and language which took them further and further from the orthodox Jewish life of their birthplace.

If his mother had lived, Al might have become a cantor. But despite her great influence on him, there seems little evidence that she was the motivating force behind the song "Mammy." He always insisted that neither this song nor another of his great hits, "Sonny Boy," had anything to do with his own life.

Right The song her son made famous — which Naomi never heard.

My Mammy!

WRITTEN BY SAM LEWIS & JOE YOUNG

COMPOSED BY WALTER DONALDSON

FEATURED BY AL JOLSON

IN The JAZZ SINGER

WARNER BROS SUPREME TRIUMPH.

6D NET.

LONDON:
FRANCIS, DAY
& HUNTER LTD,
138-140, Charing Cross Road.
W.C.2.

NEW YORK:
IRVING BERLIN, Inc.,
1607, Broadway.

AUTHORISED FOR SALE
ONLY IN THE BRITISH EMPIRE
EXCEPTING CANADA,
AUSTRALIA & NEW ZEALAND.

COPYRIGHT.

Rose Fitzgerald

JOHN FITZGERALD KENNEDY
(1917-63)
35th President of the United States (1960-63).

Rose Fitzgerald was born in Boston, Massachusetts, in 1890. Her father, who came from a prosperous family, was a successful politican who became a state senator, sat in the US House of Representatives, and was three times Mayor of Boston. In her autobiography, *Times to Remember,* Rose wrote that her father liked to cut a figure and was more spontaneous than frugal, while her mother minded the budget.

The parents sent Rose and her sister to a convent school in Blumenthal, Holland. There she became proficient in French and German, which were to be helpful when marriage and motherhood took her into the world of diplomacy.

At the convent school she appears to have been hard-working and already showed signs of the brisk efficiency that was to characterize her later life. But that she was a very normal schoolgirl is clear from a letter to her parents in which she asked them to send her copies of "Are you Sincere?," "Take me out to the Ball Game," and other popular song hits. And in another letter she told her mother: "Agnes [her sister] and I bought two captivating little hats, just the kind you and Pa like, plain and small, but oh, so coy!"

Rose was twenty-four when she married Joseph Patrick Kennedy. He was the twenty-six-year-old son of a Boston saloon owner whose father had left Ireland during the potato famine. Joseph's own father became a state senator and political boss of a ward in Boston. Thus the marriage brought together two powerful Irish-American political families.

Joseph himself was not to follow in his father's footsteps either as a saloon owner or a politician. He showed remarkable business acumen and by the time of his marriage had already gained control of a small bank in Boston. He was a

millionaire at the age of thirty and was to become one of the wealthiest men in the United States. Although he never entered politics as such, he was given several important government posts by President Franklin D. Roosevelt.

There were nine children of the marriage, four sons and five daughters. Rose Kennedy's life was dominated by unwavering Catholicism and devotion to her husband and her children, over whom she watched with unflagging efficiency. She kept a card index of their progress, their illnesses, and even visits to the dentist. She was very much the mistress of her home for her husband was often away, but she deferred to him.

The peak of her husband's career was his appointment as US Ambassador to London where he served for the significant years from 1937 to 1940. There in the British capital Rose Kennedy was presented at Court and presided as hostess at Embassy receptions. Their stay in London led to the marriage of the daughter Kathleen to a British marquis.

Rose Kennedy was in her sixties when her son John became a senator and was seventy when he was elected President, but she played an active and purposeful role in his and his brothers' political struggles. Moreover she kept her sense of humor. When John was President, she sent some photographs of him with the Soviet leader to Mr Krushchev along with a request that he should sign them for her family. When her son learned of her action he chided her gently, writing, "Dear Mother, if you are going to contact Heads of State it might be a good idea to consult me or the State Department first as your gesture might lead to international complications. Love, Jack." To this she replied with tongue in cheek that she was glad he had warned her — she was about to write to Castro.

Right Rose caught deep in conversation.
Pages 132-133
Photograph of one of America's most famous families.

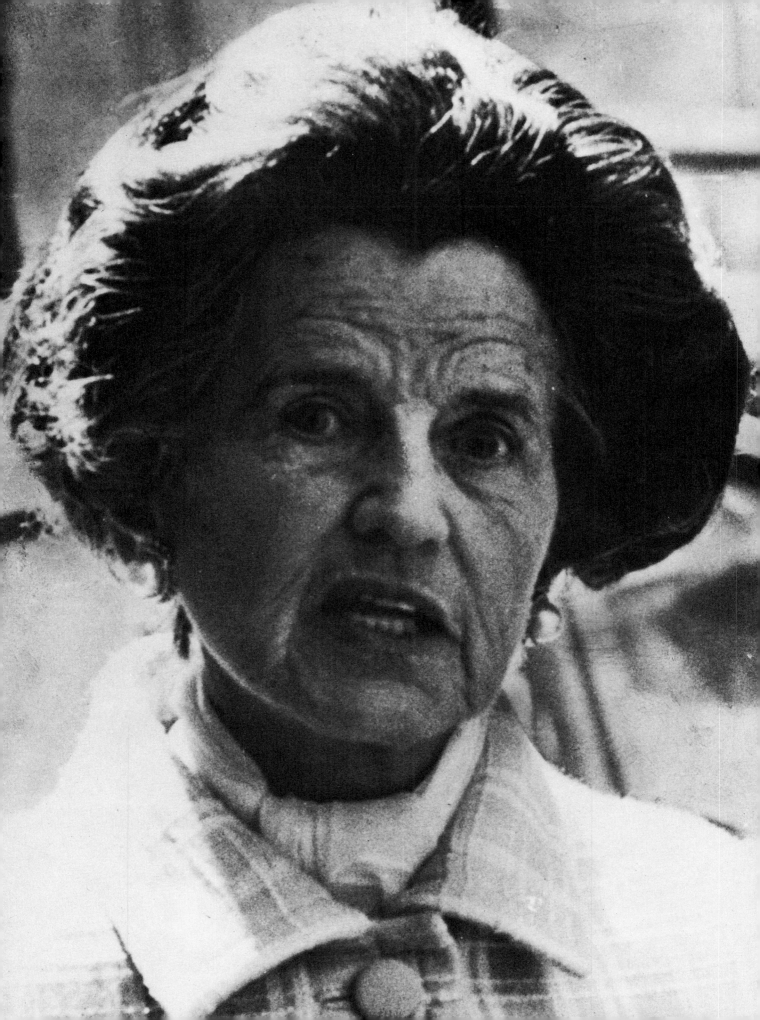

Alberta Williams King

REVEREND DR MARTIN LUTHER KING, JR
(1929-68)
A major figure in the American civil rights movement. He received the Nobel Peace Prize in 1964 and was assassinated in 1968.

On June 30, 1974, Alberta "Mama" King was once more playing the organ for the Sunday service at Ebenezer Baptist Church in Atlanta, Georgia. Her husband, Martin Luther King Sr, was the pastor of the church, and she was making a guest appearance that day (she had retired from the position of full-time organist some time before). The congregation was starting to sing "Just a Little Talk with Jesus" when a young black man entered the church and moved down into the "Amen" corner next to the organ. Seconds later he pulled out a gun and, screaming, "I'm tired of all this, I'm taking over," he shot Mrs King and two other people at point-blank range. Her husband, who was not preaching that Sunday and who had come into the church only minutes before, hurried to her side. Alberta King was rushed to the hospital, but she died within the hour. She was sixty-nine years old.

The death of "the peaceful warrior," as Mama King was called, caused sadness and anger throughout the United States and the world. Flags were flown at half-mast all over Atlanta, and the mayor described her as "one of the great women of history, a rock of ages."

Alberta Christine Williams was born in Atlanta in 1904, the daughter of the Reverend Adam Daniel Williams, one of the most influential pastors of the city. He had been a local leader of the NAACP (National Association for the Advancement of Colored People) during the 1920s, when the Ku Klux Klan was at its most destructive, and had been instrumental in securing the first high school in Atlanta for black pupils. He took over the Ebenezer Baptist Church and made it one of the strongest and most famous black churches in the South.

Alberta attended Spelman Seminary and Hampton Institute. While still a student, she met Martin Luther King, and they were married with her father's approval on Thanksgiving Day, 1926. Martin was the son of a poor drunken sharecropper on a cotton plantation. In 1916 he walked twenty miles to Atlanta, where he took a job, studied at night, saved his money, and went to Morehouse College. From there he went on to become a fervent Baptist preacher. He was a sober, thrifty man, and was immediately welcomed into the family by his father-in-law.

The Kings and Williamses each lived in half of the Reverend Williams' large white frame house on Auburn Avenue. This began as a temporary arrangement but it suited both couples so well that it became permanent. Alberta worked as a teacher until the birth in 1928 of their first child, Christine. On January 15, 1929, the Kings had a son, who was named Martin Luther Jr. Alberta had a very difficult time with the birth, and when the baby finally arrived it was so quiet that they thought it was stillborn. Their third child, Alfred Daniel, was born in 1931.

Alberta and Martin King raised their children in rigorously conventional circumstances. They were a popular family in the community, and their backyard became a gathering place for all the neighborhood children. Alberta was always ready to comfort and encourage her children, and if ever they were discriminated against she would tell them: "Always remember you are just as good as anyone."

"Bunch," as she was called by her husband, was a quiet and devout woman. She was the "soul and backbone" of the family, and an inspiration behind her son's doctrine of nonviolence. She taught him to believe in peace and freedom. Yet she was no stranger to violence and tragedy. She lost both her sons within eighteen months: Martin Luther fell to an assassin's bullet in April 1968, and Alfred Daniel accidentally drowned in a swimming pool at his home in 1969. According to one of Martin's colleagues, "Doctor King's sweetness came from her. She was sweet to the point of innocence, as choice as any woman who ever lived."

Right "Mama" King's expressive face displays her grief at the loss of both her sons.

LYDIA BEARDSALL

DAVID HERBERT LAWRENCE
(1885-1930)
English novelist and poet.
Famous for such novels as
*Sons and Lovers, Women in
Love,* and *Lady Chatterley's
Lover.*

Lydia Beardsall was born on July 19, 1852. She came of a Nottingham, England, family that had made money in the lace industry but then lost it during the depression of 1837. There was in her family a strong nonconformist tradition: her father was a Methodist preacher, her grandfather a famous hymn-writer.

In 1874 Lydia met Arthur Lawrence, a young collier with black hair and beard. Arthur was different from most of the men she had known, and different in character from Lydia herself. He spoke roughly, loved to dance, and had an energetic enthusiasm for life; she was sensitive, fastidious and puritanical. They were married on December 27, 1875. Shortly after their marriage, Arthur Lawrence returned to his old pit job and moved with his bride into a cottage at Brinsley. The first night he came home from the pit he was so covered with coal dust that she thought a black man had come into the house. This was the life of a collier's wife which Lydia Lawrence was to know for the next thirty-five years. It is clear

from her daughter Ada's account that she quickly regretted her marriage.

Despite the troubles that followed, Lydia Lawrence struggled courageously and even cheerfully to give her children the kind of life she wanted for them. Her husband regularly drank away much of his earnings, and Lydia supplemented the housekeeping money by running a small shop in the front room, selling linen and lace. She found solace in the company of the children and tried to keep them from their father's influence. She was determined above all that her sons should not go into the mines and that her daughters should not become domestic servants.

Her five children were born between 1877 and 1887. David Herbert — or Bertie, as the family called him — was the second youngest and the youngest of the three sons. He was a frail, bronchitic child, and he demanded and received much of his mother's attention. "We all petted and spoiled him from the time that he was born —

my mother poured her very soul into him," said his brother George. Having been a schoolteacher before her marriage and a writer of verse herself, Lydia Lawrence was determined that Bertie should shine academically as his oldest brother William had done. After William's death at twenty-three, his youngest brother became the chief purpose and mainstay of her existence. For Bertie's education she would make endless sacrifices, and as a young man he would go with her on holiday to Mablethorpe or the Isle of Wight. Jessie Chambers spoke of the "curious atmosphere" of the Lawrence household at this time, which she thought to be compounded of Lydia's grief over the death of William, her antagonism to her husband, and her love of Bertie. Certainly the latter always felt torn between his love for his mother and his attraction to other women: "My mother has been passionately fond of me and fiercely jealous. She hated Jessie and would have risen from the grave to prevent my marrying her," he wrote in a letter just before his mother's death.

In August 1910, while staying with her sister Ada in Leicester, Lydia Lawrence fell ill with cancer. She was brought home, and there she died an agonizing death on December 9. Lawrence had written to his publisher and urged that *The White Peacock* be published, if possible, before her death, and he afterwards described how "the very first copy of *The White Peacock* that was ever sent out I put into my mother's hands when she was dying. She looked at the outside, and then at the title-page, and then at me, with darkening eyes . . . she was beyond reading my first immortal work. It was put aside, and I never wanted to see it again. She never saw it again." He later said of her:

She is my first, great love. She was a wonderful, rare woman — you do not know; as strong, and steadfast, and generous as the sun. She could be as swift as a white whiplash, and as kind and gentle as warm rain, and as steadfast as the irreducible earth beneath us.

Page 136 The Lawrence home where Lydia ran her front room shop; and a studio portrait of the growing Lawrence family. *Below* Lydia suffering from cancer in the last months of her life; and the house where she died.

ann hill carter

ROBERT E. LEE
(1807-70)
American general who commanded the Confederate Army in the Civil War.

Ann Hill Carter was one of the twenty-one children of Charles Carter of Shirley, a rich estate on the James River in Virginia. Carter was so wealthy that each of his children was heir to a fortune. Ann, born in 1773, was brought up in an atmosphere of freedom and generosity.

The family was large and well-connected, and had plenty of social life. Among the family friends were the Lees, who lived in nearby Stratford. Ann was twenty when Henry Lee, at that time the Governor of Virginia, came into her life. Henry had had a brilliant career in the Revolutionary War as a leader of light cavalry; his exploits had earned him the nickname of "Light-Horse Harry." He had been married once but his wife, Matilda, had died in 1790. After her death Henry spent much of his time in public life and even contemplated going to France to fight in the revolutionary army there. When he first went to Shirley to visit with the Carters he fell in love with Ann's best friend Maria Farley, who was staying there at the time. To complete the triangle, Ann fell in love with Henry.

But Maria did not care for him at all and refused his proposal of marriage – although her loyal friend tried to persuade her to accept, saying: "Oh, stop, stop, Maria – you do not know what you are throwing away." Refused by Maria, Harry then turned his attentions to Ann and proposed to her too. Charles Carter tried his best to oppose the match but he finally relented, and the marriage took place on June 18, 1793.

For Ann, marriage meant moving to Richmond, the state capital, to take up her duties as the Governor's wife. Unfortunately, it meant much more than that. A friend of the family later wrote that she had just a fortnight's happiness before the defects of Light-Horse Harry's character became fully apparent, for the gallant General was a spendthrift and a philanderer. Neither his father nor his first wife had ever trusted him with the management of affairs, and though he enjoyed a considerable fortune, he did not have full control over it. The brighter side of Harry Lee's life continued for a few years. In 1799, after completing his second term as Governor of Virginia, he was elected to Congress. A few months later he delivered a brilliant eulogy

for his old Commander-in-Chief, George Washington. Now real poverty came, for Harry had been speculating in an attempt to retrieve his fortunes and lost all his money. Ann found life at Stratford, Lee's family mansion, dreary indeed. She stayed there alone while her husband vainly tried to retrieve his fortunes. She had to keep herself warm by carrying a charcoal brazier from one room to another.

The dreariness gave place to a time of alarms and troubles, with Light-Horse Harry dodging creditors and debt collectors. In this milieu Ann gave birth to four children, the eldest of whom died when a year old. Early in 1807, just before the birth of a fifth child, she wrote to her sister-in-law indicating that this baby was very much unwanted. The child was Robert Edward Lee, who was to be her mainstay and comfort in the years ahead.

In 1809 Light-Horse Harry's debtors finally caught up with him, and he spent the next two years in a debtors' prison. In 1812 he was stabbed and left for dead while defending an editor friend against readers who did not like his political views. A year later Henry Lee – disfigured, bent, and nearly blind – left Virginia for the West Indies in search of sunshine and health. In his lonely wanderings he never forgot Ann. He wrote to his son Carter, on their wedding anniversary: "This is the day of the month when your dear mother became my wife . . . a happy day, marked by the union of two humble lovers." Nine months later he was dead.

For Ann Lee, the years of separation and widowhood were marred by persistent and painful illness. Accounts of her, and her few surviving letters, show her to have been a simple, meticulous person who taught her children the qualities of character that she valued so highly. She asked her sons to be "honorable and correct" and indulge only in such habits "as are consistent with religion and morality."

In her last years Ann came increasingly to depend on Robert, the eldest son left at home. During her last illness he nursed her devotedly, gave her medicine, and spent nearly all his time with her, night and day, until at last death came.

Right A portrait of Ann, mother of the future Confederate commander, wearing a cameo portrait of George Washington.

Maria Aleksandrovna Blank

VLADIMIR ILYICH LENIN
(1870-1924)
Russian revolutionary leader, founder of the Bolshevik Party, and first Head of State of the newly formed Soviet Union.

Right Maria and Ilya with their six children.
Far right In this idealized painting the widowed Maria is comforted by Vladimir after the execution for revolutionary activities of her eldest son, Alexander.
Pages 142-143 The years of suffering gently weather Maria's determined features.

Maria Aleksandrovna Blank came from a respectable bourgeois family. Her father, a Russian of German origin, was a doctor and a landowner. He raised his daughters on a 1000-acre estate and had them educated by private tutors. He also insisted that they sleep between damp sheets ("to strengthen their nerves") and forbade them to drink tea or coffee, both of which he regarded as poisons.

In 1863 Maria married Ilya Nikolayevitch Ulyanov, a teacher of mathematics and physics at the Penza Institute for Children of Noble Families. Ilya made good progress in his profession: he was appointed an inspector of schools and later became Director of Public Schools. Most of the couple's married life was spent near Simbirsk, a town on the Volga River, where they lived in relative isolation. Here they raised six children (one had died in infancy) and managed, through Maria's frugality, to live in substantial physical comfort.

Family life has been pictured as tranquil and contented. Ilya would often read to the children — perhaps from *War and Peace,* which was then being serialized. Maria, who had been tutored in music, would play the piano while the children sang.

This domestic happiness was disrupted in 1886, when Ilya died suddenly of cerebral hemorrhage. Not long after this, disaster struck again: Alexander, the eldest son, was executed for conspiring to assassinate the Tsar, and his sister Anna was imprisoned. During this dreadful period Maria showed great courage, pleading everywhere for her son. On the eve of his execution she sat outside his cell door urging him to be brave.

After Alexander's execution Maria became desperately anxious to save Vladimir from a fate like his brother's. But he, a brilliant though erratic student, was already becoming a revolutionary. Hoping to divert him from this course, Maria bought a small farm. "Mother wanted me to run a farmstead," Lenin later said. "I had given it a try, but I saw that it wouldn't work." The family lived on the farm for just one summer.

In 1889 the family moved to Samara (now Kubyshev) where they shared a two-story house with another family. By this time the whole Ulyanov family, except perhaps Maria, had become the object of official disfavor. The house became a center of radical intrigues, and Maria, still pained by memories of her eldest son's execution, was sorely distressed. "It is a grievous pain," she wrote, "to look at my son and see his best years being wasted away."

Vladimir had been expelled from Kazan University for participating in a student protest meeting, and his applications for readmission and for jobs were consistently rejected. That he was in trouble with the authorities was made quite clear on one of his applications. Some official wrote on it: "Ask the superintendent and department of police about him. He is a rotten man."

It was only through the pleadings of his long-suffering mother that Vladimir was able to take extramural courses at St Petersburg University, where he passed his law examinations brilliantly. He was to spend a short time in a law firm in Samara, but thereafter devoted himself to revolutionary activities. His periods of exile in Siberia and then in Europe meant that mother and son saw little more of each other.

Maria died in 1916, aged eighty-one, while Lenin was in exile in Zurich. He was said to have been heartbroken and to have gone on long walks in the mountains. Leon Trotsky said later that Maria Blank was, for her son, "the source of nourishment, the playmate always there, always at hand, the author of all blessings, the source of all joys, the angel of justice in the nursery."

Frances Zuchowski

WLADZIU VALENTINO LIBERACE
(1920-)
American pianist and popular entertainer whose public image is characterized by glamor, opulence, and love for his mother.

Most people associate the name of Liberace with candelabra, glittering clothes, and mother. When the Queen Mother met Liberace, after he had made the 1972 British Royal Command Performance, she immediately asked him: "How's your mother?"

At the time of this meeting the most famous mother in show business had just celebrated her eightieth birthday. She was born Frances Zuchowksi in Menasha, Wisconsin and spent her childhood in that state. When she was eighteen she married a French-horn player, Salvatore Liberace, who had played with John Philip Sousa and with the Milwaukee Symphony Orchestra. She had four children, the third of whom — Wladziu Valentino Liberace — was born when she was twenty-eight. Wladziu, known today only by his last name, got his middle name from Rudolph Valentino, his mother's silent-film hero.

Liberace was born in West Allis, Wisconsin, an area that many Polish immigrants had found congenial and made their home. Even the severe winters had a welcome familiarity. Liberace's grandparents were farmers, and Frances inherited many of their homey ways. After she was married, she continued to go to her parents' home to wash her hair in rain water they collected in a cistern. She regularly took Liberace to the farm so that he had enough fresh air. Essentially she was a country girl who found even a small town too full of people. She insisted that her children be brought up in the country, which was an excellent idea except that her husband had difficulty finding work in the Wisconsin area, and what he did find was not very lucrative.

But Mrs Liberace showed herself equal to the occasion and opened a family grocery shop. The Liberaces lived behind it and, since both parents were good cooks, the family lived well. Salvatore found work even harder to come by during the Depression, but Frances, with great skill and devotion, always kept the home going.

She liked music, but it was Liberace's father who guided his early musical education. When Liberace was only seven, he won a scholarship to the Wisconsin College of Music where he studied for many years. (Liberace is, in fact, a very good pianist — something that his extravagant showmanship is apt to make people forget.)

Nonetheless, in one dramatic way, Frances made her son's career possible. When he was quite young, one of his fingers became infected and the doctors wanted to amputate it. She realized that this would thwart his ambition, which was, even then, to become a famous pianist. True to her background, she defied the doctors, applied an old-fashioned poultice, and the finger was saved.

Frances retained for many years her belief in the simple life. Even after Liberace was earning enough to buy her anything she wanted, she eschewed extravagance. It was a long time, for example, before he could persuade her to have a deep-freeze because she believed that food that had been frozen was unhealthy. For many years, she still preferred to wash her own hair. But after she began to make some guest television appearances and saw how glamorous professional make-up artists could make her look, she finally agreed to go to a beauty shop.

Today there is a wide gap between the home-loving Frances of Wisconsin and the Frances with a house in Hollywood Hills playing a leading role in Liberace's vast publicity network. Liberace himself says that it was probably vanity that persuaded his mother to have her hair professionally styled. Clearly, she has learned to enjoy the opulent life that her son's fame has opened up to her.

Right Frances is escorted by her proud son from a house they intend to buy. *Page 146* Frances, with her hand on her son's shoulder, shares in Liberace's popular success.

Nancy Hanks

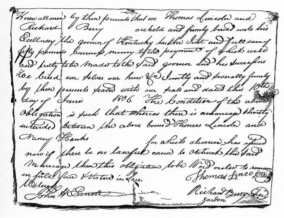

Above The marriage bond between Nancy Hanks and Thomas Lincoln.

"God bless my mother, all that I am or ever hope to be I owe to her." These words, spoken by Abraham Lincoln to his friend and biographer William Herndon, are remarkable for being one of Lincoln's few known references to his mother. She died when Abe was nine, and if he had any vivid memories of her, they were never recorded. Throughout his lifetime, Lincoln's opponents twisted what few facts were known in an attempt of dishonor his family name.

Nancy Hanks was born in Virginia sometime in 1784. Her mother, Lucy Hanks, was probably nineteen years old at the time of her birth. Nothing is known of Nancy's father. President Lincoln believed that he was a well-bred Virginia farmer or planter but no evidence has come to light to prove or disprove this opinion. At any rate, the President seems to have accepted the possibility that his mother was born illegitimate and, according to Herndon, he even had a theory that "for certain reasons, illegitimate children are oftentimes sturdier and brighter than those born in lawful wedlock."

Nancy's childhood was certainly unsettled. When she was very young, her mother brought her to Kentucky. Having a child to look after does not seem to have a had a sobering effect on Lucy. The record of the Grand Jury of Mercer Court, November 24, 1789, reads, "Lucy Hanks for fornication," and orders that she should be issued with a summons to appear. But Lucy became engaged to a young man named Henry Sparrow, and the court dropped its proceedings. A year later they were married. After a few years living with her mother and new stepfather, Nancy went, in 1796, to live with an uncle and aunt, Thomas and Elizabeth Sparrow. This couple had no children of their own and, as the years passed, clung to her with close affection. They brought her up virtuously and religiously and seem to have offered her some education.

Nancy and Thomas Lincoln were married in a neighbor's house on June 12, 1806. They were poor, but there were festivities and square-dancing after the ceremony. Thomas was born in Virginia but had moved to Kentucky in early childhood. He was able "bunglingly to write his own name." Nancy is believed to have been able to read and write, although on the one known document to which her name is signed she made her mark. They lived in a cabin in the backwoods of Kentucky. Thomas did farmwork and some carpentry. He bought a few plates and spoons at auctions, and they had enough to eat between the game they hunted and the few chickens they kept.

ABRAHAM LINCOLN
(1809-65)
16th President of the United States (1861-65), assassinated in 1865.

They may even have had a cow. The Lincolns were Baptists, but they were isolated and the preacher came by only once a month.

Sarah, their first child, was born in 1807. Two years later, Nancy gave birth to her first son, and they named him after his grandfather Abraham Lincoln, who had been killed by Indians many years before. If all the claims that have been made are true, half the female population of the county was present at Abe Lincoln's birth. A conservative estimate would put that figure in the hundreds. The facts of Lincoln's childhood and family are so few and far between that there is even debate among his biographers as to whether he was born on a mattress filled with corn husks and straw, or whether the Lincolns were wealthy enough to have one stuffed with chicken feathers. Nancy's third child, Thomas, was born in 1812 but died in infancy.

In 1816 the family moved from Kentucky to an undeveloped region of Indiana. They settled in what Abe later described as "unbroken forest," and lived in a "half-faced camp" while they built their log cabin. They moved into this before it was finished because Betsy and Thomas Sparrow

– Nancy's aunt and uncle – came out to join them, and they took over the camp. The hardships of those first years were very great. Abe learned to use an axe and helped clear the land. Just as prospects were brightening for the families, there was an outbreak of the "milk-sick," the intermittent scourge of the pioneers which, it is thought, came from drinking poisoned milk. The Sparrows both died of it. Nancy came down with the "sick" barely a month later, and died on October 5, 1818, within seven days of falling ill. She was buried in a coffin that Abe claimed he helped his father to build and, as was customary, her funeral was held several months later. Thomas married Sarah Bush in 1819 and lived until 1851.

Nancy was tall, slender, and dark-complexioned. Of her character nothing seems to be known. William Wood, a neighbor of Nancy's, and one of the few people who remembered her, said in 1865: "She was a remarkable woman truly and indeed. I do not think she absolutely died of the milk sickness entirely. Probably this helped to seal her fate." What he meant by this we are unlikely ever to know.

Right The Lincoln family's simple home.
Far right An artist's impression of Nancy, the President's mother.

Evangeline Lodge Land

CHARLES LINDBERGH JR.
(1902-74)
American aviator who in 1927 achieved fame by making the first solo flight across the Atlantic. In 1932 his baby son was kidnapped and killed.

The character of Evangeline Lodge Land is perhaps well summed up in the remark she made to press photographers who were trying to persuade her to kiss her son goodbye before he made his historic solo flight across the Atlantic. "No," she said, "I wouldn't mind if we were used to that, but we come of an undemonstrative Nordic race."

In fact, according to her son, she was of English, Irish, and French extraction. She was born and raised in Detroit and married Charles Augustus Lindbergh on March 27, 1901. Charles was a prosperous attorney who had a pleasant estate in Little Falls, Minnesota, where he held a bank directorship. From 1907 to 1917 he was a U.S. Congressman. For him this was a second marriage, his first young wife having died in tragic circumstances.

At the time of her marriage Evangeline, a graduate of Michigan and Columbia Universities, was a science teacher in Little Falls High School, and was to be a teacher for most of her life. The newly married couple built an imposing house with thirteen rooms. They called it Lindholm, and lived there for five years before it was completely destroyed by fire.

Their only child was born in 1902 in Detroit. Charles Jr was very attached to his father, but he was brought up by his mother — for the marriage was a failure and although there was no divorce the parents were estranged and led separate lives. In addition to her teaching, Evangeline also rode horses and painted watercolors. She was described by contemporaries as a fine, gracious lady, always reserved but very kindhearted. In later life she emerges as a modest person, devoted to her son and to her profession. Her son was devoted to her; during his adolescence an aunt, asked about his girl friends, said "his mother is his only girl."

By the time Charles was about seventeen his parents' separation was complete. His mother had resumed teaching physical science at Emerson Junior High School in Madison, Wisconsin, where she made a home for him and herself on the top floor of an undistinguished brownstone house. The young Charles went to the University of Wisconsin but left after two years in order to study aviation, which had become a consuming passion. "It almost broke my heart," said his mother later. To her son, however, she said: "You must lead your own life. I mustn't hold you back."

Physically, Evangeline was a woman of just over average height, "more sturdy than beautiful, efficient more than graceful," and her reserve gave the impression of a rather stiff and cold personality. By 1923 she was alone, teaching chemistry at Cass Technical School, Detroit, while her son was off flying an airplane he had bought for $500 before becoming a U.S. Airmail Pilot. Her husband died in 1924.

In 1927, when her son made his historic flight, she was temporarily and reluctantly caught up in the adulation that followed. It was to his mother that Lindbergh telephoned from Paris. Typically she slipped quietly into Washington to greet him on his return and only with difficulty was she tracked down to take her place in the national welcome which had been organized.

Within a few days she and her son were being feted, attending receptions and joining President Coolidge and his wife in a church service the following Sunday. But the modest teacher was unruffled by the glories of the moment. Asked by reporters what her future plans were she replied curtly, "I have signed my teaching contract for next year."

Evangeline remained a teacher for the rest of her working life. As she grew older she suffered from Parkinson's disease, and died on September 7, 1954.

In her will she left about $5,000 which was divided between her brother and her son with this explanation: "My son, Charles Augustus Lindbergh, is my heir and would be the natural recipient of my estate. Such a disposition would be my preference because in an inadequate way it would recognize a devotion to me which has been full and constant and which has been expressed in many material and spiritual forms."

Right Evangeline gazes upward in search of her famous son's airplane.

MARIA THERESA

Maria Theresa was a redoubtable woman. Not only was she a daughter of the Holy Roman Emperor Charles VI, but she became Empress herself and was also Queen of Hungary and Bohemia and Archduchess of Austria. Wars were fought over her and by her, and as Empress she was in her time one of the three most powerful women in Europe.

What is more, Maria Theresa somehow found time to give birth to sixteen children. All her daughters were given the first name Maria, and her tenth child, born in 1755 when Maria Theresa was thirty-eight, was named Maria Antonia. Later this name was gallicized, and Maria Antonia has gone down in history as Marie Antoinette, whose life ended at the guillotine during the French Revolution. A major contributor to this tragedy may have been Maria Theresa herself.

Charles VI was the last Hapsburg male heir. By what was called the Pragmatic Sanction, he proclaimed before his death that his daughter Maria Theresa should succeed him. The Pragmatic Sanction was accepted by the principal rulers of Europe but no sooner was Charles dead and buried than some of them, led by Frederick the Great of Prussia, went back on their word and challenged Maria's right to succeed. The year 1740, in which Maria Theresa ascended the throne at the age of twenty-three, also marked the beginning of the War of the Austrian Succession which lasted for eight years. Prussia, France, Spain, and others lined up against Austria, Hungary, Holland, and England. During the war, Maria Theresa already showed her skill as diplomat and stateswoman. She married Francis, Duke of Lorraine, who became Emperor, but Maria Theresa kept control over most affairs of State.

In her forty years as Empress Maria Theresa was a wise, astute, and respected ruler, introducing reforms and greatly strengthening her Empire. But if she was a good Empress, she was a poor mother — at least to the child Marie Antoinette. She kept her brilliant court in the famous Schönbrunn Palace, while somewhere in its rooms, away from the glittering salons, the little Archduchess led a pampered life, spoiled by indulgent governesses and music- and dancing-teachers but learning nothing to prepare her for her coming marriage to the future King of France. It is strange that her mother, who for years had maneuvered for this marriage of convenience, should have done nothing to prepare the child for its responsibilities.

So it was a pretty, frivolous young girl of fifteen, brought up in the extravagance of a splendid court, who set off in a cavalcade of over fifty carriages to join her husband in France. At the last moment Maria Theresa seems to have realized how ill-prepared the child was for she began sending messages advising her about her conduct. In a letter to the Austrian ambassador in Paris, she wrote: "I say outright that I do not want my daughter to have a marked influence in affairs. I know only too well from personal experience what a weight it is to rule a huge kingdom. What is more, I know my daughter's frivolousness and her aversion to concentrating — and she does not know a thing! All that makes me thoroughly afraid if she should try to govern a kingdom as ramshackle as France at the moment."

Maria Theresa died in 1780 at the age of sixty-three. Almost all the calamities she foresaw for her daughter were to come true in one way or another. She, however, did not live to see them.

MARIE ANTOINETTE (1755-93) Frivolous and extravagant wife of King Louis XVI of France. She was guillotined in 1793 during the French Revolution.

Far left State portrait of Maria Theresa, Holy Roman Empress.
Left A Maria Theresa silver *Thaler.*
Page 154 Portrait of Maria Theresa when a girl.
Page 155 The Empress — the hands that held a rose now hold the symbols of power.
Pages 156-157 In a 19th-century illustration Maria Theresa presents her infant son, Joseph, to the assembled politicians of central Europe.

Margaretha Ziegler

Martin Luther's mother, Margaretha Ziegler, was born in about 1463, in the small town of Möhra in the Thuringian forest of Saxony. While still in her teens she married Hans Luder, or Luther, the son of a local farmer.

In 1483 the Luthers left the farm and moved to Eisleben, where Hans began work in the coppermines. Six months after their arrival, on November 10, 1483, their second son was born in their home on the Langer Strasse. The next day he was baptized Martin, in honor of the day's patron saint, St Martin of Tours. He was to be followed by two more boys and four girls, all born by 1505.

The eight Luther children had a somewhat unhappy childhood. Although Hans Luther prospered in the mines, and indeed became a shareholder in a foundry business, he was parsimonious in the extreme. The children did not go hungry, but neither were they given money for luxuries. Both parents were stern disciplinarians. In later years, Martin Luther remembered many beatings administered by his father; on one of these occasions, when he had stolen a nut, his mother caned him until the blood welled. "Such stern discipline drove me to a monastery," he wrote later, "though she meant it well." When he became the father of a young family he remembered this, and formed the precept: "If you give whippings, keep an apple in sight as well as the rod."

Luther was inculcated from infancy with ideas of a stern God, something like his father, and with his parents' superstitions. "The devil is loose," he declared his mother whenever she heard thunder. She also believed firmly in the existence of witches. Her son later wrote that she "was so tormented by one of her neighbors who was a witch that she was obliged to treat her with the highest respect and conciliate her, for she caused such agony to her children that they would scream like unto death." Frau Luther swore that one of her sons who died in childhood had been betwitched. (The family was further depleted in 1505 by an outbreak of plague, which took the lives of two infant daughters.)

At the age of thirteen, Martin Luther was sent away to boarding school at Magdeburg, and in the years that followed his visits home were brief and infrequent. When he became a monk in 1505 his parents were extremely angry, for they — especially his father — had ambitions to see him become a wealthy civil lawyer. But by the time of their death — Hans in 1531 and Margaretha in 1534 — their son was already famous throughout Europe for his revolutionary religious teaching.

Psychologists have put forward the theory that Luther's denigration of the Mother of Christ was an unconscious rebuff to his own mother, who had mistreated him as a child. Indeed, there is only one indication that he had any affection for her: during his visit to Rome in 1510, he was anxious to say a Mass for her salvation in front of the Sancta Sanctorum chapel. Unfortunately, the crowd of worshippers was too great for Luther to take his own place at the altar, and Margaretha Luther was deprived of that benefit.

MARTIN LUTHER
(1483-1546)
Leader of the Protestant Reformation in Germany. He had been a Roman Catholic priest but rebelled against the worldly practices of the Church of Rome.

Left A painting of Margaretha by the 16th-century artist, Lucas Cranach.

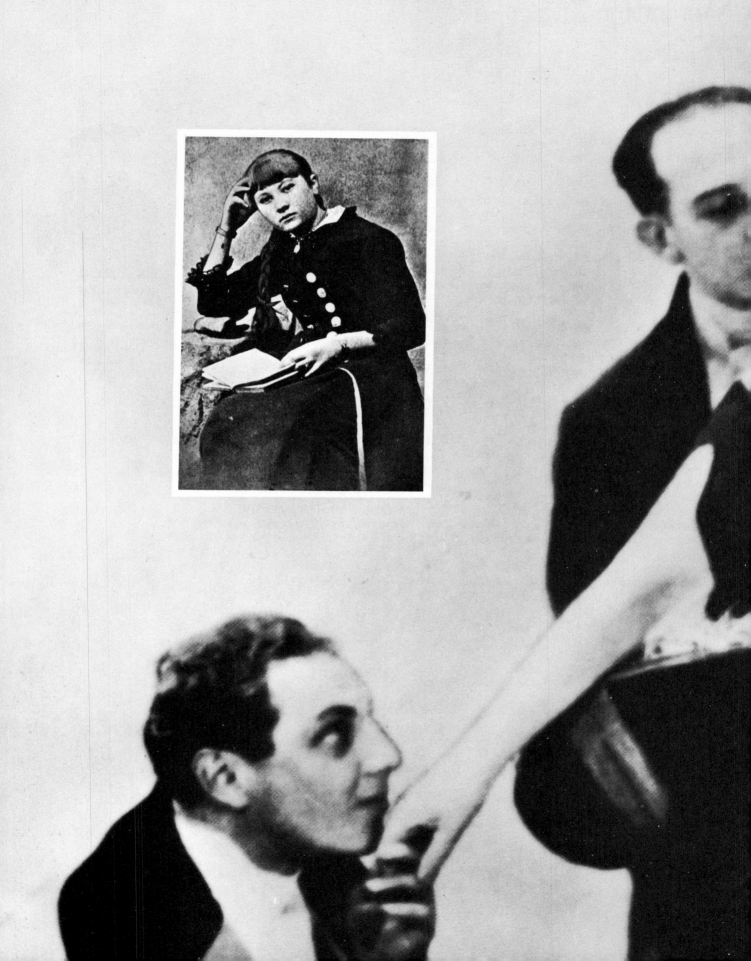

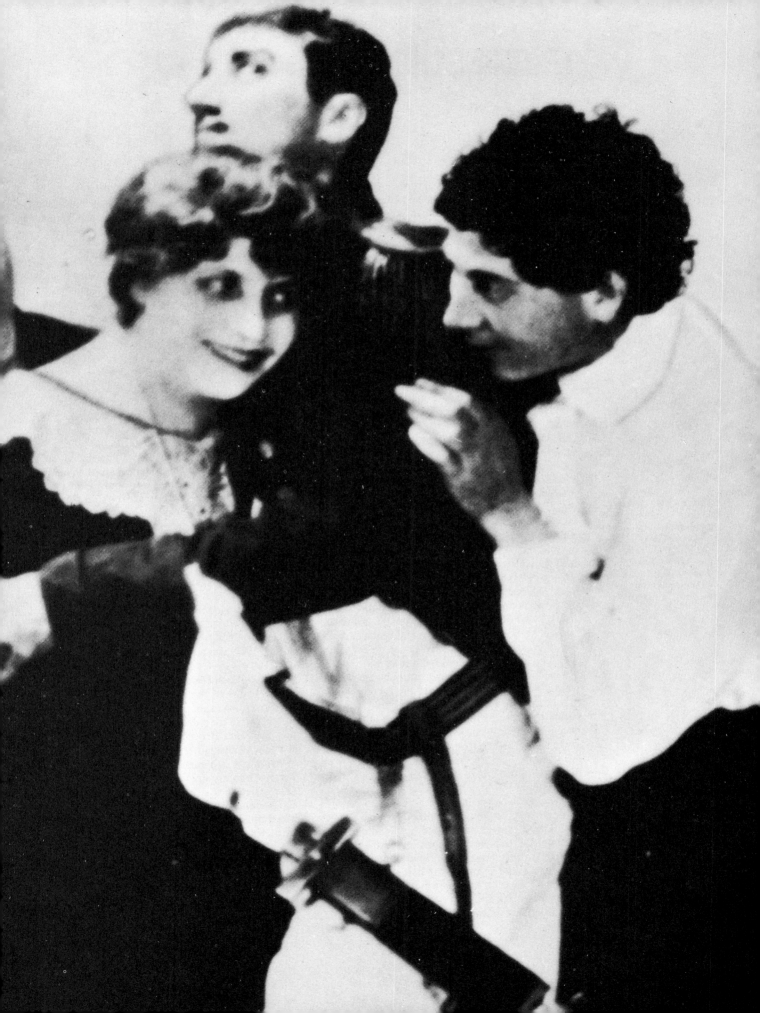

MINNIE SCHOENBERG

THE MARX BROTHERS
Chico, real name Leonard
(1891-1961); Harpo, real
name Arthur (1893-1964);
and Groucho, real name
Julius (1895-). American
comedians famous for their
films and performances on
stage, radio, and television.

Page 160 Inset
photograph shows Minnie
when a schoolgirl.
Pages 160-161 Minnie
acting in a sketch with her
famous sons.

"Age is not a particularly interesting subject,"
wrote Groucho Marx, and the Marx Brothers
have always enjoyed obscuring the basic facts
about themselves and their parents. But, almost
miraculously, something has emerged about their
mother Minnie. It is known that she was born in a
German village called Donum. Her parents were
Lafe and Fanny Schoenberg, and she was
probably born in the late 1860s.

Minnie's father was a magician, and her
mother played the harp. They left Germany,
probably sometime in the late 1870s or early
1880s, and emigrated to the United States. As a
teenager, Minnie was petite and graceful and had
auburn hair. At the age of eighteen she married
Sam Marx, a New York tailor whose efforts to
make a living were severely handicapped by his
reluctance to use a tape measure.

Minnie was a kind, dynamic woman and very
hospitable despite her money worries. Hardship
increased when she gave birth first to Chico, then
to Harpo, Groucho, and the lesser-known
brothers, Gummo and Zeppo. Minnie was not the
world's greatest cook but Sam, fortunately, was
more successful in the kitchen than in his tailor's
establishment. He could produce a gourmet meal
out of cheap cuts of meat and a few vegetables.
Life was difficult, but fun.

Not only were Minnie's parents in show
business, but her brother Al was the Shean half of
the famous comedy team, Gallacher and Shean.
Al was well off, and when her sons began to grow
up Minnie had the idea that one day perhaps they
would collect the money that came the way of
America's most successful entertainers.

She had to struggle, however, because her sons
were already showing signs of the zany behavior
that characterized their films. She persuaded
Chico to learn the piano, but his playing was
noted more for its showmanship than for its
accuracy. Harpo was coming to grips with his
grandmother's harp, but despised any orthodox
methods of playing it and, in any case, wanted to
be a butcher.

Groucho was studious and wanted to become
a doctor but, as the cost of medical school was
prohibitive, he was persuaded by Minnie to take
some initial steps as an entertainer. Although he
was far from successful, Minnie made him
persevere and eventually she had a brainstorm
that was to lead, after much fun and hardship, to
the formation of the Marx Brothers act. She
persuaded Groucho and Gummo to join in an act

called "The Three Nightingales," the third
member of which was an out-of-tune female
singer selected by Minnie. She was replaced from
time to time by other outsiders. Harpo later
joined the act, which then became "The Four
Nightingales."

Minnie often had to sit for hours and hours in
the waiting rooms of agents to get the act some
work. According to Groucho, he wouldn't have
wanted to be buried in some of the small towns
where they played. The family lived mainly on
Chico's pay, though this was an uncertain
quantity, partly because he went from job to job,
but mainly because he was an incorrigible
gambler.

Since variety acts tended to be paid according
to how many people were in them, Minnie
decided that it would be a good idea to add two
more people to the Four Nightingales. They
briefly turned themselves into "The Six Mascots,"
with Minnie and her sister Hannah as the two
extra performers. Neither had the slightest talent,
but such was Minnie's confidence that this was a
minor problem. They would strum guitars —
which they couldn't play — and sing "Two Little
Girls in Blue." Alas, in order to look like
schoolgirls, these two middle-aged women
decided to appear on stage without their glasses.
The result was disastrous. Both tried to sit on the
same chair, which collapsed. "The Six Mascots"
once more became "The Four Nightingales."

Minnie was much more successful at
promoting the act than at keeping her sons to the
script. With the addition of Chico it became more
and more wayward until eventually it was
renamed the "Marx Brothers." Minnie and
Chico began to feel that the act was good enough
for Broadway. Groucho had his doubts, but was
finally persuaded. Minnie, of course, was right,
and the Marx Brothers opened in their first
Broadway show, *I'll Say She Is,* in 1923.

Minnie was elated, though for her the opening
was not exactly uneventful. She decided to buy a
new gown. In the course of having it fitted, she
slipped and broke her leg. But a minor mishap
like that did not daunt her. On the first night she
was carried into the theater on a stretcher.

Critics, including Alexander Woollcott,
enthusiastically acclaimed these new geniuses of
buffoonery. After more stage successes they
made their first film, *Cocoanuts,* in 1929. In that
year Minnie died. She did not live to see them
attain universal fame.

HENRIETTA PRESSBURG

The mother of Karl Marx was Henrietta Pressburg, a Dutch Jew from Nimwegen. Her forebears had emigrated to Holland from their native Hungary, and there began a family of rabbis. Henrietta must have been shocked to discover, only a year after her marriage in 1816 to German lawyer Herschel Levi Marx of Trier, that he intended to become a Christian.

Henrietta was barely literate (she never mastered either the speech or the writing of the German language), and she had no understanding of her husband's views. Though brought up as a Jew, he had leanings toward the deism of the eighteenth-century Enlightenment; but it was his admiration for things Prussian that led him to enter the Evangelical Church in the autumn of 1816. At his baptism he took the name Heinrich.

By the summer of 1824, the Marxes had seven children — their first child, Moritz David, had died soon after birth. In one ceremony, Sophia, Karl Heinrich, Hermann, Heinrich, Louisa, Emilia, and Caroline were all baptized. On the register, their mother was designated a Jew, with a note to the effect that she was not a Christian only in deference to her parents' objections. A year later, after her father's death, Henrietta too became a Christian. (Her last child, Edward, was baptized soon after his birth.)

From his early childhood, it was apparent that Karl Marx had an exceptionally fertile brain. His ambitious father encouraged his studies, but his mother had no part in them. She was a thoroughly domesticated woman, caring for nothing outside her home and family circle. In later years, when Karl Marx was already immersed in formulating the doctrines that would be the political-philosophical basis of the Communist movement, she was still writing to him of nothing more than the need to dress warmly and wash thoroughly. "Obey your dear father," was her only recorded moral scripture.

When Heinrich Marx died in 1838, his widow and children had a small capital sum on which to live. Karl, the perpetual student, was a constant drain on the family's resources. By the early 1840s his mother was beginning to nag at him to find employment.

So Karl Marx left home and began his continental wanderings. When he did return to Trier in 1861, he did so with the intention of demanding money. In his two-day visit, he managed to do no more than persuade his mother to destroy two IOUs that he had given her. He wrote to a friend: "I have had an answer from my old lady. Expressions of affection, but no cash. In addition she told me something that I knew already — that she is seventy-five years old and feels that she is beginning to break up." A second visit, in 1862, was no more successful.

This visit was the last time that Karl Marx was to see his mother. She died in 1863. Having borrowed his fare from his friend and collaborator Friedrich Engels, Karl Marx went to Trier to settle the family finances. He found, to his horror, that it was not meanness which had prevented his mother from assisting him. She had only about thirty dollars to leave to her children.

KARL MARX
(1818-83)
German philosopher and economist who laid the foundations of Communism. His writings include *The Communist Manifesto* and *Das Kapital*.

Below The Marx family home in Trier.

Bluma Mabovitz

GOLDA MEIR
(1898-)
Born in Kiev, Russia, as Golda
Mabovitz. Prime Minister of
Israel (1969-74).

Golda Meir's mother, Bluma Mabovitz, was born in Pinsk (formerly in Poland but now Russian). It was within the Pale of Settlement, the area set aside for Jews to live in. It was also, as it still is, a city of woodworkers. By the time she was twenty Bluma was married to one of those woodworkers, a tall, handsome man named Moshe Mabovitz. Soon after they married, Moshe passed an examination that qualified him for a dispensation to live outside the Pale of Settlement, and he took his family – Bluma and their first-born baby girl, Shana – to Kiev, the capital of the Ukraine.

Life in Kiev was hard for Jews, however skilled they were. There was always the fear of a pogrom, and Moshe was repeatedly snubbed and cheated because he was a Jew. Even worse, the next five children Bluma bore, four boys and a girl, all died. Her seventh child was Golda, born in 1898. The last was Zipporah, born in 1902. But by then Moshe had had enough of life in Russia. He decided that he must leave and go to America. By selling his tools and other possessions he raised enough for his fare to the United States. There he hoped to save enough to send for his family. In 1903, he departed.

Bluma took her three daughters back to Pinsk to live with her father, who owned a tavern. To earn money she baked bread and trudged around with it from door to door. This provided enough for her to rent two rooms of her own, there being very little space in her father's quarters behind the inn. She carried on in this way for nearly three years, until Moshe finally sent money for the fare to America. It was not a straightforward journey. Bluma and the children were provided with false passports to cross the frontier, and Bluma had to pass for a girl of half her age. Their baggage was stolen before they even left Europe. A ship took the family from Antwerp to Quebec, and from there Bluma shepherded her three daughters onto a train for Milwaukee, Wisconsin, where Moshe was working as a carpenter for the railroad.

Bluma soon found that her husband was not making a great success in the United States. The accommodation he had provided for them was just one rented room. Bluma rose to the challenge. Within days she had found a moneylender, borrowed some cash, and rented a little grocery store with accommodation. There she installed her family, and there she kept them, well fed and provided for. Much of the time,

164

Moshe had no work.

Bluma's attitude to her family tended to be dictatorial. There were endless rows with her eldest daughter, Shana, who refused to work in the shop in addition to doing her own factory job. Shana left home several times, and left for good when Bluma forbade her boyfriend to come to the house. This time Shana stayed away, even when she developed tuberculosis. When she grew well she married her boyfriend and settled in Denver, Colorado. Bluma forbade Golda to write to Shana, but Golda disobeyed.

Golda and her mother finally quarreled about the question of education. Bluma had a number of miscarriages, and often kept Golda home from school to serve in the shop. Bluma also made Golda late for school by insisting that the girl look after the store in the mornings while she went to market. When the school authorities finally complained, Bluma rose an hour earlier to do her marketing before store time – although she was working until late in the evening. It was small wonder that she objected when Golda wanted to go on to high school and become a teacher. Teachers, she believed, could not keep their jobs after they married – and Golda was therefore training to be an old maid. Finally, she arranged a marriage for Golda, to a wealthy man twice her age. At this, Golda ran away to Shana in Denver.

Though Golda stayed away, she and her mother corresponded. Moshe refused to have anything to do with her until he and Bluma found out that Golda had quarreled with Shana and was living on her own, working in a department store. They asked Golda to return – and go to high school after all. Golda agreed. Even then, Bluma deemed it her duty to steam open Golda's letters from her boyfriend, Morris Meyerson, whom she eventually married in 1917.

But time mellows even the most dominant personalities. Shana, Golda, and their families emigrated to Palestine in 1921, and five years later Moshe and Bluma followed them. Bluma took great pride in Golda's political career, and in her grandchildren, until she died in 1951.

Right A rare family photograph of Bluma, Moshe, and their three surviving daughters.

165

Gladys with Norma Jean.

Prasedi '62

Gladys Hogan

Gladys Hogan was the second child of Della Hogan and a man named Monroe. At the age of twenty-five she was the mother of two children, Jack and Bernice, but her husband – a man called Baker – had left her, and the children were being brought up in Kentucky by some of Baker's relatives. In 1924 Gladys married a man of Norwegian extraction, Edward Mortensen, but this marriage was no more successful than her first. Mortensen had no regular employment, squandered such money as he earned, and soon left their Hollywood home for San Francisco. Gladys moved to a furnished room.

She was an attractive woman with fine features, more popular with the opposite sex than with her own. She worked in the processing laboratory of Consolidated Film Industries where she spliced together processed negatives for MGM and Paramount. Under her was a staff of five who lived in dread of being worked to death through her compulsiveness.

In 1925, Gladys became pregnant again. The identity of the father is uncertain, but some evidence suggests that Gladys knew him through her work.

Gladys wanted to move in with her mother, who was living at Hawthorne, southwest of Los Angeles. This proved impossible and her mother directed her to some neighbors, Albert Wayne and Ida Bolender. He was a letter-carrier, and both were very religious. When the baby was due, Gladys went to the Los Angeles General Hospital, where she registered as Gladys Pearl Mortensen. (She had not divorced him.) There was no lack of funds because an executive where she worked raised money for her.

The baby, the future Marilyn Monroe, was born in 1926 and named Norma Jean. It was an easy birth and, after twelve days, Gladys returned with her baby to the Bolenders to live in their rear bedroom. She soon resumed work, found herself somewhere else to live, and left Norma Jean in the care of the Bolenders. When her daughter was baptized, her surname was given as Baker.

Gladys sent the Bolenders $25 a month to care for Norma Jean, and was always regular in her payments. She visited her daughter once a week but didn't stay long if she had a date. Mental illness was now beginning to afflict her. She would laugh and cry for no reason, and her search for a stepfather for Norma Jean became so frantic that she put men off. Her father had already died in an asylum, and now her mother

met the same end. Her brother was supposed to look after the funeral arrangements but had become so withdrawn from the world that Gladys had to do it herself. Her worries were further increased by a fire at Consolidated, which had to move to Santa Monica Boulevard. Gladys didn't like her new place of work and resigned. She may have been unemployed for a time but somehow kept up her payments to the Bolenders.

In due course, Gladys got a job as a film-cutter at Columbia Pictures and also spent some time at the Bolenders' when Norma Jean had whooping cough. Despite Gladys's neglect of her daughter by normal standards, she does appear to have had some love for her and, seven years after her daughter was born, finally kept a promise she had often made, to get a house in which she and Norma Jean could live. It was a pleasant white bungalow in North Hollywood. She bought furniture at auctions and acquired a white piano, much loved by Norma Jean, which had belonged to Fredric March.

The arrangement didn't work. Gladys was used to living alone and giving vent to her strange moods, but with Norma Jean around she had to restrain herself. Also, she liked to be free for her dates. Norma Jean suffered in this new environment. The religious Bolenders had taught her to sing "Jesus Loves Me," but her performance of it in her new home was considered a great joke.

After a year, Gladys finally fell prey to the mental sickness of her parents and brother. Moods of chronic depression alternated with outbursts of hysteria. One day she became so ill that the couple who shared the bungalow had to call for an ambulance. Strapped to a stretcher, Gladys was taken to the hospital. The doctors diagnosed paranoid schizophrenia, and she was taken to the state asylum at Norwalk where her mother had died. She still had lucid moments and during them was adamant that no one should adopt Norma Jean. There was no alternative but to treat the child as an orphan, even though she knew she wasn't one, and send her to an orphanage.

Gladys recovered sufficiently to re-emerge into the world from time to time, and even remarried. But her illness eventually conquered her and she always had to be institutionalized again. Except for brief reunions she was parted from her daughter for good, and Marilyn Monroe used to remark bitterly, "I never really knew my mother."

MARILYN MONROE
(1926-62)
Glamorous American actress whose life ended in suicide. Her many films include *Some Like it Hot* and *Gentlemen Prefer Blondes*.

Left Gladys is drawn into the myth of her famous daughter's life – a pop artist's depiction of Marilyn's confused past.

167

Anna Maria Pertl

Anna Maria Pertl was born in about 1720 in the small village of St Gilgen, fifteen miles from Salzburg in Austria. The village lies on the shore of the Abersee, now known as the Wolfgangsee after the famous composer. Anna Maria was the daughter of a local official. She was neither very well educated nor intellectual, but she was practical, cheerful, and physically attractive. On November 21, 1747 she married Leopold Mozart, a German from Augsburg. Leopold had been destined for the Church, but found that music had a stronger appeal. He was a composer and violinist in the band of the Archbishop of Salzburg, and it was in Salzburg that the couple made their first home. Here their lodging was on the third floor of a handsome house facing the Löchelplatz. They were well suited to each other temperamentally, and people referred to them as the best-looking couple in Salzburg.

The Mozarts had seven children, but only two of them survived. Maria Anna, also called Marianne, or more often by the affectionate diminutive Nannerl, was born on July 30, 1751; her little brother Wolfgang Amadeus was born on January 27, 1756. By this time his father was thirty-seven and his mother probably thirty-six. Anna Maria took some time to recover from her son's birth.

It quickly became obvious that Anna Maria had given birth to a prodigy. He was soon able to play simple pieces from memory, and could compose little minuets at the keyboard before he was five years old. Nannerl, four-and-a-half years older, was already an accomplished performer on the clavier. Leopold was quick to appreciate his children's gifts; and in order to exploit these gifts took his two little ones to Munich in 1762 on the first of many tours around the courts of Europe. Wolfgang's sixth birthday occurred on this tour. His mother remained at home. In spite of losing so many babies, Anna Maria does not appear to have raised any objection to having her offspring dragged on cold, rough journeys to display their talents in one musical center after another. It never occurred to either of the parents that this hazardous, wearing, and often very boring way of life might damage the children.

Anna Maria first accompanied the family when they went to Vienna in September 1762, and then in June 1763 they all set forth on a tour of southern Germany, Brussels, London, Holland, Paris, and Geneva — a tour that lasted over three years. Leopold wrote many letters home to his landlord, describing the children's precocious performances and the reception they were given

WOLFGANG AMADEUS MOZART
(1756-91)
Austrian composer, famous from a very early age as a musical prodigy.

Left Anna's portrait dominates a Mozart family music session.

by their various patrons. The whole family became inveterate letter writers, and this correspondence reveals a little of Anna Maria's character and her earthy, unsubtle humor.

Leopold made himself responsible for his children's schooling, not that this extended far beyond musical matters. Anna Maria devoted herself entirely to their physical welfare, nursing them with stamina and fortitude when they were ill and in London also taking over the cooking because she considered the food to be so poor; at this time her husband commented that she had become very thin.

The family letters show that the Mozarts had a close-knit and easy-going relationship. Wolfgang was affectionate and responsive, and was never physically punished. In spite of Anna Maria's limited intellectual capacity, she was fully able to share the family's musical interests and appreciate Leopold's fussy commands, which did not cease even though hundreds of miles separated them. Her letters are often outspoken, coarse and illiterate, but they reveal her deep affection and solicitude for her family and the merry verbal banter that they all shared with each other and with close friends. When Anna Maria was left at home, she worried about rising prices and bad influences to which her son might be exposed while abroad; when she was on tour, she inquired anxiously about her household's state of health, never forgetting the internal economy of Bimperl, their fox-terrier bitch.

In 1777 it was decided that as Wolfgang could not gain promotion at home, he should try further afield. Leopold was refused leave by his employer, and although Anna Maria was deeply fond of her home she agreed to accompany Wolfgang alone to Munich, Mannheim (Germany) and Paris. Anna Maria, now fifty-seven years old, admitted to being homesick for Salzburg but, being an experienced traveler by this time, was able to enjoy the places she saw on her journey. She found it quite a strain, however, and in October wrote home that the effort of packing made her sweat, her feet were killing her, and she was exhausted.

In Paris, where mother and son had lodgings in the Rue du Gros Chenet, Anna Maria complained that writing letters made her arm and eyes ache. She soon became seriously ill with some unidentified disease. Although Wolfgang nursed her as well as he could with the help of neighbors, she died on July 3, 1778.

rosa maltoni

Rosa Maltoni was born in 1858 in a small village near Predappio, about thirty miles south west of Ravenna, Italy. Her father was a veterinarian who was always struggling to maintain his family's middle-class status. Rosa had a somewhat lonely childhood.

At the age of nineteen Rosa was appointed an elementary school teacher in the village of Dovia, about two miles from Predappio. She lived with her parents in Predappio and walked to work every day. Aside from these trips to the school and her weekly attendance at church services, Rosa was rarely seen in the street. She was stocky, with a dark complexion and dark hair. Her firm, square jaw — inherited by her famous son — belied a gentle expression and quiet manner.

After a time Rosa attracted the attention of the village blacksmith, Alessandro Mussolini. Alessandro, a self-educated man, was more interested in politics than in his trade. He founded a branch of the Socialist International and devoted much time to reading and writing political literature. There was an element of the clandestine in his courtship of Rosa: they passed love letters by leaving them in the notebook of one of Rosa's pupils.

In spite of the initial opposition of Rosa's parents — Alessandro was a declared atheist — the couple were married in church in January, 1880. They lived in a few rooms of the rundown Palazzo Varano in Dovia, where one room served as the classroom of Rosa's school. Their first child, Benito Amilcare Andrea, was born in 1883. His younger brother, Arnaldo, arrived two years later and a sister, Edvige, in 1888. Benito's names were chosen by Alessandro: Benito, after Benito Juàrez the great Mexican revolutionary;

BENITO MUSSOLINI
(1883-1945)
Italian Fascist leader, Premier of Italy from 1922 to 1943.

Left Two views of Predappio, the village of Rosa's birth.

171

Amilcare, after Amilcare Cipriano who fought for the Paris Commune; and Andrea after Andrea Costa, a Socialist deputy. It was Rosa, however, who insisted that the boy receive a Christian baptism.

The Mussolinis were poor, but Rosa wanted her children to have a middle-class education. Benito proved to be a sullen and rebellious child. When he was nine, Rosa sent him to a boarding school run by the Salesians, a religious order founded in the mid-nineteenth century and engaged mainly in educational works. Benito, however, was in constant trouble, and Rosa intervened many times to prevent his expulsion from the school. He was finally expelled when he wounded a classmate with a knife and threw an inkwell at one of his teachers.

Rosa never ceased aspiring to middle-class status for herself and her family, and Benito's misadventures caused her much anxiety. He finally qualified as a teacher, though not without further trouble, and went to Switzerland to seek work. In 1902 Rosa's worries were compounded when her husband's Socialist activities led to his being imprisoned. The following year, worn out and discouraged by her troubles, Rosa fell ill. She was never to recover her health, and in February, 1905, she died of meningitis. She was forty-six years old.

Rosa Maltoni e Alessandro Mussolini.

Above Carefully retouched photographs of Rosa and her husband, Alessandro. *Right* Rosa's bedroom, where Benito was born. *Far right* Rosa proudly displays her infant son — the future "*Duce.*"

Letizia Ramolino

NAPOLEON BONAPARTE
(1769-1821)
Corsican-born soldier and statesman who rose to prominence after the French Revolution. In 1804 he became Emperor of the French.

Right Letizia's youthful portrait in her Corsican home; and a marble statue glorifying the mother of Napoleon.
Pages 176-177 A proud moment for Letizia as she watches her son's coronation.
Pages 178-179 Two views of Letizia — "*Madame Mère*." The drawing of her in old age was made by her grand daughter.

Letizia Ramolino was born in 1750 in Corsica, and a Corsican she remained — in speech, outlook, and sympathies — throughout her long and eventful life. Even as a child she was renowned for her beauty, and was called "Ajaccio's little wonder" in her home town. At fourteen she was married to an eighteen-year-old law student, Carlo Maria Bonaparte. In their twenty years of marriage the couple had twelve children, eight of whom survived to maturity.

Letizia had grown up in the years of struggle for Corsican independence from Genoa, and only two months after her wedding the French moved in to govern the island. Her husband Carlo played a leading part in the resistance to the occupation, and for Letizia the following years were fraught with excitement and danger, as the family took to the hills as fugitives. At length, however, Carlo came to terms with the French. He was given high office in the government they set up in Corsica, and his noble birth was officially recognized. But in 1785 he died, leaving Letizia, a widow at thirty-four, to bring up her

children — four of them still under ten years old.

Her elder sons had already begun their careers in France and were able to contribute to the family income, and in 1793 the Bonapartes moved to France to make their home there, under the care of Letizia's second son Napoleon, who was already making a name for himself in the French army. At first, amid the alarms of the French Revolution, and on a small income, Letizia's life was hard. By the end of the century, through Napoleon's rise to power, she had a small fortune and a prominent place in fashionable Parisian society.

But it was Napoleon's assumption of the Imperial crown, in 1804, which saw the zenith of Letizia's glory. She was fêted everywhere as the mother of the conqueror and statesman, and entitled "Imperial Highness" — though better known simply as "Madame Mère." Her position was no less brilliant than that of a queen. With dignity and sensitivity she graced her position far better than any of her sons and daughters, who vied for titles and power and quarreled so bitterly

and so frequently that Letizia had continually to mediate between them and the source of all their grandeur, her son Napoleon.

If any charge can be brought against Letizia's conduct at this time, it is that she was avaricious, for she accumulated money as greedily as the Emperor accumulated foreign territory. She claimed that her avarice was simply a precaution against political reversal: even though three of her sons were kings and one of her daughters a queen, she knew how dramatically things could change. "I may one day have to find bread for all these kings I have borne," she said.

She was proved right in 1814, when the European Alliance beat Napoleon back into France and deprived him of his crown. Letizia hastened to join him in exile on the island of Elba, and in 1815 encouraged him in his plans to return to France with a new army. With Napoleon re-enthroned in Paris, Letizia presided over his court for a few weeks; but with Napoleon's final defeat at Waterloo, she left France for ever and made her home in Rome. Forbidden by her son to join him on the desolate island of St Helena, Letizia lived out the rest of her life in Italy.

Her sons Louis and Lucien and her daughter Pauline lived nearby, and her last years were cheered by the love of her grandchildren – though misfortune seemed to dog the lives of the younger generation of the Bonapartes.

When Letizia heard of the death of Napoleon, in May 1821, she was distraught with grief. Screaming, she clasped a bust of her son in her arms, fainted and was ill for weeks. Toward the end of her life, in her eighties, she became blind and enfeebled, though she always retained vestiges of her once-famed beauty and the strength of character and will that had carried her nobly through triumph and disaster. Letizia died in 1836, leaving an immense fortune. She was buried first in Italy, and her body was taken to her native Corsica in 1852. A hundred years later, that of her husband, Carlo, was brought back to the island to join hers.

Hopwood sc

LETIZIA RAMOLINI

MOTHER OF NAPOLEON

CATHERINE SUCKLING

HORATIO, LORD NELSON
(1758-1805)
Britain's greatest admiral, a national hero for his successes during the Napoleonic wars. He was killed at the Battle of Trafalgar (1805).

Not a great deal is known about the mother of England's great naval hero. His biographers refer to her as a "shadowy figure," and the lack of information is mainly due to the fact that she died at the age of forty-two, when Nelson was only nine years old.

What is known is that Catherine Suckling was born in 1726 and was in her 'teens when she married the Reverend Edmund Nelson, Rector of a group of parishes in the English county of Norfolk. Both were of good family, though hers was more exalted than his. She was the daughter of a Prebendary of Westminster Cathedral and was related to the Earls of Orford (the Walpole family). Her brother, who was to play an important part in Lord Nelson's life, was a Post-Captain (next to Admiral) in the Royal Navy.

The setting of Catherine's married life was idyllic. Parsonage House at Burnham Thorpe, where the Nelsons lived, stood in its own small estate of open lawns and fields. The Nelsons enjoyed the friendship of wealthy neighbors, some of whom were cousins. Parsonage House stood only four miles from the coast, and the children must have often savored the salty tang blown by the North Sea winds.

Here Catherine, with the help of several servants, carried out the duties of a clergyman's wife, visiting parishioners and being visited by them, and found time to bear eleven children in seventeen years. Three of them died in childhood. The sixth child, a frail and sickly infant, was born in 1758 and was named Horatio (a favored name in the Walpole family).

Catherine has been described as "a woman of considerable firmness and fortitude, though of a delicate habit, as well as of great meekness and piety." Beyond this, little is known of Nelson's mother except that she hated the French — something she probably learned from her naval brother who had fought a French squadron in the West Indies and equally likely passed on to her young son Horatio.

Catherine died on the day after Christmas in 1768 (her mother died five days later). She left the Rector with eight children, the youngest of whom was only ten months old.

Later the hero of Trafalgar was to say, "The thought of former days brings all my mother to my heart, which shows itself in my eyes."

Right A formal portrait of Catherine.

CATHERINE SUCKLING
WIFE OF EDMUND NELSON
BORN 1725. DIED 1767.

AGRIPPINA THE YOUNGER

The Emperor Nero is always identified with wanton and prodigious cruelty. His mother, if tradition can be trusted, had a career even more consistently maleficent than his.

Agrippina the Younger, born in AD15, was one of the nine children of Agrippina the Elder and Germanicus Caesar, a popular Roman general. Among her siblings was Caligula, who would, as Emperor (37-41), achieve fame for his megalomania. The children were raised by their grandmother, who was shocked by their scandalous behavior and accused Agrippina of having incestuous relations with Caligula.

Accusations like this one had already given Agrippina a dubious reputation when she married the first of three husbands, Gnaeus Domitius Ahenobarbus. They must have been a well-matched couple: Gnaeus, a patrician, was described as a murderer and adulterer and was accused of having incest with his sister. The fruit of their marriage was Lucius Domitius, born in AD37. Agrippina centered all her hopes on him, seeing in him a means of satisfying her immense ambition.

It is not certain what happened to Gnaeus, but Agrippina's second husband was Passienus Crispus. He conveniently disappeared (Agrippina was accused of poisoning him) when his wife turned her attention to a bigger prize. This was the Emperor Claudius I. That he was her uncle did not put her off for a moment; nor did the fact that he had come to power through the murder of her brother Caligula. He was thirty-nine and she was thirty-four when, in AD49, they were married.

Agrippina is described by a contemporary as possessing "beauty, majestic air, noble manners, and a lively and enterprising intellect." Immediately upon marrying Claudius she put these attributes to the service of her avarice and ambitions. Claudius became her servant, so completely dominated by her will that he set aside his own son Britannicus and made her son (now called Nero) the heir to his throne. With her son close to power, Agrippina assumed virtual control of the Empire. On one occasion she rode to the Capitol in a triumphal chariot previously reserved for religious purposes.

When Nero was sixteen Agrippina decided that Claudius was no longer necessary and killed him – or so we are told – by poisoning his stew. His death was kept secret from the public until Nero was safely proclaimed Emperor, and then Agrippina settled down to enjoy the rewards of her endless machinations.

Her enjoyment was fairly shortlived. Nero was as willful as she and resented her efforts to interfere in his love life. A crisis was reached when she threatened to replace him with the discarded Britannicus. He had Britannicus murdered and removed Agrippina's guards and all other trappings of authority. By AD59 he was completely fed up with his mother and hatched a complicated plot to get rid of her.

Pretending a reconciliation, he invited her down to the Bay of Naples and there persuaded her to take a trip on a boat specially prepared with a collapsible bottom and deck that would fall and crush her. The plot went awry and Nero had to fall back on cruder methods. His assassins were sent to his mother's villa. There Agrippina was stabbed to death as she called on Nero's men to "pierce the belly that has produced such a monster."

Years before, when she was told by a soothsayer that her son would reign but would have her put to death, she had cried: "Oh let my son kill me provided he reigns!" Her wish had come true.

NERO
(AD 37-68)
Emperor of Rome from 54-68. Persecuted Christians after the great fire of Rome (64).

Left Agrippina with her young son, Nero.

PRINCESS DAGMAR
(Maria Fyodorovna)

NICHOLAS II
(1868-1918)
The last Tsar of Russia. An ineffectual ruler, he abdicated in 1917 after the outbreak of the Revolution. He was executed with his wife and children in July 1918.

Right A gentle smile from the young Princess.
Pages 186-187 The curvaceous Tsarina retains her youthful appearance as her husband gains weight and a beard.
Page 188 Maria Fyodorovna and the future Nicholas II.
Page 189 Maria Fyodorovna arrives in Denmark during the Russian Revolution

Few women have experienced such sharply contrasting fortunes as Princess Dagmar of Denmark. When she was a child her family lived in comparative poverty. Dagmar and her sisters Alexandra and Thyra had to make their own clothes – and make them last. But in 1863, when Dagmar was sixteen, her father, Christian of Schleswig-Holstein, succeeded to the throne of Denmark, and the family went to live in the luxurious royal palace in Copenhagen.

At around the same time, Dagmar's sister Alexandra made a brilliant match with Edward, Prince of Wales, heir to the English throne. Dagmar herself became engaged to the Tsarevitch Nicholas, son and heir of Tsar Alexander II of Russia. Nicholas, however, died in 1865, shortly before the day planned for the wedding. His dying wish was that Dagmar should marry his brother Alexander. She did so, taking the name "Maria Fyodorovna" on her wedding day, according to the Russian custom of giving Russian names to imperial brides.

There could have been no greater contrast between the handsome, delicate Nicholas and his brother Alexander, now the heir to the Russian throne. Alexander was a rough, simple giant of a man. But the marriage was supremely happy, and the small, graceful, dark-eyed Maria Fyodorovna soon became immensely popular. She had five children: Nicholas, born in 1868; George, born in 1871; Xenia, born in 1875; Michael, born in 1878; and Olga, born in 1882.

The little Danish Princess became Tsarina in 1881, when her husband ascended the throne as Alexander III following his father's assassination. The new Tsar was the complete autocrat and dominated his family as he did his country. He preferred simple living, country pleasures, and hard work to elegant court functions. To Maria Fyodorovna was left the task of bringing up their children, and she paid particular attention to the eldest, Nicholas. He was a shy, awkward, and uncertain youth who stood in great awe of his father – and of his destiny as future Tsar, for which he always felt unsuited. On only one matter did Nicholas display resolution: despite his father's objections, he refused to consider marriage with anyone but Princess Alix of

Hesse-Darmstadt. Not long after the Tsar had given his permission for the match, however, he fell ill and died, and the well-meaning but weak Tsarevitch became Tsar Nicholas II.

Nicholas became Tsar in 1894, and for the next twenty-eight years his mother Maria Fyodorovna lived on in Russia as Dowager Empress. She still took part in court functions, at which Russian etiquette gave her precedence over her daughter-in-law, the new Tsarina Alexandra Fyodorovna. The two Tsarinas had no great sympathy for each other. Alexandra disliked state occasions, preferring a bourgeois home life; the Dowager loved splendor and travel, frequently visiting the courts of her relations and presenting herself as a leading social figure at home.

The two women did agree that Nicholas II should resist any encroachment on his autocratic Imperial power. Nevertheless, Maria Fyodorovna came increasingly to fear Alexandra's influence over Nicholas, especially when she fell under the spell of the notorious monk Rasputin, to whom the young Tsarina attributed mystical power.

The First World War brought imperial rule to an end. By 1916 it was obvious that Nicholas II could no longer command either his troops or his government. Numerous appeals were made to Maria Fyodorovna by those who opposed the Tsar's conduct of affairs, but by now she was unable to pursuade him to take a stronger line. When the revolutionary army swept through the Crimea in April 1917, Maria yielded to the entreaties of her sister, Queen Alexandra of England, and was taken from Russia in the British warship *HMS Marlborough*. Thus she escaped the assassination of the Russian Imperial family instigated by the Bolshevik revolutionaries.

Maria Fyodorovna's last years were spent in the royal palace in Copenhagen. There her nephew King Christian kept her short of money, telling her that she must sell the jewels she had brought with her from Russia. She was saved from this indignity by the intervention of her nephew King George V of England, who granted her a pension of £10,000 a year. Maria Fyodorovna lived on until 1928, refusing, to the end of her life, to believe that Nicholas and his family had died.

LEVITSKY. PHOT.^{phe}   À St PETERSBOURG

Fanny Smith

FLORENCE NIGHTINGALE
(1820-1910)
Englishwoman who revolutionized nursing and hospital treatment in the nineteenth century. She nursed wounded soldiers in the Crimean War.

Frances Nightingale was still on her somewhat extended honeymoon when her second daughter, Florence, was born in 1820. She had married William Nightingale in 1818, and the couple had been traveling in Europe ever since. If Florence had been her first child, she might have had the unusual name of Parthenope Nightingale for that was the name they gave to their eldest daughter, commemorating the fact that she was born in Greece. Instead, Florence was given her name after the city in Italy in which she was born.

Frances, always known as Fanny, was the daughter of a wealthy man named William Smith, who was a Member of Parliament for nearly half a century and son of an extremely rich London merchant. She was one of ten children, five girls and five boys, and she once said that "We Smiths never thought of anything all day long but our own ease and pleasure." She married William Nightingale, a schoolfriend of her younger brother, on the rebound as it were, for her father had prevented a love-marriage to a young but penniless member of the aristocracy. William was only twenty-four, she nearly thirty, but they were married within six months. He had changed his name from Shore to Nightingale only three years before his marriage, after inheriting a considerable fortune from an uncle of that name.

At the time of her marriage, Fanny was beautiful, extravagant, and pleasure-loving. Her father was a champion of the downtrodden, but she was evidently something of a snob with ambitions to be an outstanding hostess.

Soon after Florence's birth, the family returned to England and established themselves at Embley Park, a house near the New Forest. They had another country house, but it had only fifteen bedrooms and was not grand enough for Fanny. At Embley Park, William led the life of a country squire and Fanny was very much the lady of the manor. But William, a typical gentleman of his age, was cultivated and intellectually curious, and, although the two children suffered under the usual governess, he played a big part in educating the intelligent Florence.

Fanny, it seems, had little appreciation of the character and quality of her second daughter. Florence was good-looking and gifted, and clearly destined, in her mother's opinion, for a good match in the marriage market. But carefully arranged house parties, presentation at court, a London season with balls, dinners, and theater parties all brought no result. Florence's affections remained untouched, and there was developing in her a burning desire to relieve human suffering.

To Fanny this was largely incomprehensible, and Florence found understanding with her father's sister, Aunt Mai, rather than with her mother.

Fanny was a generous and charitable woman herself, but this did not extend to the realities of contact with poverty and disease, and she was horrified when her daughter proposed to become a hospital nurse. It was Florence herself who would later establish the dignity of the nursing profession but at that time nursing was regarded as something disreputable, and Florence was later to say that her parents' reaction "was as if I had wanted to be a kitchen maid."

Florence lost that round, but she was a determined young woman and made secret plans that led to her becoming Superintendent of an Institution for Sick Gentlewomen in London. It is small wonder that her mother declared tearfully, "We are ducks who have hatched a wild swan."

Florence's determination eventually made her, after Queen Victoria, perhaps the most famous Englishwoman of her time. Even before she returned from the Crimea and honors were showered on her, Fanny had changed her views about her daughter's career. After a meeting in Florence's honor in 1855, she held a reception "for notabilities" and wrote to Florence that this was "The most interesting day of thy mother's life . . . . The like has never happened before, but will, I trust, from your example gladden the hearts of many future mothers."

Indeed, she began to relish her position as mother of the famous Lady of the Lamp, but to the end failed to understand Florence's inspiration and single-minded drive, even reproaching her for not attending parties when she was overwhelmed with administrative problems and herself an invalid. Nevertheless, Florence's sense of duty overcame her lifelong contempt for her mother's attitude to life. She nursed the senile and almost blind Fanny through the last years of her life until she died in 1880, aged ninety-two.

Right Sentimental view of Fanny, the loving mother, with her two happy children.

HANNAH MILHOUS

RICHARD NIXON
(1913-)
37th President of the United
States. Political scandals
forced him to resign in 1974.

Right Hannah, Frank, and
their first three sons pose
for a studio photograph.

Hannah Milhous was born on an Indiana farm in 1885, the daughter of an orchard nurseryman and descendant of generations of farmers. Her parents were Quakers, and Hannah grew up in an atmosphere of pacifism, virtuous toil, and racial equality. Her mother still used the "thous" and "thees" of the old speech, and insisted that all their workers – Indian, Mexican, black – share their table. In this way she carried on the tradition of earlier Milhouses, who had helped escaping slaves flee north.

Shortly after Hannah's birth, a new Quaker community called Whittier had been founded in quiet farm land near Los Angeles. It was popular, and citrus fruits would grow there: Hannah's father, Franklin, decided on a new start. They moved in 1897, when Hannah was twelve. Parents, grandparents, brothers, sisters, horses and cows, all made the journey. With them went a great load of timber, doors and window-frames – all things that Franklin feared they would not find easily in "wild" California. In Whittier they bought land, built a house, planted trees, and sent the children to school. In 1903, when she was seventeen, Hannah met Francis Anthony Nixon. They were married four months later.

The couple went twenty miles south to live in the village of Yorba Linda. They bought ten acres of land, and Frank built a single-story frame house. Here Richard Nixon was born, on January 9, 1913.

Hannah chose her son's name out of admiration for the English hero-king, Richard the Lionheart. He had been preceded by another son, Harold (born in 1909), and was followed by three others: Donald (1914), Arthur (1918), and later Edward (1930). There was little money, and the Yorba Linda home was hard to heat – freezing cold at night, burning hot during the day. In the mornings the family dressed huddled round the cooking-stove. Outside, on their land, Frank had planted lemon trees. Among the family's very few luxuries was a piano Hannah bought for Richard, thinking music might be his career.

The lemon grove never flourished, and eventually the family decided to sell it. In 1922 they returned to Whittier to open a gasoline station. They had a choice of two sites, of which one was favored by Hannah. They chose the other, and oil was later found on the rejected site.

But the new venture was a success. They began stocking milk and bread for the drivers, and from this a general store grew. Hannah would be up at dawn, baking pies to sell. The children pumped gasoline, delivered groceries, and helped stock up the shelves. At breakfast there were prayers and a Bible reading; on Sundays the children went four times to church – for Sunday school, Christian education, and two services.

Then Harold, the eldest son, developed tuberculosis. Hannah refused to put him in a public hospital but took him instead to a private nursing home in Arizona, hoping that the dry air would help. For two years she stayed there with him. Frank sold half their land for medical bills, and Hannah worked in the nursing home scrubbing floors and cooking. Frank and the sons lived on canned food, eggs and hamburgers, and had candy-bar breakfasts. Arthur, the fourth son, died suddenly from tubercular meningitis. Eventually Hannah had to bring Harold back to Whittier, and he too died. "It is difficult to understand the ways of our Lord," Hannah said at Arthur's funeral, "but we know that there is a plan and the best happens for each individual."

Hannah took great pride in Richard's successes both at study and in student politics. When he graduated from Duke Law School, Frank drove Hannah and her mother the 3000 miles to North Carolina to be there.

The 1952 Presidential campaign (when Nixon was Vice-Presidential candidate) began with a Los Angeles rally, led by a Whittier delegation with Hannah and Frank at the head. But Hannah's usual role in her son's political life was to comfort and support. She looked after the grandchildren while Richard and Pat campaigned or took a holiday. Later, after Frank's death in 1956, she moved to a Pennsylvania farm where her son could escape from Washington to relax.

Hannah died in 1967, and never saw her son achieve the goal that so completely dominated his adult life – the Presidency of the United States. He did mention her in several of his speeches as President. Perhaps the most famous mention came in the last public speech he made, just after he resigned the Presidency in August, 1974. His mother, he said, was "a saint." In his moment of final defeat Nixon's thoughts turned to the woman who, he said, was the source of his own idealism.

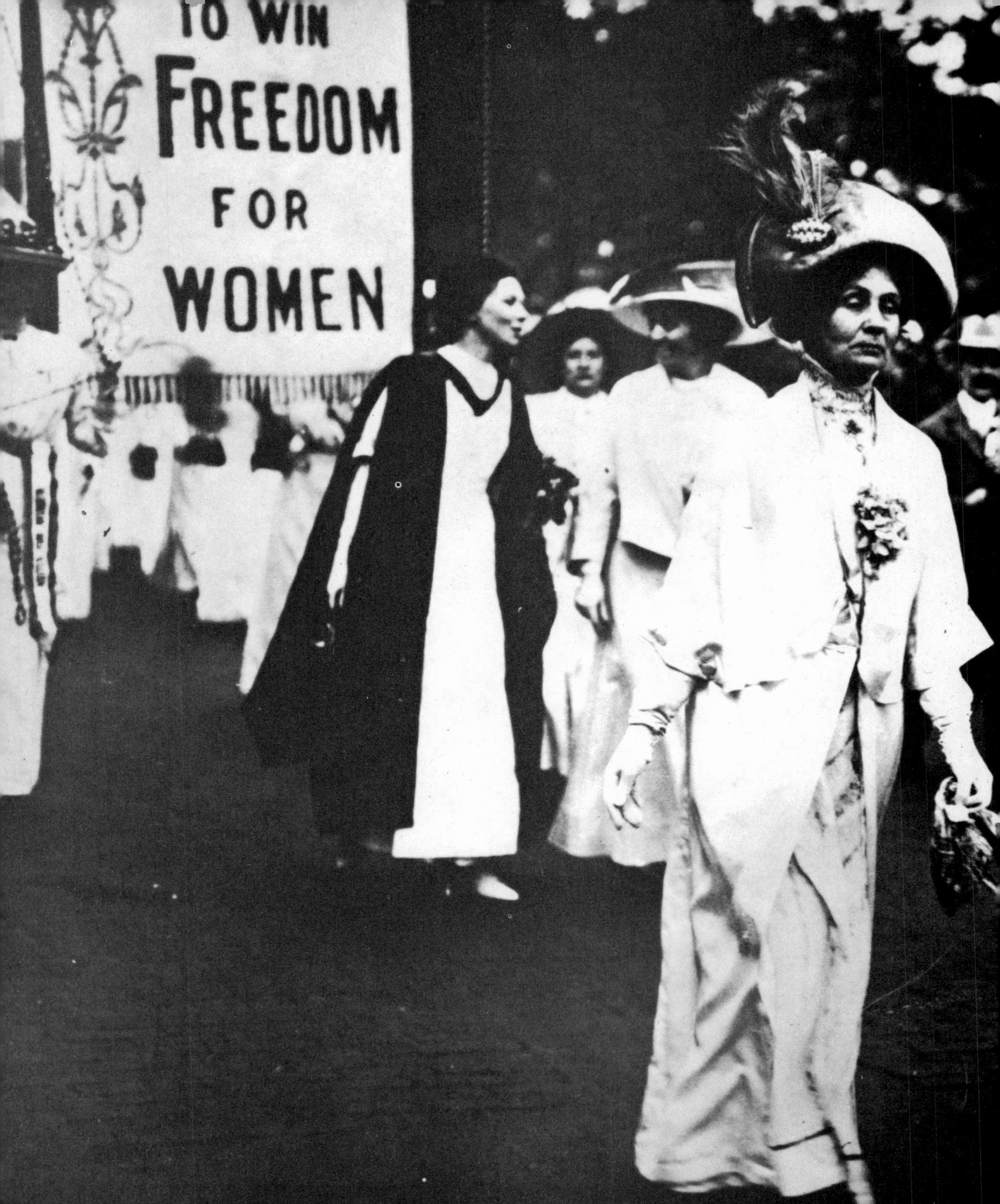
TO WIN
FREEDOM
FOR
WOMEN

Emmeline Goulden

**CHRISTABEL
PANKHURST**
(1880-1958)
Leader, with her mother, in the campaign for women's suffrage in England. She was imprisoned several times for her militant activities.

Emmeline Goulden was born in Manchester, England, in 1858, the daughter of Robert Goulden, a calico-printer. Both mother and father were early advocates of women's suffrage, and Emmeline was taken to her first political meeting at the age of fourteen. She was sent to school in Paris and returned inspired with revolutionary ideas. She fell in love with Richard Marsden Pankhurst, a barrister of forty who had joined John Stuart Mill in his fight for women's suffrage. Richard and Emmeline were married in 1879. They joined the Fabian Society and worked together for women's rights. Emmeline was also a Manchester Poor Law Guardian.

They had two sons and three daughters, but they were to lose both sons: Frank, at the age of four, and Harry, at twenty. Their three daughters, Christabel, Sylvia, and Adela, shared their mother's toughness and determination and her total involvement in women's affairs, although Christabel was the only one who remained in complete accord with Emmeline's militant activities.

In 1885 the family went to London, where Emmeline opened a fancy goods shop with her sister Mary. After little Frank died of diphtheria the Pankhursts moved to a large house in Russell Square. Another shop was opened nearby, under the same name but on more ambitious lines, in which oriental brasses and William Morris cretonnes were for sale. Christabel worked in the shop, but she was unhappy and frustrated. She joined the Labour Party and studied law. It was the refusal to admit her to the Bar after taking her degree with honors at Victoria University, Manchester, in 1905, that determined her to devote her life to women's rights.

On her husband's death in 1898, Emmeline accepted a post as Registrar of Births and Deaths. She resigned from the Fabian Society because of their refusal to oppose the Boer War. By 1903 she had founded the Women's Social and Political Union, making "Votes for Women" their slogan. Emmeline resigned from the registrarship, gave up her home, and traveled from meeting to meeting. Under her leadership, leisured women joined with working women to interrupt political meetings by the ringing of bells and the waving of banners, and they created general confusion by chaining themselves to railings and breaking windows in Downing Street.

Militants, among them a few men, planned every possible way of getting themselves arrested in order to draw attention to their cause. When imprisoned, many refused food and even drink, and that horrible reign of terror, forcible feeding, began. On March 25, 1913, the Prisoners Temporary Discharge Act, known as the Cat and Mouse Act, was introduced. Under this act, prisoners whose lives were endangered by hunger strikes were released on licence, and rearrested as soon as health was regained.

Mrs Pankhurst herself underwent imprisonment, forcible feeding, and going without sleep. On February 24, 1913 she was arrested for her connection with the bombing of Lloyd George's house and was sentenced to three years' penal servitude. Of this sentence she served forty-two days in ten imprisonments, and on one occasion was carried to a meeting on a stretcher, still on licence, and auctioned the licence for £100.

When at last Christabel saw the end of their long struggle in sight, she wrote: "The militants will rejoice when victory comes in the shape of the vote, and yet, mixed with their joy will be regret that the most glorious chapter in women's history is closed." But another fight was yet to come, before women won their right to vote. On August 4, 1914, war against Germany was declared. Six days later, all suffragette prisoners were unconditionally released. Now, under Emmeline's leadership, they devoted their energies to the war effort.

Emmeline adopted four illegitimate baby girls, and in 1916 made a home for herself and her "war babies" in Holland Park, London. After the war she sailed for Canada. In 1925 Emmeline left Canada for the French Riviera, where she and Christabel ran the English Tea Shop in Juan-les-Pins.

In 1926 this extraordinary woman, a former Fabian, became the official parliamentary candidate for the Conservative Party in Whitechapel, in London's East End. She settled in the East End, and parted with her last "war baby." Mrs Pankhurst died on June 14, 1928, aged sixty-nine, just as the Bill giving equal voting rights to all men and women over the age of twenty-one received royal assent. Her statue was erected in Victoria Tower Gardens.

Pages 194-195 Emmeline leads the way in the battle for women's suffrage.
Right Emmeline and Christabel proudly display their prison uniforms.

RUTH WILSON

George Smith Patton's mother was born Ruth Wilson, the daughter of one of the most powerful men in nineteenth-century California. He was Benjamin Davis Wilson, an enterprising adventurer from Tennessee who had been one of the first American pioneers to blaze a westward trail into California. By the time of Ruth's birth, "Don Benito" (as the Spaniards and Indians of California called him) was a well-established rancher, the first mayor of Los Angeles after California entered the American union. Ruth was brought up in luxury on her father's immense estate and as a young girl married an up-and-coming lawyer, George Smith Patton, who had an aristocratic Virginian ancestry and whom she was said to have loved since her childhood. In 1885 their only son, George, was born on the San Gabriel ranch inherited from "Don Benito." Two years later, Ruth gave him a sister, named Anne but known in the family as "Nita."

The young Pattons had an unorthodox upbringing. Their father believed that children learned best not by reading for themselves but by hearing the classics read aloud. Much of his time, and Ruth's, was spent in reading to them. Young George's father thus directed his education, while his mother's sister, "Aunt Nannie," a domineering, high-strung woman, spoiled the children terribly. She refused to allow Ruth to punish either of them, going into hysterics whenever she was thwarted. It appears that Ruth had a less forceful character.

Nevertheless, Ruth played a major role in the household. She had a large establishment to run, supervising many indoor servants and catering for the numerous cowhands who worked on the 1800-acre ranch. The Pattons always gave the impression of having great wealth, but in fact their income was severely diminished after the manager of the Wilson estate absconded with much of the family's capital. Moreover, George Patton Sr suffered from tuberculosis for many years and was unable to keep up his law practice. A large slice of the ranchland had to be sold.

Nevertheless, the Pattons had fortune enough to allow them the luxury of a summer cottage on Catalina Island, off the California coast near Long Beach. It was there that young George, still in his teens, met his future wife, Beatrice Ayer. And when he was a young army officer, the whole family traveled to Stockholm to see him take part in the pentathlon in the 1912 Olympic Games. This must have been a great moment for Ruth, for she was herself a keen sportswoman — proficient in swimming, golf, tennis, and fishing.

In maturity, George Smith Patton left California for the eastern states, and spent many years abroad in the army. But in the flush of his glory after the Second World War, he insisted on returning to San Gabriel, his birthplace, and spoke with fond memories of the Episcopal Church which the family had attended and which Ruth's father had founded.

GEORGE S. PATTON
(1885-1945)
American general in the Second World War. He was known as "Old Blood and Guts."

Left A self-assured expression from the mother of the future General.

Catherine the Great

PAUL I
(1754-1801)
Tsar of Russia (1796-1801).
Kept from the throne for
34 years by his mother, he
reversed her policies on his
accession. He was strangled
by a group of his officers.

Right Engraving of the
youthful Catherine.
Pages 202-203
Catherine's coronation;
and a court painting of this
determined Russian ruler.

Catherine the Great was born in Stettin, Germany, on May 2, 1729, and christened Sophia Augusta Frederika. Her father, Christian Augustus of Anhalt-Zerbst, was a poor German princeling.

When Catherine was ten years old she had a childhood love affair with her cousin, Karl Peter Ulrich. He was also a German but had been named Grand Duke and heir to the Russian throne. The romance was nurtured by Sophia's mother, and Sophia herself was not unwilling. "Child as I was," she wrote later, "the title of queen sounded sweet to my ears." At the age of fourteen she was taken by her mother to the Russian court at Saint Petersburg, and after eighteen months the Empress Elizabeth agreed to Sophia's betrothal with the Grand Duke Peter. As a condition of the marriage Sophia was required to adopt the Orthodox faith, and on doing so she took the Russian names of Catherine Alexeyevna.

The marriage took place with great pomp and ceremony on August 28, 1745. It was to last for seventeen years, but was a miserable failure. The Grand Duke, sickly in childhood, his face hideously pitted by smallpox, was always to remain an "unbalanced dreamer." He hated Russia, played at toy soldiers in adulthood, and was a passionate admirer of Frederick the Great of Prussia with whom Russia was at war. The marriage was not consummated for at least seven years, and Catherine found consolation elsewhere.

On September 20, 1754, after two miscarriages, she gave birth to a son who was named Paul Petrovich. It is improbable that he was Peter's child — the Grand Duke was believed to be impotent — but the child was accepted and the birth of an heir warmly welcomed. The Empress Elizabeth took over his upbringing so effectively that Catherine hardly ever saw him. In 1757 Catherine gave birth to a daughter and Peter remarked, "I don't know how it is that my wife becomes pregnant."

Catherine's character was quite different from her husband's. Although she was a pleasure-loving woman she had a very serious side to her and was a great deal better-educated than the majority of people at the Russian court. She gave her heart and mind to the affairs of her adopted country.

The Empress Elizabeth died of a stroke in 1761 and Peter became Tsar. It was typical of him that he immediately offended his new subjects by ending the war with Frederick the Great. However, when he ordered his army to fight alongside the Prussians he was forced to abdicate and then murdered in an army-backed coup d'état staged in Catherine's favor. Catherine had foreseen and planned for such an eventuality, and although she protested her innocence it was certainly her closest friends who committed the deed. Peter's reign had lasted less than six months.

Catherine had been preparing herself to reign almost all her life, and she achieved her ambition at the age of thirty-three. As Empress and Autocrat of the Russians she was to reign for thirty-four years and was to do much to westernize the Russian court. The beginning of her reign coincided with the Enlightenment in France and the West, and Catherine was interested in literature and science as well as politics. She corresponded with Voltaire and Diderot, built schools and hospitals, and encouraged the education of women. She also acquired much of Poland (getting a former lover elected King), and won the Crimea and neighboring territory from Turkey. Catherine's efforts on behalf of territorial acquisition and intellectual advance were matched by a continuing hostility toward the masses: she ruthlessly suppressed peasant risings, and actually extended serfdom. She died of a stroke at the age of sixty-seven.

Before and during her reign she had a series of publicly admitted lovers and had several children out of wedlock. When her last lover, the Prince Potemkin, accused her of having had fifteen lovers she admitted to seven but said, "God knows it was not from debauchery for which I have never had any inclination. If in my youth I had had a husband whom I could have loved I should have remained faithful to him all my life. It is my misfortune that my heart cannot rest content, even for an hour, without love."

Painted by L. Eusebj. Engraved by T. Cheesman.

Her Imperial Highness
Catherine Paulowna,
GRAND DUCHESS
of all the Russias,
Princess Dowager
of HOLSTEIN OLDENBOURG &c &c &c.

Dedicated by permission to his Excellency Prince Gagarine Chef de la Cour de S.A.I &c
by his Excellency's very obliged & obedient Servant —— L. EUSEBJ.

London Pub.d June 22.1814. by Colnaghi & C.o 23 Cockspur St. for L.Eusebj 8 Maccclesfield St. &c.

Lyubov Fedorovna Pavlova

ANNA PAVLOVA
(1882-1931)
Perhaps the most renowned
ballerina of all time. For many
years the star of the Russian
Ballet, she is specially
remembered for her role in
The Swan.

Lyubov Fedorovna Pavlova was thirty-three in 1882, when her only child, Anna, was born. Lyubov was living in St Petersburg at the time, but she came originally from Tver (now Kalinin), a town some 300 miles to the south. The man she married, Matvey Pavlovitch Pavlov, was a peasant and reserve soldier but it is doubtful that he was the father of her child. In later years Anna would never speak of him and did not like to be addressed as Anna Matveyevna, the customary way of addressing a woman whose father was named Matvey. Recent research suggests that Anna's father was Lazar Jacovlevitch Poliakoff, a member of a wealthy Jewish family of bankers and patrons of the arts.

At the time of Anna's birth the Pavlov family was poor. Matvey died two years later, and Lyubov went to work as a laundry woman. Eventually she was to become responsible for washing the linen at the Imperial Ballet School, and later still she ran a laundry of her own in St Petersburg.

Despite her poverty Lyubov kept a neat home and took care to provide a tree at Christmas, complete with candles and golden fruit, and at Easter an egg containing toys. In the summer they stayed at a *dacha* (small villa) in the countryside outside St Petersburg. Since Lyubov would not have been able to afford this herself, it may be that Anna's real father rented it for them.

In 1890 Tchaikovsky's ballet *Sleeping Beauty* was danced for the first time at the Maryinsky Theater. Lyubov took her eight-year-old daughter to see it, preparing her for the treat by telling her the story and explaining, "You are going to enter fairyland." This visit was to change her daughter's life. From that time on, Anna's one ambition was to become a dancer.

For two more years Lyubov continued to look after her daughter at home. She taught Anna to sew, and encouraged her to read fables and fairy tales aloud to her. Lyubov, unlike her daughter, had received no education and was never able to read very well.

At the age of ten, Anna was accepted by the Imperial Ballet School, which meant that all her needs, including clothing, became the responsibility of the state. Lyubov visited her every Sunday for the next eight years, and during the holidays Anna came home to stay with her.

After Anna became a celebrated dancer in the Imperial Ballet, Lyubov continued to follow her daughter's career. In 1902 Anna appeared to fall on the stage, and Lyubov, watching from the top gallery, burst into tears and hurried backstage to find out what had happened.

Soon Anna began touring abroad and in 1914 left Russia for good to take her own company on the succession of long international tours that made her name famous throughout the world. Mother and daughter were briefly reunited in 1924 when Lyubov came to England for three weeks. She stayed at her daughter's home in Hampstead, saw her dance in Bournemouth, and then went back to Russia. She was seventy-seven at the time.

The date of Lyubov's death is uncertain. Anna died in 1931, leaving no will, and three years later the Soviet Union claimed her estate in Lyubov's name. Even though she had made her home in England for twenty years, Anna was still officially domiciled in Russia and in Russian law a mother could claim the estate of her daughter if she had been totally dependent upon her. The Russians maintained that Lyubov was still alive (she would then have been eighty-seven), and the case was fought in the British courts.

Anna's business manager argued that although she did regularly send generous checks to her mother, this money was not her sole means of support. In the end, however, Lyubov (or the Soviet Union) won the case and most of the British estate went to Russia, which was at that time much in need of foreign capital. Whether any of the proceeds went to Lyubov — or even whether she was still alive by that time — will probably never be known.

Right Lyubov with her daughter

Maria Picasso Lopez

PABLO PICASSO
(1881-1973)
Spanish painter, sculptor, and
graphic artist.

Maria Picasso Lopez was born around 1860 in the Spanish town of Malaga. The Picasso family, which is thought to have been Andalusian in origin, had lived in Malaga for many years and it was there that Maria grew up. Maria's mother was later remembered by her grandson as a wonderfully imaginative storyteller. Her father, Don Francisco Picasso, was born in Malaga and educated in England. Later he became a civil servant in Cuba; he disappeared there in 1883 and was said to have died of yellow fever. Maria is known to have had at least two sisters, but the family was probably even bigger.

Maria first met her future husband when he was courting her cousin. José Ruiz Blasco was under pressure from his large family to marry and produce a male heir, and the Picasso girl had been selected as a suitable partner for him. José, however, was unwilling to commit himself to her. He kept everyone in suspense for some time before suddenly announcing his intention to marry Maria instead. Two years later, in 1880, they were married. They moved into a large white apartment house in the square in which Maria had grown up. They were a typical provincial family who attended the bullfights every weekend and went to church on Sunday.

Their first child, Pablo, was born on October 25, 1881. There was some trouble at the birth, and the midwife who was in attendance thought that the baby had been born dead. Fortunately one of José's brothers, a doctor, was present; he noticed the woman's mistake and resuscitated the child. The birth of their second child was equally dramatic. When Pablo was three years old, there was an earthquake in Malaga. José rushed home to his family and evacuated them to the safety of a friend's home. As Pablo described it to his friend Jaime Sabartés some fifty years later: "My mother wore a kerchief on her head. I had never seen her like that before. My father seized his cape from the coat-stand, threw it round his shoulders, took me in his arms and rolled me in its folds, leaving only my head exposed." Shortly after they took shelter, Maria gave birth to a daughter, Lola. Their second daughter, Concepción, was born in 1887.

José was an artist by trade. He specialized in animal and bird still lifes, and was particularly fond of painting pigeons. He was a tall, gaunt, distinguished-looking man with red hair, who was basically defeated by his life and situation. Pablo remembered him as always being depressed and lethargic. Of the children, Concepción was the one who most resembled him, and her death in 1891 left him even more broken and unhappy. He was a good teacher for Pablo and encouraged him to paint and draw everything he saw. When he realized that his young son was already a better artist than he could ever be, he gave Pablo his brushes and never painted again.

Maria was different from her husband both temperamentally and physically. She was small-boned and well-proportioned and had magnetic black eyes and long blue-black hair. Her son Pablo took after her in build. She was warm and gay and had many friends.

Within the family she was particularly close to Pablo. In her old age she was fond of telling how the first noise that he learned to make was "*piz! piz!,*" a demand for *lapiz,* a pencil. Unlike José she refrained from advising or cajoling him, and she did not object when he wanted to return to Paris in 1901. She understood that he had extraordinary talent and supported him in everything he did. On learning that he had begun to write a bit, she wrote: "They tell me that you write. I can believe anything of you. If one day they tell me that you say Mass, I shall believe it just the same."

After José's death in 1913, Maria moved in with the widowed Lola and five grandchildren. She took about twenty of Pablo's earliest paintings with her and covered the walls with them. From then until the time of her death in 1939, she wrote to Pablo often and made frequent visits to see him. During the Spanish Civil War, she wrote to him to say that a convent had been burned within a few yards of their building. She was unhappy because for weeks the room had reeked with the stench and smoke, and they had been unable to open any windows.

The summer visits to the South of France must have been exciting for her, because Pablo's eccentric guests often preferred to dress up in strange costumes rather than go sunbathing. In one photograph of such an occasion she is seen sitting on the edge of a canoe wearing a strange hat fringed with beads. Even as an old woman, her enthusiasm for life and her pride in her son were unfailing.

Right Picasso's portrait of his mother shows no hint of his future artistic development.

ELIZABETH ARNOLD

EDGAR ALLAN POE
(1809-49)
American writer of short stories, poetry, and criticism. He has been described as the inventor of the modern detective story.

Imagine sitting in a theater in Boston, Massachusetts in the year 1796. George Washington is still President. Relations with England have improved since the War of Independence ended fifteen years ago, and you have just been entertained by a concert in which appeared a young English actress "straight from the Theatre Royal, Covent Garden." There is another treat in store for you, for after the show a little girl slips onto the stage and sings "The Market Lass." She endears herself to you and the rest of the audience.

The young singer was Elizabeth Arnold, only nine years old and daughter of the Covent Garden actress. The critics were enraptured by her innocent charm. "Although a Miss of only nine years old her powers as an Actress would do credit to any of her sex of maturer age," wrote one. But he threw in a warning on the theatrical life of the time in which she was to grow up. "It is hoped that Gentlemen of the town will attend once more. But the ladies, perhaps, ought not to attend till it is known whether their ears are again to be offended with expressions of obscenity and profanity."

After the success of the Boston concert Elizabeth and her mother performed together for a time, but then her mother disappeared from the scene and Elizabeth became an actress in her own right. From the parts she played, sometimes those of boys, it is clear that she exuded a wholesome freshness, gaiety, and innocence. "Lovely child!" a critic wrote, "thy youth we know will not long continue; thy beauty soon must fade; but thy Innocence! May it continue well and support thee in every character while in the theater of this world."

But critics' dreams and the realities of the life of touring actors in the United States of the time were two different things. Actors were still regarded as little better than vagabonds. Elizabeth was certainly in regular employment in a touring company, staying in theatrical boardinghouses, enjoying short and long seasons in the cities of the eastern seaboard from New York to Charleston. And she was clearly popular,

playing half a dozen different parts, sometimes the lead, in as many plays a week. She also sang well.

In 1802, when she was sixteen, she married Charles Hopkins, a member of the company, but the marriage lasted only three years. On September 26, 1805, playbills showed Charles playing Sir Peter Teazle in *The School for Scandal*. With him, playing the part of Joseph Surface, was another handsome young actor, David Poe. Within a month Charles was dead; within six months the young widow had become Mrs David Poe.

The theatrical life continued. Play followed play. A son was born in 1807 and again, significantly, Mrs Poe did not appear on any playbill early in 1809. Then, on January 19 of that year, there appeared in the local newspaper this reference to the birth of Edgar Allan: "We congratulate the frequenters of the theater on the recovery of Mrs Poe from her recent confinement. This charming little Actress will make her reappearance tomorrow evening as Rosamonde in the popular play of *Abaellino the Great Bandit,* a part peculiarly adapted to her figure and talents."

Alas, there were not to be many more performances. Another child, a daughter, Rosalie, was born in 1810. Elizabeth began to fade away from consumption. In 1811 she was described as "very sick, having quarreled and parted with her husband and is destitute." On the same day appeared a heartrending appeal for a benefit performance at the theater. "To the Human Heart. On this night Mrs Poe, lingering on the bed of disease and surrounded by her children, asks your assistance *and asks it perhaps for the last time.* The generosity of a Richmond audience can need no other appeal."

She died on December 8, 1811, her handsome widower soon after. Edgar was removed from the theatrical lodgings, the only home he had ever known. He was brought up by a kindly family who took him to England. His mother, who had given much pleasure to many theatergoers, was with him only two years of his life.

208

209

kate porter

COLE PORTER
(1893-1964)
American composer of popular music including such songs as "Begin the Beguine" and "You're the Tops."

Right Photographic portrait of Kate — not everyone agreed with her view that she was a woman of style and sophistication.

The mother of the playwright Moss Hart said of Cole Porter's mother, Kate, "She's very nice, very, very nice, for a country woman." If the comment ever got back to Kate Porter, she would not have been very pleased. In her own eyes, she was a woman of style and sophistication.

Kate Porter was born in the early 1860s. She was the daughter of J.O. Cole, a man whose pioneering spirit had brought him considerable wealth. Cole had been brought up in the frontier town of Peru, Indiana and set out in 1850 for the goldfields of California. On his return home seventeen years later, he was rich enough to open a brewery and buy large tracts of land in Indiana, Illinois, and West Virginia.

J. O. Cole married Indiana-born Rachel Henton, and they had two children, Kate, and a son, Louis. Cole was rough, tough, and rich, but behind the hard exterior there was a sentimental streak, and he spoiled both his wife and daughter.

Kate was small and dark, had a large mouth, and was rather plain in appearance. But she had a will of her own and was determined that she should have an education suitable for the fashionable woman she intended to be. She decided to go to Vassar College, but this plan fell through. It has been suggested that her father objected to anything "Eastern," though Cole Porter later denied this. She went first to Colby Academy in New London, Connecticut, and then to Brooks Seminary, a finishing school in New York.

After she had graduated, she returned to Indiana. A somewhat haughty manner concealed a strong romantic spirit and a desire to live her life as she wished. Much to the surprise of the townsfolk of Peru, she fell in love with Samuel Fenwick Porter, who owned a drugstore, and she married him in 1884. He was charming and goodlooking certainly, but not quite the type Kate was expected to marry. For one thing, he had no money. Kate's father paid most of the bills and never thought much of Sammy.

Kate and Sammy lost two children. Then, in 1891, along came a son whom they named Cole. He was an entertaining child and Kate soon decided that he would fulfill all her dreams. A fortune-teller told her that children became famous if their initials spelled a simple word. Cole was promptly given a second Christian name, Albert, so that his initials spelled CAP.

Kate made her son wear all manner of smart clothes and even, on one occasion when he was still very young, dressed him in a wing collar and black tie. He was not allowed to play any rough games, but was given riding lessons. Above all, Kate made him practice the piano and also sent him off to have violin lessons. His music teacher was in a town thirty miles away, and between his lesson and catching a train home he had some hours to while away. On one occasion he discovered a shop that sold "naughty" books and said later that they inspired some of his more risqué lyrics, such as "Love for Sale." His father's interest in poetry may also have influenced his lyric writing, but by and large Cole did not get on with him, and his main early influences were his grandfather and Kate.

At the age of ten, Cole began to compose songs. And soon his mother had taken one to Chicago to be published, though she apparently paid the publisher for the privilege. Kate also took Cole to many plays and operas.

Later she decided to send him East to attend Worcester Academy, where he arrived with an upright piano. The Academy was chosen by Kate because she wanted Cole to have a classical education and meet important people. But J. O. Cole wanted him to remain in Indiana and learn about farming and business. This led to a violent fight between Kate and J. O., who did not speak to one another for two years. Cole, meanwhile, was not visited at school by either of his parents. J. O. managed to get him to go home briefly to do some farming, despite objections from Kate. (Kate won the argument anyway when Cole made it clear that farming was not his métier by collapsing in the heat.)

Cole subsequently went to Yale and then, at the insistence of J. O., to Harvard Law School. He had already become a francophile and toward the end of the First World War served in the French Army, where, as a foreigner, he was under the control of the Foreign Legion.

Kate's work was largely done. Cole, astonishingly like her in appearance, was a cultivated man, witty, charming, and already showing strong signs of his unique talent. She performed one more service for him when she persuaded J. O. to increase his allowance so that he could marry a wealthy international hostess.

Kate died in 1952 in Peru, Indiana, after a cerebral hemorrhage. Cole had rushed there shortly before her death and as she lay unconscious wrote the finale of the show *Can Can*.

JEANNE WEIL

MARCEL PROUST
(1871-1922)
French writer, most famous for his novel *Remembrance of Things Past.*

When Marcel Proust was born on July 10, 1871, nobody expected the weak, sickly child to live. He liked, throughout life, to blame his ill-health on the fact that he was conceived and born during the German siege and occupation of Paris in the Franco-Prussian War: his mother, he felt, had been deprived of the proper food necessary for her own and her child's well-being. Perhaps she, too, felt responsible; for certainly she devoted much of her life to nursing him.

Madame Proust was born Jeanne Weil, the daughter of a wealthy Jewish stockbroker. She was beautiful, cultured, intelligent, and well-educated – the ideal wife for the distinguished Paris doctor, fifteen years her senior, whom she married in September 1870. Adrien Proust was a man of action, independent and kind, though somewhat hasty and bad-tempered. His wife was gentle, rather shy, with a knowledge of English and German and a little Latin and Greek. She gave to her husband the security of her affection and deep respect, managing his household with elegance and efficiency. It was a very happy marriage. When Adrien Proust died in 1903, Marcel and his mother made of the doctor's study a kind of memorial shrine, leaving it exactly as it was when he had used it, except for photographs of him illustrating various stages of his life.

Marcel was their firstborn. Two years later they had another son, Robert, who was to become an eminent surgeon; but it was Marcel who became the main object of his mother's anxious love. "Mon petit loup" (my little wolf), she called him, while Robert was only "Mon autre loup" (my other wolf). Asked, as a child, what he wanted for a New Year present, Marcel replied to his mother: "Your affection." When she left him for a few days, he would weep hysterically, and one evening he was inconsolable because she had failed to come to kiss him goodnight. He called from his bedroom window to where she was entertaining guests in the garden below, and although she came at his call, he afterwards attributed to that moment his realization that love could never be perfect. At the age of thirteen, he recorded in an album that his idea of misery was "to be parted from Mama," and he was later to write to a friend: "You [are] really and truly the person that with the exception of Mama I love best in the whole world."

It was not an easy task being the mother of Marcel. From the age of nine he suffered from chronic asthma, and his life as an invalid began. Much of his time was spent in bed, and his mother acted as nurse, companion, and encourager. As he grew to manhood this dependence did not change. While Proust was in the army for a year, he wrote to his mother every day and she to him. Her letters were full of advice and homely gossip. But it was not only when he was away from home that this extraordinary correspondence flourished. When his asthma attacks were bad, he would often sleep during the day and be awake at night. Then he would leave long notes for her before he went to sleep, some of them loving and tender, others querulous and critical. This habit of daytime sleeping was deplored by his mother and was – along with his expensive tastes and wasteful spending – the cause of most of their arguments.

Jeanne Proust, a thrifty and efficient manager herself, was horrified by her son's extravagances. Despite her efforts to persuade him to enter a profession and her constant encouragement to publish what he wrote, he remained financially dependent on her until her death – a fact that they both resented.

It is difficult to know how seriously to take Marcel's charge that his mother loved him best when he was ill, but certainly he felt it to be true, and there is little doubt that he often used his asthma to win her affection. At the same time, though, he resented having to be ill: "It is hard not to have affection and good health simultaneously," he wrote to his mother in 1902. She clearly considered her role as his nurse to be of paramount importance: just before her death she said to Marcel, "I'm going back to Paris, because I'm useless and can't help you when you're ill."

Jeanne Proust remained calm and self-sacrificing to the end. She was concerned above all that Marcel should be spared the sight of her suffering. Even when she was dying of uraemia, she tried to convince him that she was well. And when he insisted on being at her bedside, she would play with him – when she was able to speak – the literary games they had played together since his childhood. She died on September 26, 1905. As Marcel sat by her body he wrote: "Today I have her still, dead, but accepting my caresses – tomorrow I shall lose her forever." Never having relinquished her Jewish faith, Jeanne Proust was buried without a church service at Père Lachaise cemetery in Paris. What a disappointment Marcel must have been to her: only a few articles published, and so much promise!

Right Jeanne with her sons, Marcel and Robert.

neeltjen willemsdochter van suydtbrouck

Neeltjen Willemsdochter van Suydtbrouck was born in Leyden, Holland around 1570. Her father was a baker. Nothing is known of her childhood except that she learned to read and acquired a thorough knowledge of the Bible.

On October 8, 1589 she was married to Hermen Gerritszoon van Rijn, a Leyden miller. Hermen was a prominent figure in town affairs and must have been quite wealthy for, in the years of his marriage, he purchased a half-share in his mother's windmill within the walls of the city of Leyden. Hermen also bought a small house near the windmill to live in with his wife. Their surroundings were simple but comfortable.

It is not certain exactly how many children Neeltjen and Hermen had, but the names of seven are known. Adriaen, the eldest child, followed his father and became a miller, and some of the other sons are thought to have had similar trades. Rembrandt, the second youngest child, was born on July 15, in a year that has been accepted as 1606. Contrary to popular belief, he was born not in a windmill but in the house his father bought when he married. The couple's only daughter was Lijsbeth, the youngest of the family.

Neeltjen outlived her husband by ten years, and after his death she and the unmarried Lijsbeth lived together. Neeltjen was about seventy years old when she died in Leyden. She was buried on September 14, 1640. In her will she left a considerable fortune, chiefly in property.

REMBRANDT VAN RIJN
(1606-69)
Dutch painter and graphic artist.

Left Neeltjen in old age — two drawings by her son.

215

Deborah Hitchbourn

PAUL REVERE
(1735-1818)
American patriot who won
fame in 1775 for his ride
through Massachusetts to
warn fellow patriots of the
British advance.

The mother of Paul Revere was born Deborah Hitchbourn in 1704, the daughter of Thomas Hitchbourn and Frances Pattishall of Boston. On both sides of her family were several generations of solid New England farmers and mariners, pioneers of Britain's American colonies. Her father owned wharves on the shoreline of Massachusetts Bay, and was also involved in shipbuilding and repair.

In 1729 Deborah married a Boston neighbor, the goldsmith Paul Revere. He was a Frenchman, a Huguenot who had left France to escape religious persecution. (The name "Paul Revere" was actually an anglicized form of "Apollos Rivoire.") He was apprenticed to a Boston goldsmith and by the time of his marriage had acquired a successful business of his own.

Deborah had nine children between 1733 and 1744, though two of them died in infancy. Paul Revere Jr, born in 1735, was her second child. He and his four sisters and two brothers were brought up in the Reveres' frame house in Boston's North End, among the city's thriving artisans.

Each Sunday Paul Revere Sr took his family to the "New Brick Church," better known as the "Cockerel Church" for its prominent weathervane. During the rest of the week the Revere children were allowed much freedom, with many Hitchbourn cousins running in and out of the Revere house. In the evenings the children would gather to hear Deborah's thrilling tales of the exploits of her ancestors: of Captain Pattishall who had been killed by wild Indians and of her grandfather Thomas Hitchbourn, who, when owed money by a shoemaker, broke into

his shop and stole two pairs of shoes in lieu of the cash that he would probably never have received.

Deborah brought a good share of money to her marriage. Her great-grandfather Pattishall had left her some land in Maine, and when her father died in 1735, he left the family a share in the wharves. When old Mrs Hitchbourn died in 1742, a clause in her will read: "To my daughter Reever [sic] named Deborah, 1½ years' rent for her house she now lives in."

Nevertheless, when her husband died in 1757, Deborah was left without ready cash, so that she had to supplement her next month's rent money with a silver thimble and some rum. She found that her son Paul, now nineteen, would not be legally eligible to own the family business until he was twenty-one, although he had been well trained as a goldsmith by his father. So Deborah was the nominal owner of the smithy and shop while Paul did the work.

Deborah still had several young children to bring up. And later, after Paul married, she helped look after his children as well — sixteen of them, by his two wives. She had her own rooms and provisions in his house in North Square.

But all was not easy in Deborah's later years, for the War of Independence involved the whole family. Paul was one of the leaders of the local committee to plan the revolt against the British, and he was prepared to go to war against them. On the night of April 18, 1775 he made his famous ride from Charlestown to Lexington and Lincoln to warn the citizens of the approach of the redcoats. Deborah died two years later, on May 23, 1777, while the war was still raging.

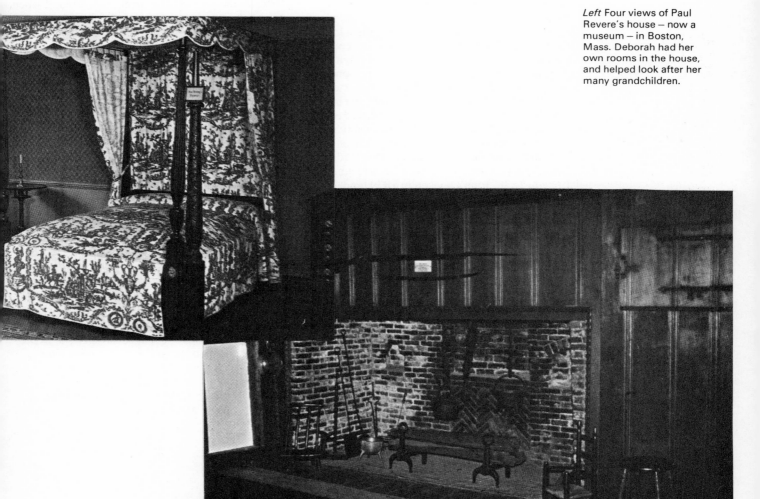

Left Four views of Paul Revere's house — now a museum — in Boston, Mass. Deborah had her own rooms in the house, and helped look after her many grandchildren.

ELIZABETH DAVISON

JOHN D. ROCKEFELLER
(1839-1937)
Pioneer of the American oil
industry and founder of the
Standard Oil Company.

When John D. Rockefeller was a boy, his mother once said of him: "I don't know what John is going to be when he grows to be a man, but I'm sure of one thing – he won't starve." She lived to see him become the richest man in the world.

Elizabeth Davison was the daughter of a prosperous farmer who lived in Niles, Cayuga County, New York. She was a spirited young woman with a legacy of Scottish ancestors, and she is described as slender, red-haired, and blue-eyed. She must also have been a young woman of great piety, determination, and fortitude.

In 1837, when she was twenty-four, Elizabeth married "Doctor" William Avery Rockefeller. It would be difficult to imagine two more dissimilar characters. Rockefeller in many ways typified the successful confidence man. As "Doctor Wm. A. Rockefeller, The Celebrated Cancer Specialist," he sold quack medicines, traded horses and land, loaned money, and at times made quite a lot of it for himself. Yet despite the differences between his character and that of his wife, their marriage does not seem to have been an unhappy one.

Rockefeller's activities meant that he was away from home for long periods. (At one time his absence was involuntary: he was indicted for the alleged rape of a hired girl and had to stay away until the case had blown over.) The Rockefellers lived at first on their farmstead in Richford, New York, and Elizabeth there bore three children: Lucy in 1838, John Davison in 1839, and William Avery Jr in 1841. Later the family bought a seven-room farmhouse at Moravia, New York. Here Elizabeth had three more children: Mary Ann in 1843, and twins who died in infancy.

Her husband's frequent and protracted absences meant that Elizabeth was left with the jobs of bringing up the children and running the farm. She allocated work to the children according to age, and much of the responsibility fell to John, the eldest son. Her husband would return from time to time, filling the house with his powerful personality and, apparently prosperous, paying off any debts incurred during his absence.

But during the absences it was the pious, hard-working, and resolute Elizabeth who shouldered the family burdens. It was said of her that her dignity verged on pride and her reticence on taciturnity, and that as a neighbor she was more respected than loved. With the children she was a strict disciplinarian. On one occasion when John was being chastized for some alleged misdemeanor and he protested his innocence, his mother replied: "Never mind, we have started in on this whipping and it will do for next time."

At the same time, she was clearly a mother of imagination. John D. Rockefeller in his *Random Reminiscences* tells how, when a boy, he very much wanted to cut down a tree that obstructed the view from the dining room window. The family was strongly opposed, but one day his mother said to him: "You know, my son, we have breakfast at eight o'clock and I think if the tree were felled some time before we sat down at table there would probably be no great complaint when the family saw the view which the fallen tree revealed."

Despite the father's errant ways and Elizabeth's rather grim approach to life, the family seems to have been a united one, most probably a tribute to Elizabeth's influence. When John married, he and his bride lived with his parents in Cleveland for six months and then moved into the house next door. As Elizabeth grew older she spent most of her time with her children and their families, always closely interested in what they were doing. And the affectionate relationship between John and his mother is evident in a letter from him asking her to come to stay: "The robins," he wrote, "already enquire for you, and we can have the whole lawn full if you will only come back to greet them."

Her grandson said once: "She always sat next to Father at table and how well can I remember often seeing him hold her hand lovingly on the table. Grandmother trusted Father absolutely and loved him devotedly."

This stalwart old lady, cherished by her family, died on March 28, 1889, aged seventy-six, in her younger son's house on Fifth Avenue in New York. She was buried at Burned Lake View Cemetery, with her two sons acting as pallbearers. Her husband, true to his old habits, was not present at the funeral.

Right Elizabeth – a strict
but well-loved mother.

ANNA HALL

ELEANOR ROOSEVELT
(1884-1962)
US delegate to the United
Nations General Assembly
and in 1946 Chairman of the
UN Commission on Human
Rights. She was the wife of
Franklin D. Roosevelt.

Eleanor Roosevelt was the daughter of Elliott Roosevelt (younger brother of Theodore) and Anna Hall. Among Anna's forebears were a signer of the Declaration of Independence and the man who administered the oath of office to George Washington. Her father, Valentine G. Hall, was the son of an Irish immigrant who had become very rich.

Anna, the eldest of his children, was born in 1863 and was seventeen when her father died. She was noted for her fair-haired beauty and her strength of character. She married Elliott Roosevelt in 1883, and their first child, Eleanor, was born the following year. There were two more children: Elliott Jr, born in 1889, and Hall, in 1891. She gave time to her children but also enjoyed the active social life of a wealthy New Yorker.

For some time little Eleanor slept in her mother's bedroom, and used to watch her dress for the evenings. "She looked so beautiful," wrote Eleanor in her autobiography, "I was grateful to be allowed to touch her dress or her jewels or anything that was part of the vision which I admired inordinately." In spite of kind intentions, Anna did not succeed in concealing her belief that Eleanor was ugly; she called her "Granny" because, she explained to visitors, she was "so old-fashioned." When Anna was with all her children, Eleanor had the feeling that she was

being left out.

But Anna was most concerned about her husband, Elliott, whose too-active business, social, and sporting life undermined his health. This was exacerbated when pain from a badly treated broken ankle led to drink, laudanum, and morphine. The firm upright Anna had little sympathy with Elliott's drinking and still less when he became violent and sought comfort elsewhere. There was talk of divorce and of having Elliott declared insane so that he could not dissipate the family fortune. Eleanor, now seven, felt neglected and had taken to telling lies to draw attention to herself, which alienated her still more from her mother.

Anna's health broke down, though she appeared to recover from a major operation. It was a short-lived recovery. At the end of November, 1892 she became ill again, probably with diphtheria; on December 7 she died. Throughout her two illnesses, she refused to allow her husband to visit her. When Eleanor came to write of this period she did not dwell upon her mother's death, but rather upon the return of her father, for whom she had a deep affection. The family dared not entrust the children to the widower. He lived alone and, less than two years later, in August 1894, he died. The care of Eleanor passed to her grandmother, Mary Livingston Ludlow Hall.

Right The youthful Anna, noted for her fair-haired beauty.

Sara Delano

Franklin Delano Roosevelt belonged to the same family as his wife Eleanor. Franklin was his mother's only child, though his father, James Roosevelt, had another son by an earlier marriage. Sara, the second Mrs James Roosevelt, was born in 1854. She was one of the nine children of Warren Delano, a descendant of Philippe de la Noye, a French Huguenot who left France and established himself in Leyden, Holland at the end of the seventeenth century. There, in 1609, he aided some of the exiled British Puritans who, eleven years later, sailed on the *Mayflower* to establish their community in the New World. One of his sons, Jacques, followed them and founded the American branch of the family.

Warren Delano owned a large tea plantation in Macao and amassed a substantial fortune. He retired early, investing his money in railways and property, including an estate at Algonac, New York, where he greatly enlarged an existing house a few miles downstream from the Roosevelts' Hyde Park. After narrowly escaping ruination in the crisis of 1857, Delano returned to the Far East and rebuilt his fortune in the opium trade.

Algonac was Sara Delano's principal home, but she was a well-traveled little girl. By the age of sixteen she had been to Macao, Hong Kong, Egypt, and France (for the Paris Exhibition in 1860), and spoke fluent French and German. She developed into a tall and slender young woman, dark-haired and dark-eyed, and was known as one of the four Delano beauties. Her height and dignified bearing seemed to emphasize a growing strength of character. Yet this strength did not prevent complete obedience to her father, at whose behest she turned down several suitors. It was Sara who took charge of the estate in her father's absence.

Sara was still unmarried at the age of twenty-six. She knew both branches of the Roosevelt family and became a close friend of Anna ("Bamie"), elder sister of Theodore and Elliott Roosevelt. She also met James Roosevelt of Hyde Park who had been a widower for four years. He was twice her age, but he lost no time in courting her. This time her father yielded. In October 1880 they were married and in January 1882 Sara gave birth to their first and only child, christened Franklin Delano; his godfather was Elliott Roosevelt, who was to marry Anna Hall in the next year.

Sara devoted herself almost exclusively to her husband and son — particularly the latter, whose growth and development she constantly watched. She closely followed his studies at home and at Groton, and even took a house in Boston to be near him when he was at Harvard. By then her husband James had died (in 1900). In 1901, as she and Franklin were about to return home from a tour of Europe, they learned of the shooting of President McKinley, and shortly afterwards of his death. Vice-President Theodore Roosevelt, their cousin, had become President of the United States.

Sara was immensely proud of her handsome and clever son and looked forward to having him by her for many years. She was dismayed when, in 1903, Franklin decided to marry his eighteen-year-old cousin Eleanor whom he had known since childhood. Franklin, who admired Eleanor's mind, was resolutely determined to marry her. Sara had to resign herself to taking a lesser role, looking after her estate and her fortune and occasionally financing some of Franklin's extravagant business ventures. She lived to appreciate Eleanor and suffer when Franklin was afflicted with poliomyelitis in 1921. She also saw him elected President in 1932, in 1936 and again in 1940. In June of 1939 she had the satisfaction of entertaining King George VI and Queen Elizabeth at Hyde Park. Two years later she suffered a circulatory collapse and died on September 7, 1941 at the age of eighty-seven.

FRANKLIN DELANO ROOSEVELT
(1882-1945)
32nd President of the United States. He was in office during the Great Depression and the Second World War.

Left A carefully posed photograph of Sara – a devoted wife and mother.

Marie Eléonore de Maillé de Carman

MARQUIS DE SADE
(1740-1814)
Infamous French writer of
pornographic literature.

Right The Condé
residence, where Marie
Eléonore gave birth to the
future Marquis de Sade.

The family of de Sade had been lords in Provence
from the twelfth century. They had been soldiers,
bishops and provincial governors, and had served
as Cupbearers to the Popes when the Papal seat
was in Avignon. In 1733 the family heir Jean
Baptiste Joseph François, Count de Sade,
married Marie Eléonore de Maillé de Carman, a
member of the royal house of Bourbon.

Marie Eléonore was born in 1712, the daughter
of the Marquis de Carman. She belonged to
another branch of the royal family. One of her
cousins was the Prince de Condé, an incompetent
minister of Louis XV, and at the time of her
marriage she was lady-in-waiting to the Princess.

Her husband, the Count de Sade, was born in
1702, and had begun his career as a Captain of
Dragoons in the Prince de Condé's regiment. By
the time of his marriage he was being entrusted
with diplomatic missions that later took him
throughout Europe. The Countess accompanied
him on many of these.

The first child of the marriage, Caroline Laure,
was born in 1737 but she lived only two years.
On June 2, 1740 the Countess gave birth to a son
– Donatien Alphonse François, the future
Marquis. (The titles Count and Marquis
alternated at each succession in the de Sade
family.)

The birth took place in the Condé mansion in
Paris, a vast old building with wings separated
by cramped inner courts, set alongside a huge
garden. At the time of his son's birth the Count
was in Cologne, where he had been sent as
Ambassador. Neither of the baby's godparents
was present at the christening, so the future
Marquis was held over the font by two servants.
Because of this he was given the wrong Christian
names. The Countess had instructed the servants
that he was to be christened Louis Aldonse
Donatien, but the ancient Provençal name of
Aldonse was misunderstood by the Parisian
servants and they forgot Louis entirely. When the
Marquis grew up he sometimes signed himself
Louis, and this caused him considerable trouble
during the French Revolution when he was
working as Citizen Sade under one name while
being denounced, mistakenly, as an *emigré*
aristocrat under another.

The Prince de Condé died in 1740 and the
Princess in 1741, but Marie Eléonore continued
to live in the Condé mansion helping to bring up
their orphaned boy. She hoped that the young
prince would become a useful companion to her
own son in the future. Unfortunately, Donatien
quarreled with him, attacked him violently, and

had to be separated from him by force.

At the age of four Donatien was sent to
Avignon to live with his paternal grandmother,
who indulged his every whim. He did not return
to Paris until he was ten, and during his four
years at a Jesuit school there the Countess was
able to see him whenever the Count's duties
brought her back to Paris.

The Count may have been an able diplomat
but he was an inefficient manager of his own
estates. After 1750 his financial position
deteriorated and he became increasingly difficult
to live with. He died in 1765, but several years
before this the Countess and he were living apart
– she in a Carmelite convent in Paris where she
was to remain for the rest of her life.

Before he was twenty Donatien had acquired a

Elevation d'une

reputation as a libertine. By the time he was thirty he had been imprisoned three times for sexual offenses and had enraged his wife's family by running off with her sister. At the time of her son's marriage the Countess had caused an embarrassing scene by refusing to part with her diamonds, which she was supposed to pass on to her daughter-in-law.

The young Marquis's debauchery continued to bring disgrace to the family name. He flogged a prostitute on Easter Sunday, 1768 – "a day," the Countess said later, "forever fated for the House of Sade." He was imprisoned again, and her protests to the King about her son's treatment in prison were coldly received. On his release he behaved prudently for a while, but in 1772 he was imprisoned again. He escaped and managed to remain at liberty only by keeping to his estates in Provence and staying away from Paris. The Countess never saw her son again.

In 1777 the Marquis learned that his mother was dying. He made the long and perilous journey to Paris but by the time he arrived she was dead. His wife's mother – who had long detested him – seized her chance. She secured a warrant for his arrest and five days after his arrival in Paris he was in prison again. He was to remain there for thirteen years.

Yet this rearrest, and the filial duty that led to it, secured the fame of the Countess de Sade's son. It was during those long years in the Bastille that the Marquis de Sade secretly wrote the books that have made him notorious.

faces de l'Escalier de l'Hôtel de Condé　　　　*I.Marot fecit*

Mary Arden

WILLIAM SHAKESPEARE
(1564-1616)
English dramatist and poet.

Much of what we know about the life of William Shakespeare comes to us through legal documents. The same is true of his mother, Mary Arden. She was the youngest of eight daughters of Robert Arden of Wilmcote, in the parish of Aston Cantelow, near Stratford-upon-Avon, Warwickshire. Robert Arden was connected with the Arden family of Park Hall, who claimed descent from King Alfred. Robert's children were all by his first wife, whose name is not known. His second wife, Mary's stepmother, was a widow named Agnes Hill. The Wilmcote farmhouse where Mary was brought up is a handsome, substantial manor house and, to judge by the inventory made when Robert died, was well furnished. Robert Arden owned not only the farmland at Wilmcote, but also farms and houses at Snitterfield, east of Wilmcote. One of these farms was let to a tenant farmer named Richard Shakespeare.

When Robert died in 1556 he left to Mary another farm at Wilmcote, called Asbies, with "the crop upon the ground sown and tilled as it is, and £6 13s 4d of money to be paid or ere my goods be divided." Mary was also made an executor of the will. She further inherited a share in the property in Snitterfield, and had already been given some other land in Wilmcote. Mary, in short, was an heiress when she married Richard Shakespeare's son, John, probably sometime in 1557. John was a prosperous glover and tanner. He owned a house in Henley Street, Stratford (probably the one now known as "the Woolshop"), and soon after seems to have bought the house next door (now known as "the Birthplace"). John rose rapidly in local affairs, becoming in turn Alderman, Justice of the Peace, and High Baliff of Stratford. The first years of

Mary's married life were therefore comfortable with help from domestic staff.

Mary gave birth to eight children. The first, Joan, was born in 1558, and the last, Edmund, in 1580. Three of the children died young. William, born in April, 1564, was Mary's third child.

Mary Shakespeare's life ran into a difficult time after about 1577, when John Shakespeare's financial affairs took a turn for the worse. This may have been due to imprudence, or possibly to disputes over religion (at one stage he was in legal trouble for failing to attend church regularly). At any rate, the Shakespeares were by this time short of money, and Mary's inheritance was disposed of in various ways. The share of the Snitterfield property was sold, and Asbies Farm was let for a small rent. Mary's other property in Wilmcote was mortgaged to her sister Joan's husband, Edmund Lambert. The mortgage was redeemed at the time stated, and when John Shakespeare later attempted to pay back the money and recover the property, Lambert retained it and managed to win a court action over the matter. This action was only one of many in which John Shakespeare's name appears – he was always suing someone or being sued.

Mary's later years seem to have been prosperous again. This prosperity may have been due to William's success as a playwright and actor in London. In 1596 John Shakespeare was granted a coat-of-arms, which he had been trying to obtain for years. In the grant of arms, the College of Heralds made much of John's marriage to Robert Arden's daughter, and also of the fact that he had land and properties worth £500. John died in 1601; Mary in 1608, probably aged about seventy.

Below, left to right Mary's birthplace at Wilmcote; Aston Cantlow church, where Mary and John are thought to have been married; the house in Stratford-upon-Avon where their son William was born in 1564; and Holy Trinity church, Stratford, where William was baptized.

BESSIE GURLEY

Bessie Gurley was the daughter of a minor Irish squire. Her mother died when Bessie was young, and she was brought up by her Aunt Ellen. Aunt Ellen, a hunchbacked spinster, was a strict disciplinarian. She raised her niece in an atmosphere of intense respectability.

Aunt Ellen taught Bessie the manners appropriate to a young lady of her day. She also instilled in her a love of flowers, animals and needlework, and gave her lessons on the piano. She made it clear that the acquisition of these virtues was essential for a marriage commensurate with her station in life.

But Bessie had ideas of her own. In 1852 she married a sociable and charming Irish ne'er-do-well. He came from a respectable family but had no fortune and, worst of all, he was a drunkard. This last she soon discovered on opening a cupboard and dislodging a cascade of empty bottles. Aunt Ellen, a woman of spirit, was furious at the marriage. She disinherited Bessie and bitterly sent her as a wedding present a bundle of IOUs signed by her niece's father.

So the young couple embarked on a life of poverty in a small rented house, not quite a slum, in unfashionable Synge Street on the outskirts of Dublin. Despite their poverty, there were soon more mouths to feed. Bessie gave birth to two daughters and, on July 26, 1856, to a son who was christened George Bernard.

According to her son, Bessie was a poor mother and a bad housekeeper. About her he said, "I should say she was the worst mother conceivable, always, however, within the limits of the fact that she was incapable of unkindness to any child, animal, flower, or indeed to any person or thing whatsoever." Meals were erratic and ill-cooked, and the children were left largely to fend for themselves. All his life Bernard Shaw resented the absence of maternal guidance and the failure of his parents to give him the education he thought he should have had. "She was not a bad wife or bad mother, she was simply not a wife or mother at all. Like my father she was a hopelessly uncoercive person: and we as children had to find our way in a household where there was neither hate nor love, fear nor reverence, but always personality."

Bessie possessed a very pure mezzo-soprano voice and was passionately fond of music. To help their financial situation the Shaws took in a lodger, a man named Vandeleur Lee who taught singing and had devised a "Method" involving special study and use of the larynx. Bessie fell under his thrall and became a disciple. In time the whole family, with Lee, moved from Synge Street to set up a joint household in Hatch Street, Dublin.

Then in 1872, Vandeleur Lee decided to move to London and launch his "Method" there. Bessie and her daughters immediately packed up and followed him, leaving the adolescent boy and his alcoholic father in lodgings in Dublin. Bernard Shaw never believed that there was a love affair between his mother and Lee and thought the move to London was no more than a characteristic Bessie-ism. He was probably right, for she soon discovered that Lee was a charlatan and immediately parted company with him.

But she did not return to Dublin – indeed, she never saw Ireland again, and only saw her husband once again when, years later, he paid a brief visit to London. She established herself and her daughters in a house where she earned a modest income teaching music. Eventually her son came to London and there began his career, first sharing their comparative poverty, then buying for her a house in Fitzroy Square where he worked in an untidy study, feeding on just the sort of scrappy and occasional meals that his mother had served in their Synge Street days.

Bessie eventually settled down and for many years taught at the very respectable North London Collegiate School for Girls. She died at the age of eighty-eight. At her funeral the only two mourners were George Bernard Shaw and the undertaker, who rebuked Shaw for his flippant behavior. The undertaker was himself in tears, and Shaw thought he was putting on a hypocritical act until he discovered that he had for years been his mother's closest friend.

GEORGE BERNARD SHAW
(1856-1950)
Irish wit, playwright, and critic. Among his best-known plays are *Pygmalion* and *Saint Joan.*

Left Bessie in the garden. *Below* Bessie relaxing in old age. She was described by G. B. S. as "the worst mother conceivable."

Mildred Stoughton Spock

Few individuals in this century have had so profound an effect on the raising of children as Dr Benjamin McLane Spock. His book *Baby and Child Care* was published in 1946; since then it has sold over 25,000,000 copies in twenty-six languages.

The mother of Dr Spock was Mildred Louise Stoughton. She was born in New York City in October, 1876. In 1900 she met Benjamin Ives Spock, a lawyer who was general counsel for the New Haven Railroad. They were married not long after meeting.

Benjamin and Mildred had six children, of whom Benjamin McLane, born in May 1903, was the first. Benjamin has referred to his mother as "tyrannical": she was completely devoted to raising her children but she did so, says he, with "a rod of iron." She was not religious but had an intense moralism; she idealized marriage, and disapproved of sex.

Not long after the publication of *Baby and Child Care,* Dr Spock invited his mother to visit him and his family. He had been apprehensive about what she would think of the book. "A young man's book on childbearing might be thought of as a possible criticism of his mother," he writes, especially when the book contains "new-fangled ideas" on the subject. Spock's apprehensions proved groundless: when asked for her opinion on his book she simply said, "Why, Bennie, I think it's quite sensible."

Mildred Louise Stoughton Spock died in 1968 in a nursing home in Hartford, Connecticut.

DR BENJAMIN SPOCK
(1903-)
American doctor famous for his book *Baby and Child Care*.

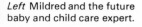

Left Mildred and the future baby and child care expert.

231

EKATERINA GHELADZE

JOSEF STALIN
(1879-1953)
Dictator of the Soviet Union
for nearly a quarter of a
century.

Right Ekaterina – she
wanted Josef to be a
priest.

Ekaterina (Keke) Gheladze was born in about
1856 in a Georgian village. Her parents were
poor serfs – her father a potter. When she was
nine, after the abolition of serfdom, the family
moved to Gori; here, when Kate was eighteen,
she married the twenty-two-year-old Vissarion
(Beso) Ivanovich Djugashvili, who was newly
arrived from a village in the Caucasus. He had set
out to find his fortune, and had come to Gori to
set up as a shoemaker.

At the time, Gori had a population of about
6000. Its meandering streets were dotted with
orchards and lined with peasant huts. The
Djugashvilis found a home on the outskirts: an
old adobe shack with brick-built corners and a
leaking roof. It had a kitchen and one other room,
lit by two small windows and floored with bare
brick chips over which, on rainy days, mud and
water would flow in from the courtyard. It was
furnished with a small table and stool, a couch
with a straw mat as a mattress, and an ancient,
noisy sewing machine. Wooden bowls caught the
rain that dripped from the roof.

At the time of her marriage Keke Djugashvili
was a pretty girl with chestnut-red hair, who
could probably neither read nor write. While Beso
tried to earn money making shoes, she paid the
rent and kept them alive by working as a
washerwoman, cutting and sewing and scrubbing
floors. Also, between 1875 and 1878, she bore
three children, all of whom died in infancy. On
December 21, 1879, when she was twenty-three,
she bore a son, who was christened Josef.

She set her mind on his becoming a priest, for
Beso's attempt to raise them into the
lower middle classes was drifting into drunken
failure. The house was full of quarreling and
violence. It is said that Josef once joined in by
throwing a knife at his father. Eventually Beso
left home to become a worker in a Tiflis shoe
factory (which later gave Stalin "proletarian"
status).

With Beso gone, the mother and son moved
into a priest's house, where Keke worked as a
domestic. Neighbors respected her because her
life had been so hard. She sang folk songs to Josef
and kept him well fed. In 1889 she managed to
get him into the local church school – having to
work for the school as cleaning woman,
laundress, and seamstress as part of the
agreement. Constant sewing had ruined her
eyesight, but her patience had saved Josef from
having to be apprenticed at ten to a shoemaker or

carpenter. Only a few years before, all schools
had been barred to serfs' sons.

She was to be disappointed by her son's choice
of career. In 1892 she was happy to hear him sing
solo chants at Mass in the Gori church. Ten years
later she was being questioned by police about his
part in a clash between police and strikers in
Batum. Josef Djugashvili metamorphosed into
Josef Stalin; and, after 1917, was one of the few
leading revolutionaries to have had really poor
parents.

After Stalin's ascendancy, Keke was given two
rooms in the former Viceroy's Palace at Tiflis.
Here she lived modestly under police guard. Once
a commissar joked that the guard had been
strengthened recently, to prevent her ever giving
birth to another Stalin. The commissar was shot
after a special show trial. Once she visited the
Kremlin, but longed only to get back to the
Caucasus and later refused to live in Moscow.
She never learned to speak Russian. She missed
her son, who came to see her only twice, but
contented herself with sending him his favorite
walnut preserve, and once wove him a blanket. In
her dim little bedroom, furnished with an iron cot,
she kept a great pile of newspapers, every one
with a speech by, or a report or photograph of
Josef.

She was a modest old peasant woman, with
pale freckled skin and silver-rimmed glasses, who
tried to live up to her son's position. Once
Svetlana Alliluyeva, Stalin's daughter, saw her in
a spa in the Caucasus, dressed all in heavy black
in spite of the great heat. When she was asked
why, the old woman said: "I have to . . . don't
you see, everyone around here knows who I am."
When interviewed by *Tass* journalists in 1932,
her face glowed with real joy and pride when her
son's name was mentioned.

Stalin did visit her once more, not long before
her death, and she bluntly told him that she
wished he had become a priest. He chose to be
pleased with the irony of this. But as she grew
older, her religiosity attracted too much notice.
She was said to have turned one of the rooms into
a private chapel, complete with icons. Stalin had
her taken back to Gori, where she developed
pneumonia. She died in Tiflis on June 7, 1937,
without being allowed to see a priest. Stalin did
not come to the funeral. She was buried secretly
at night, without ceremony, and later the grave
was marked with a simple granite slab and no
cross.

Marya Nikolayevna Volkonskaya

Two shabby sentinels, muskets shouldered, paced back and forth at the entrance gates of the great house, Yasnaya Polyana. They were a reminder to the little girl within those gates of the dignity of her father, Prince Nikolai Sergeyevich Volkonsky – as was the little band of serfs that solemnly played a Haydn symphony outside his window every morning. Not that she needed these reminders. Her mother had died two years after Marya was born, and Prince Volkonsky, a proud and dynamic man, devoted much of his time to the education of his only child.

Princess Marya Nikolayevna Volkonskaya, heiress to all this grandeur, was a plain, rather dull child, but she acquired a broad education from her cultivated father. In addition to French she learned English, German, and Italian, as well as music and mathematics. Yet under the unemotional exterior that she learned to keep in her father's presence, Marya was a romantic and a daydreamer. She was not, however, so romantic as to suppose that her short figure and heavy-browed face would ever win her a suitor, and was thrilled when a marriage was proposed for her with the son of a neighboring Prince. But before the marriage plans were far advanced, the young Prince died of typhoid. Marya determined to lead the life so common to only daughters – that of caring for her aging father.

Prince Volkonsky died in 1821. Marya was then thirty-one, and her secluded life with an old man had made her look much older than she was. She was mistress of the family estates – with 800 serfs at her beck and call, and nothing to do. Encouraged by friends, she went to live in Moscow, where she could go out into the society her father had shunned since falling out of favor with Tsar Paul back in 1800. Old maid though she was, she still hoped for marriage. And very soon her friends had found a bridegroom for her.

His name was Count Nikolai Ilych Tolstoy. He came of a family that was almost as old and distinguished as her own . . . even if the name "Tolstoy," which means "the stout," came from the nickname of a corpulent ancestor. Count Nikolai was five years younger than Marya. He had served in the Russian army against Napoleon, but resigned his commission when the family finances appeared to be in difficulty. He could be the life and soul of any party, but since

his father had died, deep in debt, Nikolai had attended no parties. He was now working as deputy director of an orphanage in order to provide for his mother and a distant cousin, Tatyana (Toinette), who kept house for them. Count Nikolai needed a rich wife, Princess Marya wanted a husband. A marriage was arranged, and it took place on July 21, 1822.

Their first child, Lev (Leo), was born a year later, and soon afterwards Count Nikolai gave up his post and went with his wife to live at Yasnaya Polyana, her old home. His mother and Toinette went with them. There Count Nikolai settled into the life of a landed proprietor, supervising the estates, organizing the serfs, and hunting. His high spirits were restored, and soon this marriage of convenience blossomed into love: letters exchanged between the two when Nikolai was absent on business begin "My tender friend," and Marya wrote many poems telling of her affection for her husband.

Marya derived her greatest happiness from her children. She was a born storyteller and, like her father before her, she made it her duty to supervise the education of her children. Her eldest son was the apple of her eye, and she was determined that he should grow up both talented and brave. Marya was able to devote all her time to her family because Toinette took charge of the household, as she had in Count Nikolai's bachelor days. At first Toinette was wildly jealous of Marya, but Marya's kindness and affection soon won her over, and the two women spent many happy hours together.

On March 14, 1830, Marya gave birth to her fifth child, a girl, whom Marya named after herself. The birth, like all the others, took place on a black leather divan which is still preserved at Yasnaya Polyana. Marya's health declined rapidly after the birth of her last baby. On August 16, 1830 she said farewell to her family. Leo, not yet two years old, was frightened at the sight of his dying mother, and was taken away crying. She died soon afterwards.

Count Nikolai survived his wife by seven years. After some time, he asked Toinette to marry him and be a mother to his children. But Toinette, who had always loved him deeply, had an even stronger affection for Marya's memory and refused to take her place.

LEO TOLSTOY
(1828-1910)
Famous Russian novelist, author of *War and Peace* and *Anna Karenina*.

Left Silhouette of Marya – the only known portrait.

carrie brown

SPENCER TRACY
(1900-67)
Star of many Hollywood films,
including *Edward My Son,*
Captains Courageous, and
Boys Town.

Carrie Brown came from an old and
distinguished Massachusetts family. One of her
family founded Brown University. She was
good-looking and, as a young woman, had plenty
of wealthy admirers. Several of them would
probably have married her, and there were
suggestions that she was marrying beneath her
when she chose a swarthy, Irish-Catholic
business executive named John Tracy. But her
instincts were right. He turned out to be an
excellent husband who made enough money to
keep his wife and children in comfort. Soon after
being made Sales Manager of the Sterling Motor
Truck Company, he bought an
impressive-looking house in a tree-lined street
near Lake Michigan. In time they had a son,
Carroll, and then, in 1900, another boy who was
named Spencer.

Carrie was soon aware that she had produced
a tough customer. She said that he talked,
walked, and fought early. He had a quick temper
and was forever scrapping with the Polish,
German, Italian, and Irish children who inhabited
Milwaukee. All the same, Carrie adored him, and
he was affectionate in return.

There were further worries for Carrie and John
when Spencer took a violent dislike to school.
Carrie sometimes burst into tears when Spencer
had played truant, and for a time he would show
remorse. But soon he would misbehave again,
and his parents were forever having to find a new
school for him because he had been expelled from
the previous one. He once said he only went to
school to learn the subtitles of silent films. But
Carrie persevered in her efforts to persuade him
that education was essential, and firmly resisted
his suggestions that he be allowed to leave school.

1916 was an unhappy year for Carrie. Her
husband decided to move to Kansas City, where
he thought there was a good business
opportunity. She never liked her new home, and
there were further difficulties when Spencer was
expelled from yet another school for fighting.
Fortunately for Carrie, John's business idea was
a flop and they returned to Milwaukee.

When Spencer was seventeen, he went to the
Marquette Academy, which he liked, and Carrie
was delighted to see some improvement in both
his schoolwork and his manners. But her peace of
mind was soon disturbed again when he told her
that he was going to play his part in the First
World War by joining the Navy. He was only
away, as it turned out, for a few months, and in
this time he came to appreciate both his parents.
Nonetheless, this didn't prevent him from

shocking them both by saying he wanted to go on
the stage. This idea was temporarily abandoned
while Spencer attended the Northwestern Military
and Naval Academy. There, to Carrie's delight,
he met a wealthy, well-mannered cadet, Ken
Edgers, whom he greatly admired. Edgers spent
several Christmases with the Tracys, and referred
to Carrie as his "Winsconsin mother."

Spencer then went to Ripon College, but in
1922 finally persuaded Carrie and John that
acting was the only thing he was really interested
in, and they allowed him to go to the American
Academy of Dramatic Art. Carrie, loyal as ever,
accepted his decision and prophesied that he
would do well.

In the late 1920s John (now working for
General Motors) and Carrie moved to New York.
Spencer, after the early hazards of an actor's
career, was on the brink of stardom. Less
happily, Spencer was married and had a
three-year-old son who was completely deaf.
Carrie spent a lot of time helping Spencer's wife,
Louise, with the difficult task of bringing him up.

There was further grief for Carrie when her
husband died of cancer. However, this indirectly
led to Carrie's being reunited with her children. In
1931 Spencer Tracy signed a film contract that
guaranteed him an annual minimum income of
$70,000. Overwhelmed by so much money,
Spencer asked his brother Carroll to come to
Hollywood to help him handle it. Carroll agreed,
and Carrie came with him.

Carrie, distinguished and gracious in old age,
lived on until 1942. This was just long enough to
see one of her dreams come true. Because of her
grandson's disability, she and her daughter-in-law
had set their hearts on opening a clinic for deaf
children. In 1942, with the help of many
voluntary contributions, the John Tracy Clinic
was started in the University of Southern
California. It was to develop into one of the
world's leading clinics for deaf children.

Pages 236-237 Carrie
with her actor son.

JANE LAMPTON

When twenty-year-old Jane Lampton married John Clemens, on May 6, 1823, she was not motivated solely by devotion to him. Jane was a beautiful and witty young woman, famous throughout Kentucky for her charm and gaiety. She had many suitors, but she was in love with a Lexington physician. After they quarreled one night, Jane impulsively agreed to marry John Clemens if the wedding could be arranged immediately. It could be, and Jane remained loyal to her husband for the rest of his life.

The life that Jane led with her husband was a mobile one. He was a born optimist, always moving from place to place and embarking on new enterprises which would lead, he was sure, to prosperity. Having trained in law, he worked for a while as circuit clerk of the court in Jamestown, Tennessee, where he bought seventy-five thousand acres of land, declaring: "Whatever befalls me now, my heirs are secure. I may not live to see these acres turn into silver and gold, but my children will." This land was to remain the hope of the Clemens family for many years to come. While John Clemens was speculating, his wife was bringing up a family: three sons and two daughters, of whom Samuel (later to take the pseudonym of "Mark Twain") was the youngest. They moved from a series of small clapboard houses to an elegant mansion referred to locally as the Crystal Palace, then back to more modest dwellings, according to the fluctuations of John's fortunes.

John Clemens spent little time with his growing family, and never joined in the games and amusements that his wife so enjoyed with the children. In later years Mark Twain remarked that he could not remember ever having heard or seen his father laugh, while of his mother he said, "She had a sort of ability which is rare in man and hardly existent in woman — the ability to say a humorous thing with the perfect air of not knowing it to be humorous."

The picture we have of Jane Clemens is engaging: "Her long life was mainly a holiday to her," and "She always had the heart of a young girl," said her youngest son. She was fearless, charitable, and kind-hearted. She refused to kill flies and punished the cat for catching mice. Samuel relates how one day the family bet among themselves that they could convince her, "the natural ally and friend of the friendless," to defend even Satan himself. Sure enough, after abuse of the Devil had poured forth, Jane Clemens pointed out that even though all they said was perfectly true, Satan had hardly been treated fairly, since he was the most miserable sinner and nobody ever prayed for him! This strange combination of gentle kindness and strict morality was to have an important influence on Samuel's character. At his father's death in 1847, his mother took him to see the body, saying: "Promise me . . . to be a better boy. Promise not to break my heart." And when he was about to leave home she made him solemnly swear that he "would not throw a card or drink a drop of liquor" while he was gone.

Samuel had been her most difficult child, but she had a great weakness for him: "He drives me crazy with his didoes when he is in the house, and when he is out of it I am expecting every minute that someone will bring him home half dead." Yet this troublesome child was a great support to his mother, going out to work at the age of twelve, after the death of his father, to help ease the family's financial burdens. Away from home, he wrote to his sister Pamela: "Tell Ma my promises are faithfully kept; and if I have my health I will take her to Kentucky in the spring — I shall save money for this."

He always spoke of her with warmth and affection. "Poor old Ma, asking in haste for news about people who have been dead forty, fifty and sixty years," he commented when she was becoming senile. When she died, in October, 1890, Jane Clemens was "well along in her eighty-eighth year." Her son called her a "most gentle spirit," and used her as a model for Tom Sawyer's Aunt Polly.

MARK TWAIN
(1853-1910)
Pen-name of Samuel Langhorne Clemens, American author and humorist. He is best known for his novels *The Adventures of Tom Sawyer* and *The Adventures of Huckleberry Finn*.

Left Mark Twain's birthplace in Missouri. *Pages 240-241* Two photographs of Jane, who was described by her son as a "most gentle spirit."

Irene Clemens

Hassall

Cor. Main and Third Sts.,
KEOKUK, IOWA.

Anna Cornelia Carbentus

VINCENT VAN GOGH
(1853-90)
Dutch painter.

Anna Cornelia Carbentus was born in 1819 into a family of cultured tradesmen in The Hague, Holland. Her father, William Carbentus, was a flourishing bookbinder: he had bound the first Constitution of Holland and thereafter became known as "Bookbinder to the King." As a young woman Anna drew skillful pen-and-ink sketches and painted charming watercolors, mainly of flowers.

In 1851 Anna married Theodoras van Gogh, a country parson whose parish was in Brabant. Their married life proved satisfying and happy. She cheerfully and energetically shared his work, visiting parishioners, caring for the sick, and taking food to the poor. Her warmth, kindness, and concern made her much loved throughout her husband's parish. She loved animals and plants; she and her husband took long walks in the surrounding countryside collecting botanical specimens. At thirty-three Anna bore her first child, a stillborn son who was named Vincent. The following year was born another son; this one lived, and he also was named Vincent. He was to be followed by five other children: Anna, Theo, Elisabeth, Willemien and Cornelius. These five were loving and, apart from concern over their delicate health, caused no real worries for their parents.

Vincent, however, was troubled and troublesome from a very early age. He had inherited several of his mother's good characteristics – her skill at drawing and letter writing, her good health and sturdy appearance, her passionate interest in nature. Yet he was strangely tormented. Some writers have pointed out the psychological effects on Vincent of being given the same name as his stillborn brother. And the empathy that motivated Anna to work so energetically for the people in her husband's parish seems to have caused anguish in her talented son.

Anna always supported Vincent in whatever he did, always loved and tried to understand him. But understanding was finally, by her own admission, impossible. She once wrote: "I am always so afraid that wherever Vincent may be, or whatever he may do, he will spoil everything by his eccentricity, his queer ideas and views on life." Vincent himself once wrote: "They dread having me in the house as they would dread having a large, savage dog. He runs into the room with muddy paws, he is rough, he's in everybody's way, he barks loudly. In short, he's a dirty beast. He might bark – he might go mad." These words were written to describe the attitude toward himself that Vincent imputed to his parents.

After her husband's death, Anna grew lonely in old age. Yet she retained her interest in the life around her, and was active until her death at the age of eighty-six.

Right Flower basket by van Gogh's mother; and a photograph of Anna.

VICTOIRE, Duchess of Kent

QUEEN VICTORIA
(1819-1901)
Queen of Great Britain and
Northern Ireland from 1837
to 1901.

Queen Victoria's mother was Princess Victoire Marie Louise of Saxe-Coburg-Saalfeld. She was born in 1786, the daughter of an impoverished German duke, Francis of Saxe-Coburg-Saalfeld, and grew up in the small town of Coburg, near the modern border between East and West Germany.

At seventeen Victoire married Prince Emich Charles of Leiningen, twenty-three years her senior, a man embittered by his family's losses at the hands of the invading French. In 1814, after ten years of not altogether happy marriage, Victoire was left a widow with two young children.

In 1818 she married again, this time to an Englishman, Edward, Duke of Kent, one of the sons of King George III. She was again almost twenty years younger than her husband, but their brief marriage was very happy, despite the fact that Edward had sought a wife (after living a quarter of a century with his French mistress) merely to provide heirs to the English throne. In fact, Edward and Victoire had only one child, the future Queen Victoria, born in May 1819; in January 1820 Edward died of pneumonia.

Victoire was left a widow for the second time, almost penniless in a foreign country. She remained in England only for the sake of Victoria, who, on the death of her grandfather the King, stood third in line to the English throne. The Duchess came to lean heavily for advice and support on Sir John Conroy, the comptroller of her small household. But her trust was misplaced. Conroy was ambitious on his own account, and set out to make the Duchess and her daughter wholly dependent on him so that he might, at Victoria's accession, be awarded a position of power and influence.

Conroy fed Victoire's mistrust of the English royal family and kept her isolated from them, fearing their ability to thwart his plans. He also undermined the Duchess's confidence in her brother Leopold (from 1831 King of Belgium), whom he saw as a rival to his pretensions. It was largely through Conroy's machinations that Parliament awarded the Duchess a regency for her daughter should Victoria become Queen before she came of age.

But while the Duchess was always Conroy's pawn, the Princess Victoria refused to submit to his domination. She came to despise her mother for her weakness in aiding Conroy's ploys, and hated him for the breach he created between her and the royal family.

To the very eve of her accession to the throne in 1837, Victoria had to combat Conroy's threats and cajoleries. She refused to give in to his demand that she take him on as her private secretary when she came to the throne. And once she was Queen, Victoria showed clearly that she would have none of him. At the same time, she took revenge on her mother for her years of unhappiness, allowing the Duchess only the formal respect due her, and slighting and rebuffing her in private.

Many years passed before the Queen and the Duchess were on better terms – a situation postponed largely by Conroy's remaining in the Duchess's household until 1839. The peacemaker was Victoria's husband, Prince Albert of Saxe-Coburg-Gotha. Just as Albert eased the Queen's way in politics, so he brought stability to her volatile emotions, and gradually drew his mother-in-law back into the family circle.

Having been thwarted in her aim to be everything to her daughter, and to share in her power, the Duchess resigned herself to the lesser role of domestic confidante to Victoria, and proved an admirable grandmother to the Queen's many children.

By the time of her mother's death, in March 1861, Queen Victoria had all but forgotten – and had certainly forgiven – the quarrels of her adolescent years. In the summer of 1861 she began the building of a mausoleum in the grounds of Windsor Castle, to house her mother's remains, and for the rest of her life Queen Victoria went frequently to mourn at the Duchess's tomb.

Right Flattering portrait of
Victoire, aged 56.
Page 246 Photograph of
Victoire in old age.
Page 247 Portrait; and the
mausoleum built by Queen
Victoria for her mother in
the grounds of Windsor
Castle.

H.R.H. The Duchess of Kent
1841
From the portrait by John Lucas at Windsor Castle

Marie Marguerite Daumard

VOLTAIRE
(1694-1778)
Adopted name of François
Marie Arouet. French man of
letters, author of *Candide* and
the *Philosophical Dictionary*.

Voltaire's literary output was prodigious in size and remarkably diverse in range of subject. Yet he has little to say about his parents. Even in a brief autobiography, written characteristically in the third person, he makes no mention of them. He has little to say about his childhood. "I think nothing is more insipid," he wrote, "than the details of infancy . . ." He affected to take no interest in his ancestry, and in his *Mémoire sur la Satire* he wrote: "The author of *Henriade* (himself) need care little what his grandfather was." Nor can documents fill in all the gaps left by what he chose not to tell: many registers were destroyed during the French Revolution and in civil disturbances in 1871.

But there can be no doubt about the identity of his mother, Marie Marguerite Daumard, who married François Arouet in June 1683. Madame Arouet gave birth to six children in the first eleven years of her marriage, three of whom died in infancy. The survivors were Armand, born in March 1685; Marie Marguerite, born probably in

1691; and three years later, in 1694, Francois Marie.

Marie Marguerite Daumard was the daughter of a high official of the *Parlement* of Paris, a combination of a court of law and a body that registered and promulgated the edicts of the King. He was therefore a member of the so-called *noblesse de la robe* (nobility of the gown) to which senior magistrates could lay claim. He was, moreover, descended from a minor provincial noble family, and so could claim to belong to the *noblesse de l'épée* (nobility of the sword), the true nobility of birth. Marie was therefore brought up in a respectable and would-be aristocratic home. She married a man in the same circle of senior state officials as her father. But François Arouet was not of noble ancestry: his father was a merchant and his grandfather a tanner. Arouet began as a notary, became a *conseiller du roi*, and finally a high official concerned with tax collecting.

Below Paris in the 18th century. Marie lived with her husband in the Ile de la Cité (left of the print).

It is unlikely that Marie Marguerite's marriage was a happy one. She was a vivacious and immensely sociable woman, whereas François Arouet was dour and irascible. Voltaire never believed that his mother's husband was his father; he believed himself to be the son of an army officer named Rochebrune (sometimes spelled Roquebrune), who was also known as a writer of songs. In a conversation with his niece Voltaire is reported to have claimed that "what was to her [his mother's] honor was that she preferred an intelligent man like Roquebrune, musketeer, officer and writer, to his putative father who was, by nature, a very commonplace man . . . ."

Marie Marguerite Arouet knew how to use her aristocratic connections to advance the social status of herself and her family. She secured as godparents for her eldest son, Armand, the Duchess of Saint-Simon (whose son was the famous diarist) and the Duke of Richelieu. She did not look so high for her youngest son, whose godparents were Marie Daumard, her sister-in-law, and François de Châteauneuf, a worldly priest who moved in high society. Among Châteauneuf's friends was Ninon de Lenclos, famous for her wit and beauty, whose salon was frequented by many free-thinkers.

Marie was never poor. She managed a substantial home on Paris's left bank, and seven years after the birth of François Marie her husband was granted an official residence on the Ile de la Cité, in the Rue Jérusalem where now are the buildings of the *Palais de Justice*. It was a house of ten rooms, and François Arouet also owned a country house of fourteen rooms. Both houses were richly furnished, and Monsieur and Madame Arouet must have led an active social life. But Madame Arouet did not live to enjoy the fruits of her husband's increasing prosperity, for she died in the same year that they moved to the Rue Jérusalem.

MARY BALL

GEORGE WASHINGTON
(1732-99)
Commander-in-chief of the
American forces in the War of
Independence, and first
President of the new republic.

Great figures gather great legends about them, and George Washington's legends have been remarkably persistent. American schoolchildren still hear of his inability to tell a lie, and of how he threw a silver dollar across the Potomac. Legends have also proliferated about Mary Ball, George's mother. Her legends are not so famous or so dramatic as those of her famous son, but they do show how a connection with greatness can lead to distortions of historical fact.

George Washington's mother was Mary Ball, born in 1707 or 1708, of a prosperous Virginia family which had been in America for little more than half a century. Early accounts of her life claim that Mary visited England as a young woman, and there met and married Augustine Washington. More recent evidence suggests that she spent the whole of her life in Virginia, and that after the death of her parents she lived for several years at the house of her guardian, George Eskridge, a wealthy landowner and lawyer. In 1730 she was married to his neighbor, Augustine Washington.

It is a proof of Mary's attachment to Eskridge that she named her first child George after him, rather than following custom and naming him Joseph after her father. (Augustine Washington already had two sons by his first wife – Lawrence, and his namesake, Augustine.)

George Washington was born on February 11, 1732. Over the next seven years Mary had five more children, four of whom survived to maturity. The family's life was rich and leisurely.

Mary was only thirty-five when her husband died. He left the bulk of his extensive property to his two sons by his first marriage, but a still substantial estate went to his widow to provide for the younger children.

Despite the traditional image of the fond, proud mother, it is likely that Mrs Washington was a rather forbidding, authoritarian, selfish woman. In his letters, George always addressed her as "Honored Madam," and one of his biographers asserts that her children were eager to leave home as soon as they were able. At the age of only fourteen, George begged permission to join the British Navy, but his mother refused to allow it. Nevertheless, George soon left her and went to live with his brother Lawrence, whose property, Mount Vernon, he later inherited.

While George was making his name as a military commander in the War of Independence, Mary Washington remained at home in Fredericksburg, Virginia. On one occasion, when soldiers came to commandeer her horses for the army, on the express order of George Washington, Mary refused them, saying that they were needed more urgently for work on her farm. Another time, when her son's fellow officers were praising his exploits at Princeton and Trenton, she remarked: "Ah, dear me! This fighting and killing is a sad thing! I wish George would come home and look after his plantation!" But her most inopportune stroke was her demand during the war years for a pension from the Virginia Assembly, on the plea that she was destitute. This was blatantly untrue, as George was quick to point out. Not only had he paid her a substantial sum for the house that was too big for her after her children left home, but he was paying an excessive rent for her lands and the use of her slaves.

George Washington was at Mount Vernon in April 1789, when the news came that he was to be the first President of the United States. Preparing to leave immediately for the north, he called on his mother to tell her of his appointment. It was the last time that mother and son were to meet: the following September Mary Ball Washington died of cancer.

Right Sentimental
departure – George gives
his mother a goodbye hug.
Page 252 Mary's house at
Fredericksburg; and
Mount Vernon, the most
impressive of the
Washingtons' homes.
Page 253 Mary's cousin's
house, "Bewdley"; and a
portrait of Mary when a
young woman.

MOUNT VERNON.

ANNE HILL, Lady Mornington

ARTHUR WELLESLEY, DUKE OF WELLINGTON
(1769-1852)
A brilliant British soldier whose military career culminated in the defeat of Napoleon in 1815. He later entered politics and became Prime Minister.

Right Portrait from life.
Below Anne in old age.

Anne Hill was the daughter of a wealthy and well-connected Irishman who had once been a Dublin banker. She was sixteen when, in 1759, she married Garret Wesley (later changed to Wellesley), who had the year before succeeded his father as Lord Mornington.

Anne's husband was an attractive man. He was passionately interested in music, was himself a composer and conductor, and was later to become Professor of Music at Trinity College, Dublin. He was not a wealthy man but he was a generous one, for he renounced any dowry from his young bride saying that she could spend any personal fortune on jewels for herself, executed a jointure of £1,600 a year, and allowed her £500 a year as pin money.

The bride was described at the time as "a fine young woman . . . rather a little clumsy, but with fine complexion, teeth and nails, with a great deal of modesty and good humor." It was a happy marriage. Lord Mornington played the organ and conducted concerts in their Dublin home, Mornington House, where there was much hospitality and entertainment.

Anne bore six children of whom two died in infancy, and Arthur, the future Duke, was the sixth, born on May Day, 1769. Richard, the heir, was Lady Mornington's favorite. He was superficially more brilliant than Arthur, whom he overshadowed.

Arthur was twelve when he was packed off to Eton in 1781, the year that his father died. Lord Mornington's passion for music and his often charitable hospitality had left the family in comparatively reduced circumstances, and Arthur spent less than three years at Eton. Then his mother took him to Belgium, where they lived in Brussels for a year, and it is strange to think that the pair may have wandered over the fields at nearby Waterloo. But a year of Brussels was enough for Lady Mornington, who put Arthur into the Royal Academy of Equitation at Angers, France.

There he acquired a polish that had been entirely missing before. "I vow to God," said his mother before he entered the Academy, "I don't know what I shall do with my awkward son, Arthur." When he left, she said: "He really is a very charming young man, never did I see such a change for the better." Lady Mornington was then very willing to pull strings on behalf of her youngest son. He entered the Army, earning ten shillings a day as *aide-de-camp* to Lord Buckingham, and from then on made his own way.

He seems to have maintained a dutiful if rather remote filial devotion, sending Anne a shawl during the height of the Peninsular campaign, and their relationship is probably summed up by a laconic letter she received from him in Portugal: "It is a long time since I heard from you. But I hope that you are in good health. I was not very well some time ago; but I am now quite recovered."

On the eve of Waterloo, Wellington was horrified to find that his mother, then over seventy, had joined the society throng that had flocked from London for a ringside seat at the coming battle. He sent her to safety at the port of Antwerp. In the blaze of glory that enveloped Wellington after Waterloo, Anne Hill fades from sight.

Mrs. Susannah Wesley.
Mother to the Rev. John Wesley.

Williams Del.   Owen, Sc.

S Wesley

Mother of the Revd John Wesley

London, Published by John Wesley, 78 Fleet Street E.C. May 1st 1863.

Susanna Wesley

JOHN WESLEY
(1703-91)
English clergyman who
founded the Methodist
Church.

Susanna Wesley has been called "the Mother of Methodism" because so much of her character and faith went into the religious movement initiated by her son John. Her father, Dr Samuel Annesley, was an Anglican clergyman whose nonconformist principles caused him to lose his living, though he continued to preach. She was born in his house in Bishopsgate, in the City of London, on January 20, 1669. Susanna was her parents' twenty-fifth and youngest child.

Few girls in the period received a good education, but Susanna was her father's pupil in Latin, Greek, and metaphysics as well as in more basic studies. She must have learned some theology from him, too, for at the age of thirteen she rejected her father's creed and became a devout Anglican.

One of the many theological students who frequented the Annesley house was young Samuel Wesley, and in 1689 or 1690 Susanna married him. The couple settled in London, where Samuel had a curacy.

Less than two years later, they moved to Lincolnshire where Samuel was given a living at Epworth. Here Susanna raised her large family — nineteen children, of whom ten survived to maturity. John, the famous founder of Methodism, was Susanna's fifteenth child. Of the children who survived to maturity, only two others were boys: Samuel, thirteen years older than John, and Charles, four years John's junior. The brothers were brought up in the company of their sisters, for Susanna would not allow her sons to play with the rough village boys.

The upbringing of the Wesley children seems harsh by today's standards. Susanna insisted on complete obedience: "The first thing to be done is to conquer their will," she wrote, "and bring them to an obedient temper. . . . The subjecting of the will is a thing which must be done at once and the sooner the better." She and Samuel shared the tuition of the children, all of whom received their careful attention.

Life in the Wesley household was made difficult by constant debts. On one occasion the Reverend Samuel Wesley was imprisoned for debt in Lincoln Castle, and Susanna had to beg the Archbishop for help. Samuel was not a popular man in his parish: twice the house was

set on fire, and on the second occasion, in 1709, the whole rectory at Epworth was razed. Young John was the last member of the family to escape.

Epworth Rectory had not been long rebuilt before Samuel was called away to London to attend the Anglican Convocation. In his absence, Susanna began to hold services in the rectory, refusing to attend those held by a curate whose doctrines she despised. At first only her children and the Wesleys' few servants attended, but later her congregation swelled to some 200 strong. Samuel, in London, was alarmed at such news from home, and Susanna had to use her considerable powers of persuasion to show him the necessity of doing what she had done. Many years later, the young Methodist Church took the radical step of admitting women as lay preachers.

This was not the only point of contention between Susanna and her husband. There were occasional bitter disagreements over politics as well as religion, for Susanna was an ardent Jacobite and High Tory while Samuel was loyal to the Hanoverian dynasty. "It is an unhappiness almost peculiar to our family that your father and I seldom think alike," wrote Mrs Wesley to one of her children. It is interesting, in view of their intellectual differences, that Samuel once wrote that he always "bore an undisputed sway" over his wife; "Nor was't her task but pleasure to obey."

In 1731 Samuel Wesley fell from a moving wagon, and from that time his health was never very good. He died in April 1735. After Samuel's death, Susanna first went to stay with her daughter at Gainsborough, and then paid visits to the rest of her family. Her last years were spent in the house that her son John had leased in London. In 1742 she knew herself to be near death, and she called her children to her. "Children," she said, "as soon as I am released, sing a psalm of praise to God." Susanna Wesley was "released" from life on July 23, 1742. She was buried in Bunhill Fields, the cemetery opposite the small church now called Wesley's Chapel. Her sons later collected the prayers that she had written, in the devotions of generations and those prayers are still used in Methodist services.

Pages 256-257 Susannah Wesley — "the Mother of Methodism."

ANNA MCNEILL

Anna McNeill was the daughter of a North Carolina doctor. Little is known about her childhood; in 1830 she married Major George Washington Whistler, a New Englander. They went to live for a time in his home state of Massachusetts, and it was there that Anna had her four sons, including James Abbott, born in 1834. The couple also had two children from a previous marriage of George's.

Anna was an intensely devout woman. Her primary concern about her children seems to have been whether they kept the Sabbath. Prayers and Bible readings were conducted every day without fail, and on Sundays she forbade her sons to read any book except the Bible. She once said that she preferred her top-floor bedroom to all other rooms in the house, because up there she felt closest to her Maker.

George Whistler had left the Army for a career as a civil engineer, and in 1842 he received an appointment to supervise the building of a railroad in Russia. Anna followed the next year with her sons (one of whom died on the journey), her stepchildren, and an Irish maid.

In St Petersburg the young Whistlers had to amuse themselves by reading American newspapers and, of course, the Bible. Anna just sewed. (It was round this time that James began to show signs of great talent as a draughtsman, although Anna still thought that music lessons were more important for him.) Anna worried a great deal about the creeds of the Orthodox Russian Church. She imported religious tracts printed in Russian and went around St Petersburg handing them out to soldiers she saw in the street. The troops grabbed them eagerly, which pleased Anna. She had no way of knowing, of course, that the illiterate soldiers could use her tracts for rolling cigarettes.

When cholera broke out in St Petersburg Anna took her sons to England. Once she had the boys settled with various relatives she returned to join her husband in Russia. He died there in 1849, and in July of that year Anna and her sons returned to America. Their income had fallen drastically after George's death and Anna tried to impress upon her sons a belief in the virtues of frugality. She also tried to get them the best education she could afford.

On James, however, her efforts were largely wasted: he failed his Army exams, walked out of one job in a locomotive works and another in the U.S. Office of Coastal Survey, and resisted Anna's efforts to turn his interests toward architecture. Finally she had to acquiesce in his setting off for Paris to study art. He left the United States forever in 1855. She commented at the time, "What can I do now for my Jimmie but pray, believing!"

Anna had married a Northener but she was born in the South, and when the Civil War broke out she supported the Confederacy. The South was not fighting for slavery, she said, "but in defense of its homes." When it became clear that the South was going to lose, Anna — by now a frail fifty-six years old, with weakened eyesight — slipped through the Union and boarded a ship bound for England. She was going to join James, who had moved from Paris to London.

She installed herself in James's Chelsea house, and his mistress was packed off out of sight. He escorted his mother to church on Sundays, and she organized refreshments for sitters and buyers. Soon the odors of American cooking drifted through the house. The daughter of a rich patron wrote happily of "hot biscuits and tinned peaches and other unwholesome things."

But Anna had also to learn to compromise. She found her "withdrawing room" littered with paints and canvasses, and put up with having the windows open in midwinter so James could sketch the Thames. She stopped entering the studio uninvited after she found the parlormaid posing naked. She was thankful that the girl was, at least, standing up. Swinburne was a caller at their house, and Anna (happily ignorant of his sexual aberrations) took to mothering the sickly young man.

A row over James's mistress sent him sailing off to Chile to dabble in the skirmishings of a minor war. But on his return in 1871 he painted the famous portrait of his mother, which he called *Arrangement in Grey and Black No. 1*. "What can or ought the public to care about the identity of the portrait?" he said. Yet later he admitted: "One does like to make one's mummy just as nice as possible."

He had taken a new mistress, and for several years his house was liable to sudden changes of atmosphere. One day Anna might be away, and her formal entertainments would be replaced by livelier celebrations. The next she would be back and those present might be favored with a lecture on the sin of painting on Sundays. Eventually she had to leave London because of failing health, and the mistress moved in. Anna died on January 31, 1881, and at her funeral Whistler broke down: "It would have been better had I been a parson as she wanted!"

JAMES McNEILL WHISTLER
(1834-1903)
Distinguished American painter and graphic artist who lived most of his life in London.

Pages 260-261 Whistler's famous portrait of his mother, which he entitled *Arrangement in Grey and Black No. 1.*

JANE ELGEE

OSCAR WILDE
(1854-1900)
Irish wit and writer, noted for his eccentric and unconventional behavior. Among his works are the play, *The Importance of Being Earnest* and the novel, *The Picture of Dorian Gray*.

Jane Francesca Elgee was the daughter of Charles Elgee, a solicitor in Wexford (Ireland). According to her own testimony she was born in 1826. Other authorities give the year as 1824.

While in her teens Jane was already playing a leading part in the Young Ireland movement, and writing inflammatory poems and articles in *The Nation*. She wrote first under the pen-name of "John Fenshaw Ellis," and then as "Speranza," which she took from her adopted motto, *"Fidanza, Constanza, Speranza"* (Faith, Faithfulness, Hope). Her article appealing to the young men of Ireland to take up arms against the Crown was cited in an unsuccessful prosecution for sedition against the editor, Charles Gavan Duffy.

At the age of twenty-five she married Dr William Wilde, an eye-and-ear surgeon eleven years her senior. He built his own hospital in Dublin, and was knighted in 1864. They had three children: William, born in 1852, who became a journalist; Oscar Fingal O'Flahertie Wills, born in 1854; and Isola, born in 1859, who died in childhood.

Sir William was burly and amorous, and his wife was no angel either, as Jack Yeats, the artist, darkly hinted in a letter to his son William. "She could afford to be wise and tolerant" to her erring spouse, as indeed she was throughout their life together. Lady Ardilaun, a neighbor, considered that "they were strange people, not fit to bring up boys."

The family lived a free-spoken and bohemian life in their dingy house in Merrion Square, Dublin. Entertaining, however, could be formal. Even in the afternoon, Lady Wilde would "receive" by appointment only. She would lie on an empire couch, dressed in a low-cut evening-gown of ruby-red velvet, and quote lines of her own poetry. Her salon was always conducted behind closed shutters, even by day, and in candlelight. In later life, by keeping her drawing room in almost total obscurity, and with the aid of heavy cosmetics, flowing drapery, and eccentric head-dresses, she gamely fought her battle against time. She invariably wore a gold laurel wreath in her hair, and her bosom was usually decorated with a series of large brooches containing family portraits. Steering her somewhat bulky figure among her literary lions, she put them through their paces like the competent lion-tamer she was, a performance that everyone seemed to find enjoyable. The darkness of the scene has been described as Rembrandtesque, although the novelist Gertrude Atherton, reporting a visit, assumed that the gas had been cut off.

Lady Wilde aimed to be accepted, both in Dublin and afterwards in London, as a second Madame Récamier. Asked how she managed to get together such an interesting group of people, her answer was short and to the point: "By interesting them."

Lady Wilde was a prolific writer and an authority on Celtic myth and folklore. Among her published works are: *Poems by Speranza* (1871), *Ancient Cures, Charms and Usages of Ireland* (1890), and *Notes on Men, Women and Books* (1891). She was, like Oscar, a brilliant linguist, and made translations from French and German. One of these, *Sidonia the Sorceress,* 1849, was reprinted by William Morris at the Kelmscott Press. Rossetti was enchanted by it, and Edmund Gosse said, "It is hardly a paradox to say that this German romance did not begin to exist until an Irish woman revealed it to a select English circle."

After her husband's death, Lady Wilde moved to London. On May 24, 1890 she was awarded a Civil List Pension of £70 a year, in recognition of her services to literature.

The mutual affection of mother and son lasted from Oscar's childhood and survived the scandal of his imprisonment. She died while he was still in Reading Gaol, and was buried in Kensal Green cemetery in 1896. After his release, he wrote to Robert Ross, "I quite see that whenever I am in danger she will in some way warn me." Later, in *De Profundis,* he wrote: "No one knew how deeply I loved and honored her. Her death was terrible to me; but I, once a lord of language, have no words in which to express my anguish and my shame."

Right Lady Wilde — described by a neighbor as "not fit to bring up boys." *Page 264* Caricature of Lady Wilde and her husband, Sir William. *Page 265* A photographic portrait of Lady Wilde.

Susan Catherine Koerner

THE WRIGHT BROTHERS
Wilbur (1867-1912) and
Orville (1871-1948).
American inventors and
builders of the first successful
airplane, which made its first
flight in 1903.

Susan Catherine Koerner was born in Virginia in 1831. Her father, John G. Koerner, was born in Germany but had emigrated, because of his independent spirit and dislike of the autocracy of his homeland, to the United States. He had great mechanical aptitude and soon made a name for himself in his adopted country as a maker of farm-wagons and carriages. In America he married Catherine Fry, who was American-born but of Swiss descent.

Shortly after Susan's birth, the Koerners moved to Union County, Indiana, where her father continued to make wagons and also built up large farming interests. Mr Koerner, a man of some learning himself, saw to it that Susan had a good education, and she graduated from a small college in Hartsville, Indiana. She was an excellent mathematician and displayed considerable interest in science. She also had great charm, and was considered by her neighbors to be rather "smart".

These attributes were soon noticed by a young preacher of the United Brethren Church, Milton Wright, who was not only a man of religion but a teacher. He had been at the same college as Susan, though a few years earlier, and subsequently taught there. In 1859, when he was thirty-one, three years older than Susan, they married. During the early years of their marriage, they lived at various places in Indiana and had three sons, Reuchlin, Lorin, and in 1867, Wilbur.

When Wilbur was two, the Reverend Milton Wright became editor of *The Religious Telescope,* a weekly newspaper run by the United Brethren. This involved a move to Dayton, Ohio, where Mrs Wright gave birth to two more children — Orville, who was born in 1871, and a daughter, Katherine, who was born three years later. The Wrights lived in a new seven-room house on the West Side of Dayton, across from the Miami River.

Right Room in the
Wrights' home at Dayton —
with a hearth built by
Wilbur and Orville; and a
photograph of Susan.

Both Mrs Wright and her husband were mechanically minded. He invented a crude, early typewriter. The toys they bought for their children were of a scientific nature. Orville on one occasion received a gyroscopic top, and even more important for the future was the gift of a toy helicopter. Susan and her husband always encouraged any sort of scientific activity, and Mrs Wright didn't even mind when her kitchen was used as a laboratory.

Susan's love of science once saved Orville from being punished. When he was five she sent him to a kindergarten, and after a month she went to ask his teacher how he was getting on. To her horror, she was told that after a few days he had not been seen again and the teacher had supposed that Orville's parents had taken him away. It was then discovered that Orville had spent his time at the house of a young friend where there was an old broken-down sewing-machine. Orville and his friend had tried to get it going by dripping water from a feather into the oil holes. As Orville's truancy had been occasioned by scientific curiosity, his misbehaviour was overlooked.

The Reverend Wright subsequently became a bishop, and this involved moving in 1878 from Dayton to Cedar Rapids, Iowa. However, Mrs Wright's health was beginning to fail. Three years later the family moved to Richmond, Indiana, where she could have the companionship of her sister. In Richmond, Orville took another step toward becoming a pioneer of aviation, by making a study of the construction and flying of kites.

In 1885 the Wrights returned to their house in Dayton. Four years later, in 1889, Susan died. In her last days she was constantly attended by her son Wilbur.

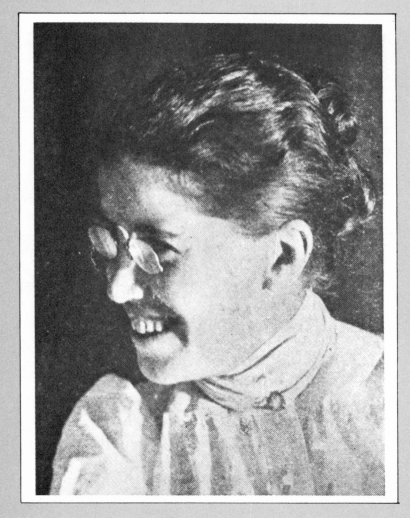

267

ACKNOWLEDGMENTS

Louisa M. Alcott Memorial Association, Concord
Popperfoto
Odense City Museum, Odense
Mansell collection
Max Jones
Jane Austen Memorial Trust
J. G. Moore collection
Beethoven-Haus, Bonn
The Bell Family Courtesy National Geographic Society
Radio Times Hulton Picture Library
Mansell collection
T. Rourke, *Simon Bolivar* (Michael Joseph)
SCALA istituto Fitografico Editoriale
Mansell collection
the Brontës Society
The Scottish National Portrait Gallery
John Murray
Chicago Tribune
Sir Charles Chaplin
Mansell collection
photo Harlingue-Viollet
Radio Times Hulton Picture Library
The Trustees of the Wedgwood museum
The Trustees of the Dickens House
Mansell collection
photo George B Briggs, United States Department of the Interior
Bibliothek der Eidgenossische Technische Hochschule, Zurich
Dwight D Eisenhower Library
Mansell collection
Mansell collection/Archive K/Keystone Press agencies
Margot Fonteyn
Henry Ford Museum
Sigmund Freud copyrights
Alexandre Dumas, *Memoirs of Garibaldi* (Benn)
Collection Viollet
Editions du Seuil and Bibliotheque Nationale, Paris
Museum Dahlem, Berlin
Ohio Historical Society, Ohio. Mansell collection
Popperfoto
M Meyer, *Henrik Ibsen* (Hart Davis)
National Portrait Gallery, London. Mansell collection
University of Hawaii at Manoa, Honolulu
Virginia Department of Conservation and Economic Development
Radio Times Hulton Picture Library
EMI Music Publishing Ltd
Popperfoto
The Associated Press Ltd
H. T. Moore. Nottingham Public Libraries
Washington-Curtis-Lee collection
Washington and Lee University, Virginia
Novosti
Popperfoto
Lincoln National Life Foundation, Fort Wayne, Indiana
Anne Morrow Lindbergh, *Bring me a Unicorn*:
Diaries and Letters of Anne Morrow Lindbergh
1922-1928
(Harcourt Brace Javanovich, Inc.)© 1971, 1972